Transformations in Personhood and Culture After Theory

Literature & Philosophy

A. J. Cascardi, General Editor

This series publishes books in a wide range of subjects in philosophy and literature, including studies of the social and historical issues that relate these two fields. Drawing on the resources of the Anglo-American and Continental traditions, the series is open to philosophically informed scholarship covering the entire range of contemporary critical thought.

Already published:

J. M. Bernstein, *The Fate of Art: Aesthetic Alienation from Kant to Derrida and Adorno* (1992)
Peter Burger, *The Decline of Modernism* (1992)
Robert Steiner, *Toward a Grammar of Abstraction: Modernity, Wittgenstein, and the Paintings of Jackson Pollock* (1992)
Mary E. Finn, *Writing the Incommensurable: Kierkegaard, Rossetti, and Hopkins* (1992)
David Jacobson, *Emerson's Pragmatic Vision* (1993)
Reed Way Dasenbrock, ed., *Literary Theory After Davidson* (1993)
Gray Kochhar-Lindgren, *Narcissus Transformed: The Textual Subject in Psychoanalysis and Literature* (1993)
David P. Haney, *William Wordsworth and the Hermeneutics of Incarnation* (1993)

Transformations in Personhood and Culture After Theory

The Languages *of* History, Aesthetics, and Ethics

Edited by
Christie McDonald and Gary Wihl

The Pennsylvania State University Press
University Park, Pennsylvania

Library of Congress Cataloging-in-Publication Data
Transformations in personhood and culture after theory : the languages of history, aesthetics, and ethics
   edited by Christie McDonald and Gary Wihl.
       p.   cm.—(Literature and philosophy)
   Includes bibliographical references and index.
   ISBN 0-271-01010-X (cloth : alk. paper).—ISBN 0-271-01011-8
   (pbk. : alk. paper)
   1. Postmodernism. 2. Criticism.   I McDonald, Christie, 1942–   .
   II. Wihl, Gary, 1953–   . III. Series.
   B831.2.T73   1994
   001.3—dc20   93-23859
                                                                    CIP

Copyright © 1994 The Pennsylvania State University
All rights reserved
Printed in the United States of America

Published by The Pennsylvania State University Press,
Barbara Building, Suite C, University Park, PA 16802-1003

It is the policy of The Pennsylvania State University Press to use acid-free paper for the first printing of all clothbound books. Publications on uncoated stock satisfy the minimum requirements of American National Standard for Information Sciences—Permanence of Paper for Printed Library Materials, ANSI Z39.48–1984

Contents

	Preface *Christie McDonald and Gary Wihl*	vii
	Acknowledgments	xiii
1	History Without Empiricism/Truth Without Facts *Nancy F. Partner*	1
2	How Old Is Our Cultural Past? *Judith Schlanger*	13
3	The Humor of the Present *Isabelle Stengers* Translated by Richard Cooper	25
4	Naming the Landscape: Leisure Travel and the Demise of the Salon *Nancy Austin*	35
5	Beauty, Language, and Re-Presentation: Notes Toward a Critique of Aesthetics—With Special Reference to Architecture *Karsten Harries*	61
6	Making Space: For a Poetry of Architecture *Mary Ann Caws*	79
7	Intentionality Without Interiority: Wittgenstein and the Dynamics of Subjective Agency *Charles Altieri*	85
8	Changing One's Beliefs *Jacques Schlanger*	117
9	Theories of Gender *Rosi Braidotti*	133

10	Stories of Gender *Sarah Westphal*	153
11	Three Renaissance Madonnas: Freud and the Feminine *Mary Bittner Wiseman*	165
	Notes on the Contributors	187
	Index	189

Preface

The word "transform" has a rich etymology rooted in definitions of character and condition. In English "transform" dates back to 1382. It combines the prefix *trans* (to or on the far side of, beyond, over) with the Latin *formare* (to form). The term first meant "to change the form of something, to metamorphose," but came to mean also "to change in character or condition, to alter in function or nature." As it is used in this collection of essays its central importance lies in the determination of a perspectival shift rather than a radically new or revolutionary insight into social relations. To shift perspective is to see the familiar anew without, however, giving up the sense of familiarity. By touching the familiar, transformation provokes curiosity, flexibility, and intellectual community. These essays grasp this process of transformation: they situate the practices of the historian, the aesthetician, the ethicist, and the cultural critic in the everyday fabric of life that the discourse of transformation may invoke and capture.

Nancy Partner, Judith Schlanger, and Isabelle Stengers expand the meaning of transformation in the vocabulary of the historian. Nancy Partner begins with the classical definition of history as a literary genre alongside poetry and rhetoric. Pragmatic in origin, as a type of writing that served secular needs, history has always been linked closely to actual life and decision making within the polis. Neither records of unadorned "facts" nor grand stories about human origins and ends, early history writing captured what still counts about those narratives we call histories: "In practice, even the most rigorous modern historians have always, and quite candidly, relied on honest authorial intentions, public integrity of method, and good faith as a pragmatic agreement that serves the same purposes as a demonstrable epistemology" (Nancy F. Partner, "History Without Empiricism/Truth Without Facts," 4). As a literary practice, reading and writing history allows an increasingly complex political constituency to present transformation in a personal, experiential vocabulary. Seeing history in this way expresses transformations in multilayered, multitonal artifacts, whose status is neither confirmed nor denied by epistemological issues of truth or fiction.

Judith Schlanger and Stengers enrich the pragmatics of history writing by considering the concept of cultural time. Why do classical writings receive the veneration of later cultures? Does veneration depend on temporal distance? For Schlanger, these questions can only be answered in terms of personal memory. Memory, like Partner's genre of history, is a flexible tool for description rather than an epistemological method. Memory cannot be taught, yet it must be acquired in order to mark out what Auguste Comte called the "trente ans pour penser." "It makes some sense," writes Schlanger, "to see ourselves as somewhere in the middle of a range of some thirty years which is more or less the scope of what we encompass at any point, the scope of our intellectual concerns, projects, and activities" ("How Old Is Our Cultural Past?" 15). The everyday language by which we are taught what to venerate and what to hold near is part of the vocabulary of the memory by which we order, shift, and locate our important projects. In terms of genre, the map of our memories has shifted from the classical exercise of imitating standard topics to the language of the novel. By the novel Schlanger refers not to the fictionalization of the past, but to contemporary analyses of experience. Experience, memory, and levels of relevance provide the patterns by which we construct our "thirty-year" frames and by which we transform our lives, like novels, into bridges between different registers of cultural value.

Responding to Schlanger, Stengers highlights the practical effects and problems of the discourse of memory. She asks, if we separate history from chronology, then where do facts speak? She endorses the elimination of teleology from history, but questions the notion of history as a strictly human construction of events, and further seeks to discover what gives a mixture of narratives their coherence. Using a test case from the history of science, specifically the Devonian controversy in geology, she searches for the actions that made the story possible yet are not part of the story and an explanation of the controversy that follows from the facts but at the same time takes into account the importance of heuristic innovation and narrative plurality. Schlanger and Stengers suggest that multilayered narratives and factual discoveries are reconciled in stories about human temporality.

One of the most enduring legacies of the philosophy that inaugurated modernity is the concept of the aesthetic. Grounded originally in an inquiry into the human faculties of imagination and feeling, it endures in the vocabulary applied to works of art and architecture. Nancy Austin and Karsten Harries take the traditional terms and issues that have been handed down from aestheticians and wrest from this material a perspective on the beauty of familiar experiences. Nancy Austin reexamines the genre of the landscape in the Parisian Salons from 1865 to 1880 and finds that the acceptance and popularization of this genre did not depend on innovations in technique and composition. The landscape painting of the impressionists, for example, is best seen in the context of popular railway travel and the public's direct access to the views named and depicted by popular magazines and travel guides. The railways did not create a taste for the landscape genre, but they did make it increasingly difficult to dictate the public's artistic taste within the narrow confines of the Salon once the perception of landscape depended on popular traveling experiences. Impressionism therefore was not a criticism of industrialization or an attempt to free art from commercialization. Just the opposite: Austin relates how some of the most astute impressionists, such as Claude Monet, discovered the appeal of their art outside of the aesthetic criteria of the Salon juries.

Karsten Harries questions the meaning of aesthetic formalism. Like Austin, he argues that aesthetic experience depends on the viewer's familiarity with everyday surroundings. He makes works of architecture central in his argument because they include both functional and decorative elements. For him the beauty of architecture cannot be dissociated from the properties that make a work of architecture work as a mere building. He insists that the traditional definitions of the purity and beauty of architecture on the level of ornamentation rather than structure are too narrow to explain what makes architecture an art form. He believes that architecture needs to be returned to the immediate surroundings in which we actually occupy and construct functional places. For him, the incorporation of architecture into public space occurs textually rather than aesthetically, as buildings become expressive. By turning from aesthetic object to text he does not mean to reject the traditions of architectural thought; he finds that idealization and self-presentation may be treated textually even though they first gained currency in the writings of architectural aestheticians. What do these terms mean? What sort of transformation do they perform? Harries writes that buildings become texts available for public discussion and use when they deploy a play of surface transformations or translations that are captured in the appearance of building materials ("Beauty, Language, and Re-Presentation," 75–76). A support is transformed into a column, a stone column into one of richer material, and therefore a function into an expression, not only doing its work but calling attention to its ability to shine forth an image of itself. In this manner, the beauty of architecture is removed from a special, autonomous domain of form and becomes a solicitation for the viewer's attention. Harries sums it up in the metaphor of a person whose beauty cannot be described as aesthetic but who creates an aesthetic impression by being particularly noticed.

To respond to Harries, Mary Ann Caws moves from architecture to writing by establishing an analogy between visual and verbal modes of expression. As an experiment in prose, she exchanges images of architecture and poetry in an act of personal transformation and recollection.

Charles Altieri and Jacques Schlanger analyze what we ordinarily mean by the depth of a person's identity and beliefs. Altieri poses a Wittgensteinian picture of intention and agency as an answer to structuralist and analytic treatments of the human subject. He rejects from the outset both the Derridean interpretation of human intention and subjectivity as inevitably divided from or absent to itself and analytical philosophy's search for knowledge in the form of impersonal propositions. Altieri believes that if we are to have an ethical outlook, then we must have an expressive mode that allows human agents to authenticate and position themselves in a social world, to contribute values to that world, and to have that contribution acknowledged and endorsed. Altieri returns to Wittgenstein to argue that subjects have no deep interiority where values are centered. Through an examination of the most prosaic particles of ordinary speech, such as deictics and first-person grammars, Altieri outlines a picture of the subject's immanence in speech, an immanence that once grasped allows us to see human subjects within a varying field of ordinary and familiar perceptions.

The same metaphor of surface and depth takes on central importance in Jacques Schlanger's autobiographical essay on losing faith in God. What transformation could be more profound? For Schlanger, coming to terms with the experience of losing God is discovering first the difference between deep and superficial belief. The difference is shown in various ways: on the basis of authority, in relation to a personal stance, and in the gradual awareness that beliefs go hand in hand with sets of practices. The practice of a belief, the set of actions that accord with it, is perhaps its most essential aspect. In losing God, Schlanger discovers, the world and oneself are not transformed in any profound way. In fact, the practice of following God endures for a long time after the cognitive recognition of the loss. What does the transformation therefore signify? It signifies the transformation of what was previously conceived as something deep and beyond exposure into a practical test for all of a person's guiding beliefs. Like Altieri, Schlanger finds that the depth of the subject's beliefs actually belongs on the surface of habits, practical activities, and small shifts in personal perspective.

The last three essays in this collection concern the transformations wrought by and on the concept of gender. Rosi Braidotti sets up an overview of feminist theory by tracing its recent genealogy from de Beauvoir, through poststructuralism, and into recent popular discourse about women's images. In the course of each transformation, universalist categories of gender break apart and proliferate. In the collapse of universalist ethics, Braidotti locates a genealogy specific to women. For her, popular music is the emblem of a new style of theory and history. Multiple contradictions between race, class, and gender, previously submerged in the universalist mode of historical analysis, are found and expressed as memories and stories rather than as theories of the human subject.

Responding to Braidotti, Sarah Westphal strengthens the purpose of story and narration as a mode of feminist analysis and revision. For Westphal, stories do more than reveal the multiplicity of contradictions that surround issues of gender. They dismantle the very concept of genealogy or origin, which continues to hold a place of privilege even within Braidotti's revisionist, populist analysis. Stories are distinguished from genealogies, according to Westphal, by the absence of founding figures. In this context, the absence of a Marx or a Freud, who would guarantee the founding of feminist theory, does not weaken feminist theory, but rather points up its nongenealogical development. By this account, which harmonizes with and extends Braidotti's, "The definition of theory becomes more elastic, accessible, and connected to lived experience" (Sarah Westphal, "Stories of Gender," 157) and includes voices that have hitherto been excluded from Eurocentric feminist theory, such as women of color and native peoples. Westphal captures this aspect of gender transformation in Benjamin's image of history collapsing into the fragment, which "multiplies the movement's potential sites of resistance" (160).

In her essay Mary Wiseman questions the conceptual link between genealogy and gender with reference to Freud's analysis of the Madonna figure. Through a close reading of key texts in the Freudian oeuvre, in which images of the Madonna (the paradigm of the desired yet maternal feminine) cross with key definitions of personality development, Wiseman shows Freud's consistent inability to locate attachment in relationships between women, such as that between mother and daughter. With the assistance of Kristeva's analysis of Bellini's *Lochnis Madonna*, Wiseman goes beyond Freud's adaptation of the Oedipus myth to locate female developments of gender. Wiseman concludes with a commentary on Dora who stands out as the singularly unhappy victim of Freud's indifference to the maternal function. His case history of Dora makes her a "stranger" to her own analysis, a strangeness we can now appreciate as part of Freud's own inability to find a language for the maternal function within a theory of gender.

These essays define transformation by blending the familiar with the conflicted and plural. "Transformation" refers to the shifting ground in our present culture between the familiar and the unfamiliar. It is a pragmatic term rather than a theoretical one. We view these essays as examples of new intellectual "genres" rather than "theories." If they do belong to a post-theoretical, intellectual genre of writing, it is because they blend philosophical vocabularies with expressions of curiosity, novelty, and plurality. The languages of the historian, the aesthetician, and the ethical philosopher join forces with the language of the literary critic. The result is an affirmation of intellectual community within our increasingly plural culture.

Acknowledgments

The editors gratefully acknowledge funding from the Social Sciences and Humanities Research Council of Canada for the preparation of this manuscript. The University of Montreal and its Department of French have provided constant assistance in communications and organizational support for this volume. Roger Prichard, Vice-Principal (Research) of McGill University, generously provided a grant in support of research for the volume.

Our work on this volume has been greatly facilitated by Nicole Piché, Administrative Assistant, Department of French, University of Montreal, and Renée Hulan, a doctoral candidate in English at McGill University.

1

History Without Empiricism/Truth Without Facts

NANCY F. PARTNER

> To insist on the fact that as the picture is reality, so the novel is history. That is the only general description (which does it justice) that we may give of the novel. But history also is allowed to represent life; it is not, any more than painting, expected to apologize. The subject-matter of fiction is stored up likewise in documents and records, and if it will not give itself away, as they say in California, it must speak with assurance, with the tone of the historian.
> —Henry James, *The Art of Fiction*

> Soldiers fired guns into the air in celebration today in Baghdad after Iraq ordered its forces to stop fighting and declared the Persian Gulf war a great Iraqi victory....
> "Victory is not how many tanks or planes we or the enemy used," said Al-Thawra, the newspaper of the ruling Baath Party. "It's all steel that can get ruined. Victory is the face that you acquire in the history books."
> —*New York Times*, 1 March 1991 Report from Baghdad

In 1884 when Henry James published his deeply considered defense of realist fiction, it was fiction and not history that still needed to be defended. Fiction still needed a defense against the ancient charges that it was morally shallow, spurious, negligible in value, a gimcrack of fleeting verbal lies. The committed practitioner of a serious art, James was perfectly able to recognize the ancient stream of contempt wherever it surfaced, in the condescension of critics, or in novelists who built escape-hatch apologies into their stories ("Reader, we know this is only a story..."). James embodied, in the totality of his work, both fiction and criticism, the authentic realist commitment: that the art of fiction be, as much as the writing of history, grounded in the real.[1]

The analogy with representational painting, which James assumed would be regarded as a true mirror of reality, is a weak point of his argument—he never paid more than cursory attention to painting—but not a hopelessly weak point. He insists merely that "*as* the picture is reality [my emphasis], *so* the novel is history," that is, *as* a picture is a technically achieved *visual* artifice committed to reality, *so* the novel is a technically achieved *verbal* artifice committed to reality.[2] The grounding point, the ultimate standard implicit in his discussion, the *thing* about which there can be no dispute or quibble, is history. In James's aesthetic algebra of proportions, picture stands in relation to visible reality as the novel stands in relation to history. The relation is one of reality-committed representation, not identity. Long realist fictions, as much as history, are depictions of life, and fictions that apologize, that want to have it both ways, and admit to being "only stories," betray their very nature, and thus betray artistic integrity, and life itself. This is the interior credo of the Jamesian novel, organized around a center in which words indubitably can represent life, in a world in which the idea that history should ever be, under any circumstances, "expected to apologize" is the merest absurdity.

When a newspaper of public record (at least in Iraq) speaks with assurance, "with the tone of the historian," in unapologizing cynical contradiction of what still passes for common reality, we are told how far history has fallen and how constantly now it *is* expected to apologize. It is probably true that most historians, whatever they think of the alleged "great Iraqi victory" in the Gulf War, would give some sort of wry assent to the newspaper's claim that "victory is the face that you acquire in the history books" and its underlying premise that history does not mirror the face of reality. The relation of the portrait to the sitter (and this accidental evocation of James's analogy with pictures seems a nasty little joke) could not be more uncertain, shifting, or deeply compromised than it appears to historians now. The analogy between fiction and history, which James conceived as built on the strongest reality principle, would seem to have become literally true but insane. As the categories of fiction and history collapse together in so much postmodern critical thought, history seems to do nothing but apologize lately. Somewhat in the spirit of the Iraqi "victory" celebrations, it often enough transforms its anxieties into belligerence and normalizes its failures into ordinary professional activity.

An instance of this apology cum denial behavior took place at the 1990 meeting of the American Historical Association and was considered important enough to be reported at length in the *American Histori-*

cal Review.[3] A panel of well-qualified experts assembled to discuss Peter Novick's ironic requiem for academic history, *That Noble Dream*,[4] or more precisely, the last chapter of it, evocatively titled, "There Was No King In Israel," in which we historians are depicted in a state of accelerating disintegration, suffering from deep foundational collapse and loss of nerve with respect to matters epistemological, ontological, teleological, pedagogical, professional, and collegial—in short, enjoying our complete entry into that currently celebrated state of "postmodern" freedom. This state of liberation from institutional or disciplinary constraints seems to be what Novick had in mind in quoting the final passage of Judges about the absence of a king in Israel when "every man did what was right in his own eyes."

The panel members (J. H. Hexter, Linda Gordon, David Hollinger, and Allan Megill) made some interesting comments (variously aggrieved, irritated, contemptuous, complaining) on their particular enjoyment of our postmodern syndrome, almost none of which, excepting Allan Megill's pure narrativist analysis, were acknowledged by Novick as even approaching a correct reading of his text. All of which led him finally to lament, ironically of course, "the deplorable decay of scriptural literacy in this secular age," since no one anywhere seems to have understood the crucial verse from Judges 21:25 as he does. And this hermeneutic imbroglio can serve as an exemplary microcosm or synecdoche to teach us: (1) the ultimate futility of attempting to anchor meaning in an appeal to authorial intention since no one pays any attention to the author even when he is alive, present, and vociferous; or (2) the need to go back to biblical exegesis and learn how interpretation really works; or perhaps (3) that the danger of quoting lines from other writers' books is that they may take a terrible revenge by writing us into their stories, no matter how we protest. (Strong narratives, like sharks, tend to devour lesser fish.)

The "postmodern" freedom from orthodoxy, hierarchy, and consensus, which is supposed to open exhilarating vistas of "rich possibilities" to us, actually, on the evidence so far, seems to inspire most historians with acute nonspecific anxiety, diffuse anger, and abreaction denial. We may recall that among the rich possibilities open to premonarchical Israel when every man was free to do "what was right in his own eyes," the one they quickly chose was to demand that a king be put over them. Many historians would have chosen a title for Novick's chapter 16 from Genesis 11, the Tower of Babel. The quarrel continues on a dozen different fronts in endless indecisive skirmishes,[5] often in a mean-spirited tone of exasperated contempt on all sides, and reenacts itself in miniature in university history departments.

And yet it is all very curious. No one in this continuing debate has demanded any sort of metaphorical king. No one has argued for single-version history, or grand-narrative history that will blot out the claims of alternate versions, especially when the alternate versions are those of women, slaves, colonized natives, marginalized others. I have heard no one demand that we construct covering laws, or vindicate the vulgar triumphs of the powerful, or celebrate the pure culture of the Folk. No one, to my knowledge, has insisted that we make only assertions whose negations can be negated, à la Karl Popper. No one has even asserted that we *should* continue to present our work in the armature of evidence we call the textual apparatus, because no one is *not* doing that.

So what is it that we are quarreling about? The *feeling* of crisis, albeit of the slow-motion or ambulatory nervous breakdown kind, is real enough, but the issue is elusive. It is usually, if pompously, located in a "crisis of epistemology" brought on by semiotic linguistic theories and deconstructive textual criticism that radically undermine the empiricist assumptions of traditional historiography. But it is impossible to find any historian, Rankean, Foucauldian, whatever, whose actual working techniques have been altered in the slightest by epistemological doubt. In fact, I do not think we really have, fundamentally, a crisis of epistemology. Even in theoretically sophisticated circles, once the modern semi-objectivists and the modern semi-relativists finish explaining their actual, true, and considered positions, it is hard enough to tell one from the other. In practice, even the most rigorous modern historians have always, and quite candidly, relied on honest authorial intentions, public integrity of method, and good faith as a pragmatic agreement between writer and reader that serves the same purposes as a demonstrable epistemology (just as Richard Rorty has claimed).

The theoretical assaults on empirical history in the wake of semiotic linguistics and antireferential literary analysis are *theoretical* operations, *meta*discourses, which have had, and will have, no substantial effect on historical research and writing (Novick, Hayden White, and Frank Ankersmit have acknowledged this repeatedly). This is not mere cultural lag, false consciousness, or naive delusion. Philosophy (that is what we are talking about) is always *about*, is always a metadiscourse addressed to practice, the systematic exercise of the mind's strange ability to reflect on itself. Surely we have noticed by now that attempts to conflate metahistory with history (and there are some very self-conscious, expressly theoretical, hermeneutically exposed books being written now) only result in the creation of new layers of yet finer metadiscourse to discuss them, thus preserving the structural and cultural distinction between them. What many historians still cherish as "real" history is nowhere evaporating into any realm of ethereal hermeneutics.

This ought to be comforting to contemplate, at least for historians with traditional sympathies. But there is an indubitable and pervasive anxiety in our profession addressed to some kind of slippage that, it is felt, ought to be controlled and somehow stopped. This cannot, humanly speaking, be a crisis of competing theories of linguistic referentiality. What it feels like is a crisis of moral seriousness. Historians seem to feel the threat of being trivialized, of being banished from the centers of serious grown-up concerns of power and politics, of being exposed as *writers*, and worse yet, as writers of literature. The "tone of the historian," the calm, unapologizing voice of serious purposes engaged with wholly adequate instruments which Henry James coveted for the novelist seems now hopelessly lost to historians.

The word "history" has two current colloquial uses that we habitually conflate. The first amounts to a vague gesture that asserts our belief in the uninterrupted actuality of past persons and events; this establishes a category, THE REAL PAST, which is nearly empty but essential to all human purposes. The second is the specific name for a complex cultural artifact of language describing past events and asserting a truth claim as the condition of its writer/reader contract.[6] This establishes a category that is full, susceptible to analysis, and available for knowledge. The recent, specifically modern refusal to call this artifact "literature" is an interesting cultural neurosis involving many interlocking strands of counterphobic denial, displacement, fear of identity dissolution, and gender anxiety. And yet historians are determined practitioners of the "reality effect" and custodians of the representational virtue of prose: the claim that sometimes, under certain publicly shared, self-imposed disciplines, extended mimesis in language can be accepted as a portion of justified belief about the real world.

We professional historians have a vested interest in confusing the two meanings of "history" partly because that allows us to finesse the problems involved in our claims to truth and factuality and mainly because it allows us to pretend that we are not centrally involved with writing, with literature, with (the ultimate threat) fiction.[7] One of the core problems is that even empiricists who believe that historical facts are "given" and not made, present in reality and not fabricated in any way, must concede that *time* itself is not presented to experience in units, segments, centuries, or anything but pure sequence and must be subjected to aggressive and artificial treatment before "events" can be located at all.[8] Facts can only exist (that is, be located, described, subjected to verification) on a grid of constructed chronology—and the one we use is breathtakingly artificial. But then any one would be. Even in the irresistible power of our chief origin myth, when God created light and fish and animals and ourselves, he neglected to control time.[9] That was left for us. And we called it narrative.

When the narrative approaches with a truth claim as its covering condition, we call it history, and it is made of words. It is "literature" because to confound literature with fiction alone is merely a category error; constructions of language exhibiting a certain degree of formal elaboration *or*, but not necessarily, fictionality, are what the category "literature" contains. Aristotle began this lucid definition when he mentioned the art that achieves a mimesis of reality with language alone (without music, that is) in prose or verse, and which, to his day, had no name.[10] This art includes drama, epic, and all forms of prose fiction, philosophy, judicial oratory, discourse of policy, and, whether we like it or not, history. And history, as long as we are parsing definitions, is always narrative. Again, just as literature is not only fiction, so narrative is not only sequential storytelling in the traditional modes. Narration renders time (that is, the sequence of events) meaningful. Historians never depict static "being"; they depict things "having come to be" and "in process of becoming" always already implicated in what "will become." Historians depict "process" even when they are, for the moment, laying out cross-sections of it. There has been no "return to narrative" in our discipline because history never went anywhere away from it. There was no such place to go.

Nothing seriously important is changed by regarding history as literature, as opposed to some form of knowledge acquisition (science, craft, formulation, discipline, and so on) that is verbal only in a secondary or accidental aspect. The cultural purposes and motives of history—the creation of meaningful knowledge of the past—remain. I am convinced the only rational hope for grounding history in a defensible truth claim (as a textual intention), and maintaining a distinction between history and fiction that can sustain more than cursory examination, depends on accepting that first category definition of history: literature. Then we have something demonstrable to talk about, which is certainly an improvement on irascible metaphysical waffling about "facts" that evaporate whenever we approach. Our turf is *literary historicity*: the precise conditions under which realist depiction becomes a candidate for inclusion in our knowledge of actuality. This project ought to compel our serious attention and respect. But it does not (except on the margins of the profession) and, I will even admit, it never has. The intimate combination of complex language and actual event, especially political event, has provoked suspicion and despair as long as there have been history and politics as we understand them.

To return to our roots—so fashionable now—the most impressive fact of the noble history of classical historiography is that the ancient Greeks almost forgot to invent it. At least they did not trouble themselves with accounts of actual events in prose until very late, culturally speaking, only after epic, lyric, tragedy, comedy, philosophy, public oratory, and legal argument were well developed. Once history, the mimesis of actuality in narrative prose, existed as a genre, the issues of accuracy (truth to actuality) and the intellectual and linguistic protocols for regulating historicity in prose were treated with boredom and manipulative indifference most of the time, wherever history was written. Sub specie aeternitatis, or at least the 2500 years of it relevant here, historical accuracy interested the Greeks for a moment in the fifth century B C., then no one at all in any rigorous sense until perhaps the seventeenth century, and with increasing intensity into our century. Not an impressive record, but worth thinking about.

The most interesting thesis concerning the late but impressive arrival of historiography on the Greek cultural scene is that suggested by Moses Finley in his brilliant essay, "Myth, Memory, and History." The question he confronts is why the Greeks suddenly required a new cultural form beginning with inquiry into the past and resulting in a continuous narrative that proposes human, secular explanations for complex events. "The new impulse," Finley suggests, "came from the classical polis, and in particular the Athenian polis, which for the first time, at least in western history, introduced politics as a human activity and then elevated it to the most fundamental social activity. A new look at the past was required."[11] Homer was never denigrated, but epic would not *do* for this new situation. I am selecting out a few facets of Finley's complex argument, but what Thucydides in particular wanted to "extract from events" was "the essence of politics and political behavior, the nature and consequences of power."[12]

Democratic politics (albeit in its early and exclusionary form) and history were connected activities from their beginnings. The impulse to write under the constricting protocol of literary historicity—thinking and writing within the limitations of our own local historicity (within human experience extended only by evidentiary reasoning)—is never very strong at the best of times. The mind *wants* fiction; that is, it wants to know beyond the mean and intolerable limitations of evidence. "Not-Fiction" is in essence a protocol of evidentiary discipline enacted in precise linguistic forms. History obeys that protocol, imposes the fictions of form alone on the raw sequence of time, and yet achieves narrative. (These are pure genre definitions; the actual cultural product is usually a far more contaminated thing.) The impulse to think and use language in this self-denying way is rare and sporadic, culturally fragile, and subject to severe epistemic slippage. Considered over *la longue durée,* the surprising thing is that it should ever have been attempted at all.

And yet there seems to have been something about life in a polis where citizens (however few) had to make decisions with real consequences that gave literature with an incorporated reality principle its first impetus. The Greeks, incidentally, immediately used their new literature to let us know just how profoundly nervous they were about conducting their political life with language alone, how nervous they were about all those debates, those endless speeches in the agora, those impossible decisions to be made by such imperfect men, who were manipulating real power with labile words. Herodotus, who celebrated democratic Athens for saving all of Greece from the autocratic Persian empire, also describes in admiring detail how the great general, Themistocles, creator of the Athenian navy, becoming disgusted with tedious debates and persuasion, lied to everyone, Greeks and Persians alike, played dirty tricks that would put the CIA to shame, and ruthlessly manipulated events to force the Greeks to stay and fight at Salamis. Herodotus has not a murmur of disapproval.[13] After all, because of these tricks the Greeks won.

Thucydides left us the chilling scene in which the vicious demagogue Cleon goaded an uncertain forum of Athenian citizens to execute or enslave the entire population of Mytilene with taunts that Athenian men were weaklings, just too, too clever for action; that they had become "regular speech-goers, and as for action, [they] merely listen to accounts of it," inebriated with words, they had become "victims of [their] own pleasure in listening," blind to facts, *unmanned*, as he heavily suggests.[14] Cleon was brutal and crude, but I think he speaks with the nervous energy of the author's real fears.

The recoil of historians from the "threat" of being writers is deeply connected to the despairing suspicions inevitable to every attempt at a free and uncoerced polity—a polity of words. The fear that language can unhinge the "reality effect" from reality, manipulate us with strange pleasures of the mind, confuse us, and render us unfit to recognize and describe reality, much less act on it, was a deep and specifically political anxiety long before Ferdinand de Saussure's seminar. Centuries after the

Greeks, Dr. Johnson summed up this attitude in his aphorism: "Words are the daughters of earth, but things are the sons of heaven." The gender anxiety here (fear of a duplicitous, superficial, and unstable Feminine) is just as available to women as to men, because it has nothing to do with sex and everything to do with culture.

But at least the Greeks had described the cultural territory in which the ability of words to convey what actually took place was crucial both to political life and to the literature that recorded and analyzed that life. Something very interesting had happened, but the issue disappeared, from literature and philosophy, as quickly as democracy disappeared from antiquity. (The Romans only began to write history in time to record the failure of their Republic.) If Moses Finley's ideas about the beginnings of Greek history writing have any extension beyond the classical experience, it might be that there is something about life in a polis, or a republic, or a constitutional monarchy that makes the protocol of historicity in language take on enough importance to be worth the effort. Or put the other way, that there is something about life in a monarchy, or a monastery, or a distant or totalitarian bureaucracy that drains some of the vital interest, the life, out of knowing what actually did happen. Fiction, after all, is a permission to the mind to act on its deepest and most compelling impulse—to *know* beyond the intolerable limits of life experience. History is a self-denying ordinance, a protocol of accepted restrictions and minute limitations; there has to be some overriding, collectively endorsed reason for accepting such a curb. Something palpable and living has to rest on it beyond an abstract notion of truth. What can it matter in a totalitarian state, where so little matters—to so few? The mind can turn to so much better purpose, to the perfections of religion, philosophy, or utopian visions, perhaps of revolution and an enforced millennial era. Citizens need a literature that is "history"—subjects do not.

The anger expressed openly or obliquely whenever history is threatened with literary redefinition (no longer "a record of fact" but "a discourse claiming to be fact") has to be connected with the anger nearly everyone feels with a politics, large or small, that is at once chaotic and rigid, exclusionary and impervious, secretive and shambling. The link between the citizen and the free state is the historicity of language, and we all attack it and fear for it with deep ambivalence. It is all we have and that infuriates us. In the modern age, the mark of a totalitarian regime is its ability and will to control information, to prevent the formation of anything resembling a disinterested record, and to substitute an ideologically constructed account. Only societies governed by their citizens need a clear protocol for establishing descriptions of events that all parties are compelled to accept, so that raw power does not define reality, and we currently are in a failure of nerve over precisely that.

The establishing conditions of literary historicity are not the overrefined occupation of a jaded culture. The ungrounding of history from the comfort of unexamined empiricist foundations has made it important again, politically important, that we actually begin to know what we are talking about when we use the words "fiction" and "history." The "face in the history books" is supposed to be the face of reality, even in a postmodern age. All the peoples of the Eastern bloc countries during the last half century knew what true literary historicity was *not* as they learned to disbelieve their government-controlled media, but with only a keyhole access to information, they only knew enough to make them deeply cynical, not enough to enable them to know anything. If language is all we have, then we must come to terms with it, because people who know just enough to believe nothing are just as impotent as the ones who believe everything they read.

NOTES

1 "The Art of Fiction" was first published in *Longman's Magazine*, September 1884; it was recently reprinted in Henry James, *Literary Criticism*, selected by Leon Edel (New York: The Library of America, 1984). James's classic essay, perhaps not as well read now as it is well known, does not propose that fiction has to be documentary in technique to speak "with the tone of the historian", the assurance and justified reality effect of the novel proceed from the mind and technical capacity of the writer.

2 By an "artifice committed to reality," I mean to focus attention on the *intention* of the maker, an intention understood through its intelligible effects, not on a (never to be) proven absolute correspondence between mimesis and reality.

3 The discussion took place at the 1990 meeting of the American Historical Association and was printed in *American Historical Review* 96 (1991). 675–708, as "AHR Forum: Peter Novick's *That Noble Dream*. The Objectivity Question and the Future of the Historical Profession "

4 Peter Novick, *That Noble Dream· The "Objectivity Question" and the American Historical Profession* (Cambridge. Cambridge University Press, 1988), and reprinted twice in 1989, again in 1990, and 1991. Much of the fascination with this book lies in its being the first modern detailed survey of "us," historians in America, our specific origins and how we came to be ourselves. Much of the controversy, however, concerns (1) whether Novick is precisely correct in his depiction (part 4) of how we are now, and (2) some ambiguity in his tone, whether he approves or condemns this state of affairs, and whether he is right or wrong to do so, whatever his feeling really is. The author has enthusiastically assisted in the controversy by sometimes denying what seems to be the unproblematical meaning of his statements, as in the "no king in Israel" quibble.

5 As just one publicly available example, see the exchange between F. R. Ankersmit, "Historiography and Postmodernism," *History and Theory* 28 (1989) 137–53, and Perez

Zagorin, "History and Postmodernism. Reconsiderations," *History and Theory* 29 (1990) 263–74, as well as Ankersmit's "Reply to Professor Zagorin," *History and Theory* 29 (1990). 275–96, in which both historians treat each other as if beneath notice, pointedly ignoring each other's statements and concerns.

6 The most rigorous and lucid explanation of the precise conditions under which texts are classified correctly as fiction or history is that of Meir Sternberg, *The Poetics of Biblical Narrative Ideological Literature and the Drama of Reading* (Bloomington: Indiana University Press, 1985), chap 1. "For history-writing is not a record of fact—of what 'really happened'—but a discourse that claims to be a record of fact Nor is fiction-writing a tissue of free inventions but a discourse that claims freedom of invention. The antithesis lies not in the presence or absence of truth value but of the commitment to truth value" (26) Sternberg is the only critic I have yet found who draws a firm distinction between the verifiability of statements *in* a text and the governing conditions of the entire text, and thus is able to make sense of textual genre.

7 One of the most contentious ideas introduced into scholarly discussion of the essential nature of history has been that narrative, or indeed any intelligible, complex sequence in prose achieved through selection and linguistic devices for expressing comparison and emphasis, is a *form of fiction*, a formal fiction in the sense of a thing made and not found Historians both concede and resist this indubitable insight because it seems to many to threaten the status of historical knowledge; any taint of "the made" as opposed to "the found" opens this threat This idea, of the "fictionality" of linguistic structure, even a linguistic structure containing no freely invented statements, is the core of Hayden White's ongoing discussions of written history, presented with special nuance and precision in *The Content Of The Form Narrative Discourse and Historical Representation* (Baltimore Johns Hopkins University Press, 1987), especially chap. 1, "The Value of Narrativity in the Representation of Reality"

8. The artificiality of time-made-intelligible, that time sequences displaying the signatures of plot are always and invariably creations of the human mind, is central to Aristotle's discussion of literature in the *Poetics* and the reason that book remains central to all discussion of language and reality in the Western tradition

9 The Genesis story presents the idea of the cycle of the week, but offers no anchor for locating subsequent events on a larger scale of time None of the historians of antiquity attempted that with the exception of Thucydides when he used "the first year of the war" as the fixed point from which he located all subsequent events Had the brilliance of this device been recognized in antiquity, all Western history might have been dated from the first year of the Peloponnesian War.

10 Aristotle, *Poetics*, trans. Gerald F. Else (Ann Arbor University of Michigan Press, 1967). "There is further an art which imitates by language alone, without harmony, in prose or in verse. ... This form of imitation is to this day without a name" (1.1 1447a29–1447b10) The word "literature" in its older colloquial sense of "all complex verbal compositions (which may be but are not necessarily fictional)" is the concept that covers Aristotle's definition

11 Moses I Finley, "Myth, Memory and History," in *The Use and Abuse of History* (London: Chatto & Windus, 1975), 30.

12 "Thucydides found himself caught up in contradictory pulls, which he was never able to resolve. He accepted the need to narrate events in sequence, but on the other hand he wished to extract from the events the essence of politics and political behaviour, the nature and consequences of power That, if he could achieve it, would be a 'possession forever', among other reasons because human nature is a constant and therefore recurrence is the pattern" (Finley, "Myth, Memory and History," 31)

13 Herodotus, *The History*, trans David Grene (Chicago University of Chicago Press, 1987); the main sequence of events is 8 56–8 123 Hearing that the Acropolis had been burned, the Athenians at Salamis wanted to leave, their allies wished to return to their cities as well

After arguments seemed to be failing, Themistocles sent a servant to the Persians to tell them that he was a secret adherent of the Persian cause, and invited them to attack soon, which they did while the Greek naval force was still intact at Salamis Themistocles admitted his tactical trick to Aristides, and told him to tell the Greeks that they were encircled and would have to fight their way out It seems clear that Herodotus admires this manipulation of events because Themistocles' strategy was, after all, the best one for defeating the Persians.

14. This sequence recounting the suppression of the attempted revolt of the subject city of Mytilene stands in clear analogy with the speech of Pericles at the funeral rites for the first dead of the war Pericles' speech specifically celebrates the polis in which policy was rationally debated and the ability to imagine different points of view did not undermine Athenian ability to act and fight with resolution once a decision was made. A year later, after more deaths, the plague, and the death of Pericles, debate had become a debilitating play of emotion, and Thucydides gives the demagogue a fearful plausibility: "The blame is yours, for stupidly instituting these competitive displays. You have become regular speech-goers, and as for action, you merely listen to accounts of it. .." (Thucydides, *The Peloponnesian War*, trans Rex Warner [Harmondsworth, U K.. Penguin Books, 1954], 214)

2

How Old Is Our Cultural Past?

JUDITH SCHLANGER

ONE HUNDRED YEARS

When I suggested this title, I certainly had no intention of looking for a numerical answer. What I wanted to do was explore the question of cultural memory and, to be more specific, the link between value and time. But it so happens that although nobody would look for a numerical answer nowadays, a figure has been tagged to cultural memory. I refer to Horace's notion that we can be sure of a work if it has been around for one century: "Est vetus atque probus centum qui perficit annos" (If it has rounded up to one hundred years, a work is old and serious") (Horace, *Epistles* 2.1., 39).

This has been quoted all along to support the notion that the judgment of history has the final say in cultural matters. As far as cultural value is concerned, time will indeed tell. A new work has to go through what has been called the test of time, and if it does, then its survival will guarantee its worth, and its worth its survival. It is a circle in which duration is both a delay and a sign, a test and a reward.

It so happens that this long-standing use of Horace's line takes it completely out of context. For about a hundred verses, the *Epistle* discusses the question of the old and the new and cultural value. How does the age of literary works (their being ancient or novel) relate to their appreciation? How is the recognition of present accomplishments different from the judgment of previous works? What is our problem with novelty? Why does admiration look backward to what is already here and has been with us for a long time? What gives the distance of the past its privilege? Why are we more critical toward a contemporary writer than toward an ancient classical writer we have studied at school? And why do we make so much of archaic fragmentary texts, the more obscure the better? How are we to understand the double standard of literary judgment: veneration for the old and distrust toward the new?

Horace asked all these questions from the standpoint of a "modern." With the Greeks, admittedly, the oldest works are also the best; it was not so with the Romans of Horace's time, and it was sheer prejudice to reject the present and to prefer the past. This conservative prejudice took then and still takes several shapes: inertia (what was important when I was young cannot become obsolete); snobbishness (it is chic to prefer what is out of reach and difficult to grasp); hostility and envy (dead authors are a weapon against the living). Appreciation, admiration, rejection, said Horace, all belong to the present; we decide now. Each period is empowered to judge its present and its past. However, this does not make the situation more secure, and poets are in bad shape anyway. For Horace, nothing is more uncertain than success that depends on the judgment of the public, as public taste is subject to change and error. The theater is a good example: where there was previously a taste for crude situations, there is now a taste for pageants and showy decorations. Thus present-day judgment is either conservative or vulgar, and the contemporary poet loses both ways. This gives Horace's analysis its tragic nuance: recognition and fame all hang by rights on present-day appreciation, but without Augustus, there would have been no true judge, which means that adequate judgment can only be mythical.

At some point in this discussion, Horace makes fun of the notion that works, like wine, mature while they wait. If the only good author is a dead author, and posthumous reputations are the only ones to trust, what is the right delay? One hundred years? Here comes the logical paradox known as the sorites: if you take out just one month or year, just one grain of wheat, just one hair, when is the century no longer a century, when does the heap of wheat become a handful, when does a horse no longer have a tail? How can a century, or any measure of time, be a meaningful criterion? How can time pertain to success and value?

So the point is not whether to wait or not to wait. The point is not whether this much-quoted line tells us that we should or should not wait in order to be sure of a given work's importance. What is at stake here is the very strong linkage, the essential linkage between value and time, appreciation and survival, this linkage that defines cultural memory. How are we to understand the time component that comes with cultural value? How old is "old"? What age is "serious"? What does the past tell us about value?

I would like to understand Horace's hundred years and his discussion of the old and the new through another measure of time. Auguste Comte suggests that everyone (or, as he puts it, every man) has a period of thirty years in which he can think. How are we to understand that? If we take it as a measure (thirty years? not twenty-nine and a half? never thirty-one?), then it does not tell us anything especially meaningful about intellectual life.

But these thirty years become a much more interesting idea if we see them as a kind of umbrella hovering over us, something like the temporal range of the mind. I am not speaking about the range of psychological memory but about everyone's private world of intellectual and professional interests. It makes some sense to see ourselves as somewhere in the middle of a range of some thirty years which is more or less the scope of what we encompass at any point, the scope of our intellectual concerns, projects, and activities. We may not stand always right in the middle of our own spotlight: where we stand depends on what kind of thing we do at one period or another; and it also changes, presumably, according to age. It is easy to assume that when one is very young, most of one's interests and projects look ahead, but that age tends to make a mind assert its feeling of continuity with its own previous intuitions and ideas and anticipate less.

If we take Comte's remark to indicate the territorial expanse of our thinking at any point, then I think it becomes wiser and less arbitrary. It points to a rather illuminating distinction between intellectual time and biographical time. It shows the thinking mind as closely linked to a person's lifespan, of course, but it also shows that intellectual time is nevertheless a specific time that has its own ways of dealing with duration and age.

I would like to understand Horace's hundred years and his discussion of time and culture along the same lines as Auguste Comte's thirty years; that is, to take them out of one time (the chronological time of history) and bring them into another (the nonsequential time of memory). Let me try to show this through a specific example.

ONE CENTURY AGO

My example is one of the numerous schoolbooks published in late nineteenth-century France in the wake of the education reform of Jules Ferry in 1881. That is, at a time of considerable turmoil and expansion in the field of education (with the institution of compulsory schooling for boys and girls), which was also a time of institutional reshuffling for literature, a reshuffling of the conceptual approach to literary studies and of the ideological role of literature as a main subject.

For the teaching of literature, this is an interesting period but a difficult time. My schoolbook is a book of transition between established but crumbling views and new conceptions that have not yet built an alternative body of knowledge. This intermediate position does not mean that the book stands somewhere in the middle, between frameworks, in some neutral place, more bland in its outlook than any of them, or partly this and partly that. It means, on the contrary, that it tries to hold everything together and, therefore, carries the full weight and confusion of both views. Trying to modernize, save, and restore an old model is a huge intellectual investment we do not pay much attention to, because in the long run it is always bound to fail, and we tend to ignore the strength, attention, and wit that have been invested into rearguard invention. The book's position is complex, too complex: this makes it unwieldy, difficult, and therefore unsteady and short-lived.

The work of a teacher named A. Henry, this (now obscure) schoolbook, "ouvrage autorisé par M. le Ministre de l'instruction publique (1881)," is one of the numerous schoolbooks that were issued and tried out in the schools and colleges, all subject to official (governmental) approval. What I have seen is its tenth edition in 1890.

The book sets out to provide a "Cours critique et historique de littérature... dans les trois langues classiques,"[1] following official instructions from 1885. Literature in the three classical languages, Greek, Latin, and French: this is a far cry from what the regular outlook was some two centuries earlier when Racine wrote to his teenage son not to read French literature as long as he was a pupil because it was too easy and a waste of time. By the end of the nineteenth century, French literature had become a major subject; however, the notion of a common approach to the three literatures (and of a common treatment of all three) points to a moment when legitimacy comes from both sides: French literature seems more intelligible when seen as part of the classical tradition, and the classical tradition more relevant when related to French literature.

The material is organized according to the old classical grid of the literary genres, although the grid has been modified (distorted, adapted) in several ways. Within this grid, each genre is dealt with not only in chronological order but also with some consideration of the historical grounding and succession of the works so that the textbook is both systematic (in a way that was already obsolete when the book was published) and historical (the blurred shape of what is about to win the day).

That is not an easy stand, nor is it entirely inadequate. For instance, this approach is able to bring to the fore a large amount of nonfictional prose, such as formal political or academic discourse, forensic or religious or intellectual eloquence; that is, it can deal with a large amount of the nineteenth-century literary production that we fail now to perceive and describe, since we have no categories for it. The textbook is far from being absurd; nevertheless, it is quite awkward, and I will point to two of its problems.

One is a problem in overall proportions, a matter of architectonics. According to the classical grid of categories, the epic poem is a major form and therefore should also contribute an important section of the book, but French literature happens to have a problem (a very interesting problem) with the epic form. From Ronsard to Chateaubriand, there were so many debates about the epic poem that the view of what an epic should be became too heavily loaded with normative constraints. The site (a French epic worthy of inclusion in the book) was emphasized, and there was a general agreement that it should be taken up by an important work; much had been elaborated on the norms and constraints of this work and still the site remained empty. Not that a number of epic poems had not been written all along, but the normative dimension was so overwhelming that every writer's prime concern was to conform to it, and no work was deemed worthy of the category. Expectations were so tight that success was impossible.

The best contender to the title was Voltaire's *Henriade*: at the beginning of the nineteenth century, *La Henriade* had indeed made it according to the teachers. But if the teachers admired the book, the writers did not, and the book was demoted. By the end of the nineteenth century, the general assessment was that French literature had no great epic poem.

After describing the obvious Greek and Latin epics, and the best French tries, the book resorts to four modern foreign epics (Italian, Portuguese, English, German). This is about the only description of foreign literature. In order to fill out the contents of an important form with a proportional number of pages, the book had to import foreign successes, but it did so reluctantly since it saw the lack of all-around self-sufficiency as a weakness for French literature. We find ourselves in a logic of national literature in which there is no discussion why French should be the third "classical language," on a par with the other two. This *Cours critique et historique de littérature* is not interested in the plurality of national literatures (an attitude that at that time was not confined to the French-speaking world). The notion is that one should find everything at home in one's own tradition anchored in the classics, which are, precisely, not foreign.

That was the first problem, the problem of having an important form lacking adequate contents. The second problem I want to point to is exactly the opposite: having an important, massive production outside the classical grid. I am referring, of course, to the novel, and the nineteenth-century problem of what to do, at a theoretical level, with the genre of the novel is clearly not specifically French. How does this textbook deal with the novel?

The novel comes as a short addition to the last chapter, a chapter devoted to the genre of letter-writing: "We have still to deal with the Novel. One should think that a book specially dedicated to young people is not the place to dwell on this kind of work." But the teachers have been officially directed to point out to the students the overwhelming growth of the novel in the nineteenth century: "Therefore let us talk about them and fill a blank for which this unassuming book has been reproached more than once. [Which indicates that the first editions managed to avoid the subject altogether.] But shall we be taxed with austere puritanism, if we first remind the pupils of the drawbacks of reading this kind of work?"

Up to now the book has been in a didactic mode. Here it switches to a moralistic diatribe against the novel as frivolous fiction and against novel reading for teenagers, in or out of school. This view was neither new nor surprising at the time, and it takes up two pages out of the six that deal with the novel. The next couple of pages take us through some Greek and Latin romances as well as through the French novel up to the nineteenth century. And the last two pages flash past nineteenth-century novels, in unhappy compliance with official regulations.

I will not comment on what is selected, omitted, admired, explained through this sketchy run. I will come directly to the last remarks of the chapter (and of the book). While trying to assess the contemporary French novel of the 1880s ("However, how can we not include Gustave Flaubert, when his friends keep saying that he is a milestone in the history of the novel in our age." This is not very enthusiastic, especially when followed by a mention of similar claims from M. Jules Verne's admirers), the book concludes: "Lastly, we would personally regret not to add that the heads of the family, confronted with the wild imaginings, the abjection, and lewdness of 'naturalism,' take comfort from reading with their children Cardinal Wiseman's *Fabiola*, or the pure and engaging stories of Mr. Jules Girardin or Mrs. Colomb." Which brings in Wiseman's *Fabiola* and concludes with yet another foreign import at a time (the Fachoda decade) when no Frenchman would willingly admit to British superiority of any kind—so great is the need for a solace for the awfulness of naturalism and an antidote to a novelist "abject and lewd," too low to be named: Zola.

My question is, what did it take for the French nineteenth-century novel to receive pride of place in high school? Take for instance the reluctantly named Flaubert and the aggressively unnamed Zola. Since then (and that was several upheavals ago), nineteenth-century novelists have indeed become "serious" authors, modern French classics, and therefore part of French literary education. But what did it take for this to happen?

I am not asking how it did happen; mine is not a historical question. Nor am I addressing the sociopolitical and ideological aspects of the transformation. I am looking at a more abstract level, asking what had to change in the overall poetic setup for this to take place. It is not enough to say that the French modern classics have been substituted for the Greek and Latin classics in the sense that one body of works or one population of names has been replaced by another. In order for this to happen, much more had to change—not only the terms but also the relations between the terms, not only the contents but the expectations.

CLOSENESS AND DISTANCE

I will point (quite briefly) to some of the transformations entailed by the new status of Flaubert, Zola, and others as modern French classics. The first is the general pedagogical outlook. Let us take the purely symbolic point in time of Rousseau's *L'Emile* in 1762. Up to then, the teaching of letters (both at the elementary level and at the more complex level of *belles-lettres*) did not even try to bridge the distance between the student and the subject. To the contrary, teaching was deliberately built around an artificial world, the world of pedagogical distance.

School tasks were defined to avoid any contiguity with real-life experience; they were meant to be far-fetched. Look at this ancient Egyptian assignment (found among the Fayoum clay tablets): "A boy, who has just killed his father, takes flight to the desert, where he fears wild beasts and the wrath of the gods. Give voice to his feelings." Or look at Diderot's first assignment at the Collège d'Harcourt at age ten: "Nero has ordered his mother killed; Agrippina's last words—'Strike my belly'—are reported to him. Show what goes through his mind." And not only are the themes not realistic (one hopes), but since the Renaissance, this very consistent pedagogy draws from a world that is by definition far away, out of reach and closed.

For about the last two centuries (or symbolically, since *L'Emile*), this approach has been challenged by another ideal pedagogy, a pedagogy of closeness and relevance, which would bring the subjects near the child at the center of her or his world. I am not saying that this other ideal is in fact implemented. It certainly was not implemented in turn-of-the-century France, but by the 1890s pedagogical distance had become an issue. The debate about the educational status of the French modern classics has not been a debate about the novel, but a quarrel about Latin—a quarrel about the world of distance, its language and contents, and about the necessity of temporal displacement.

Another point concerns the teaching of literature. Up to the late nineteenth century, it was a rhetorical preparation, a preparation in applied poetics. The student of literature went through a kind of apprenticeship and acquired a practical, technical craft. As can be seen from the examples I have just mentioned, the pupil was asked to compose pieces that were directly and closely related to the main body of literature. The idea was to learn to write more of the same. This was supposed to be a schooling in literary appreciation through the writing of literature.

By the end of the nineteenth century, this practical approach gave way to an intellectual approach. Since then, to be trained in literature was to be trained in critical writing and critical distanciation. One is not asked to use or imitate some aspects of a work, but to comment on it. However realistic the work, its thematic closeness is offset by its intellectual treatment. Flaubert or Zola can be brought into the classroom if the assignment is not to rewrite a love scene but to analyze one.

My third remark also points to a shift in closeness and distance. Kant once remarked that it is a very good thing that the models of taste should be monuments in dead languages. This was indeed understood to be the ideal situation. In a situation in which one is shut off from the world of models by a radical gap in language and civilization and in which it is obviously impossible to add to its monuments, one is free. The setup provides both nurture and freedom.

Because the ancient classics were out of reach in so many ways, they were utterly at one's disposal. They could be cannibalized for parts like an old car. The proper demonstration of admiration for the classics was to plunder them. There is a story about Milton's widow that ties it up nicely. She was asked some very leading questions by Milton's admirers, such as, "Was it not the case that her husband asked to be read the classics very often?" "Was not her husband used to expressing great admiration for the classics?" And Milton's widow answered indignantly that her husband did not have to read the classics, as he had no need to steal from them since the Holy Spirit had spoken to him every night. This answer is in perfect agreement with the general understanding at the time that inspiration must come *from* somewhere and that looting to get it is fine.

Not so with the modern classics. Whereas the Greek and Latin classics were radically cut off and therefore as close as one cared to bring them, the modern (national) classics were near—and therefore set up as out of reach.

Modern classics were set up as such in the wake of the romantic view that they were works of genius and that such works do appear from time to time and will continue to do so in a mysterious way. In what sense were they to be called models? Their greatness was not seen as the greatness of perfection, but as the greatness of genius—genius itself being seen as unique, extraordinary, and indeed anomalous. Perfection may be brought to practical use by ordinary persons but not so genius. Instead of a cultural distance, genius sets up a heroic distance. One has to relate differently to a work of genius, for its relevance and its fruitfulness are oblique.

The Greek and Latin classics were relevant methodologically, as models (with somewhat mixed results), and substantially, as sources. The great moderns, however, were enigmatic beacons, illuminating rather than providing. With Flaubert, for instance, the point could not be, quite obviously, to draw from his work in order to write something akin to what he wrote, but rather to wish to play the same kind of role and to win the same kind of reputation, as well as to share an overwhelming concern for deontology. Thus, the moderns were relevant as paradigms (the writer as a major figure, a role model) and axiologically, in terms of attitudes and values.

OLD PRESENT, NEW PAST

The institution of the modern French classics was a multiple shift: a shift in closeness and distance, a shift in the nature and level of relevance, a shift in expectations and focus. All those adjustments and transformations dealt with distance and the regulation of distance. In fact, they were shifts in memory. This brings us back to the distinction I suggested earlier between historical time and cultural time.

Historical time displays a linear past, a past organized by its chronological order. Historically, what happened twenty centuries ago stands further away from us than what took place one century ago: Horace is further than Comte and Flaubert, and the *Cours de littérature* nearer than both. But this scheme does not pertain to the time of cultural memory, for memory is not organized along those lines. Whether Comte is perceived as close and Flaubert as distant, does not depend on the calendar. Whether the obscure French schoolbook I have brought in is interesting, and what kind of survival it can hope for, is not a matter of dates, but of focus.

Most philosophies of culture in the twentieth century do not elaborate any more on the timelessness of the great works of art whose scope and value are universal. They define the classic in relation to time, in terms of survival and duration: a masterpiece is a work that does not remain embedded in its original context and therefore becomes transhistorical or dyschronic. This is supposed to be the specific property of the classic or the masterpiece.

To mention just a couple of examples: the young Georg Lukács, in his early aesthetics, stresses the paradoxical mode of existence of the great work of art. On the one hand, it is the perfect expression of its own time, the most acute incarnation of the historical moment; on the other hand, it is endowed with the strange property of staying always new. The masterpiece does not age: it stays newborn all along, never losing its "freshness." The great work of art therefore belongs to divergent temporal dimensions, which makes it a paradoxical historical being.

Gadamer's notion of a specific experience, temporal but nonhistorical, which enables us to meet ancient works somewhere on neutral ground, deals with the problems that arise when the past is understood as the display of successive periods, events, and monuments.[2] Where the distance is considered to be a given, what has to be explained is the transgression of the sequential order; that is, how we can cross the past, or how parts of the past can escape and join us.

But within memory, to put it bluntly, there are no meetings across time since the contents of memory are by definition simultaneous. What has to be explained, therefore, is the distance; that is, the fact that the contents can have different time tags. Here the distance is not a given, but a construct; indeed, meaningful distance is part of what is at stake.

One rather striking illustration of a dyschronic past is Eric Hobsbawm's *Invention of Tradition,* which shows how the main political traditions of present Europe were instituted about one century ago but with special time tags.[3] Some of them have been initiated as having always been there. This goes for nonpolitical institutions as well, such as folklore. One of the most enjoyable parts of the book refers to the Scottish kilt and tartan, invented by the mid-nineteenth century for commercial purposes and implemented *as* traditional and medieval— with total success in changing everybody's memory of the Scottish past. A similar point can be made with another example, a political example not drawn from Hobsbawm's book. The official implementation of the cult of the Emperor in the 1920s in Japan was a novelty that was expressly set up *as* traditional and immemorial.

Why is it possible to create the new as old and how does it work? It works because this spurious antiquity is accepted from the start not as a delusion (although it becomes a delusion very quickly), but as a qualifier, as a tag among other tags. That is, because cultural memory has a dyschronic organization. The contents of memory exist through focus and status; they exist as major or minor, central or peripheral, close or distant, relevant or obsolete, establishment or underground, among or above, invaluable or junk, and so forth.

The past of memory is not laid out behind us in its proper sequential order: it is none other than today's contents. The past of memory takes place now, here, currently, right away. Some of its contents are tagged as old, or very old, or brand new, and old can mean always reliable, already passé, delightfully archaic, younger than ever, boring as usual. By calling a work old in Horace's sense, as "old and serious," old and important, old and relevant, we point to the fact that it is present in a special way that we want to emphasize: to have been around for one hundred years means to have been received and received as already transmitted. Or, to put it differently, it is a third-generation immigrant. If something has been handed down, not only once, but twice already, then it has "always" been around.

I am not suggesting that the world began one hundred years ago, but that the past of cultural memory is not as remote as its historical contents. In the time-and-value linkage of culture, existence—survival—is not duration, but enactment. The historical contents may have been drawn from far away, but the issues are enacted or reenacted now. Thus memory can have both a long reach (for the past is a wealthy dimension) and a short span (as problematic concerns change so quickly).

One last point. The historical chronological past of cultural monuments and the present past of cultural memory entail very different attitudes. If we look at the past as at a huge body of accomplishments, then of course what we see is overwhelmingly rich and valuable. It is also a self-sufficient landscape, to be known, cherished, and admired through knowledge and contemplation. In relation to such a treasure, the present moment seems quite shallow. It now appears as not only fleeting but also poor, unless it draws its depth and scope from this previous wealth. In this view, the present time has no weight and no privilege as its only cultural legitimacy is to be, to paraphrase T. S. Eliot, the present moment of the past.

Not so with the present past of memory. It tells a story of shifts and turmoils, of decisions, resurrections, and loss, a rather ruthless story that does not call for a contemplative attitude but builds a precedent for change. This is a past in which existence means attention, in which focus means survival, and in which memory is a conquest. This is a past that draws on our strength, an ever-changing past, fascinating and new.

NOTES

1. A Henry, *Cours critique et historique de littérature à l'usage de tous les établissements d'instruction secondaire ou la poésie et la prose dans les trois langues classique* (Paris. Librairie Belin, 1890).

2 Hans-Georg Gadamer, *Truth and Method* (New York: Crossroad, 1975), 263–67

3. See Eric Hobsbawm and Terence Rauger, eds., *The Invention of Tradition* (Cambridge. Cambridge University Press, 1993)

3

The Humor of the Present

ISABELLE STENGERS

Translated by Richard Cooper

Judith Schlanger raises the question in "How Old Is Our Cultural Past?": What is it that "dates" the kind of judgment pronounced on the French novel by an author of a late nineteenth-century literature manual? What has made it possible for us to read these novels as comprising part of our present, whereas the text that comments on them belongs to an outdated history, an object of investigation in a history of ideas no longer our own. Schlanger makes clear that she is not asking a historical question to which a narrative can respond. Nor does she question the sociopolitical and ideological determinants of historical change to which narratives point. She tells us that she will pose the question at a "more abstract" level. My commentary is an attempt to think through this abstraction with her.

An initial remark: the abstraction with which we are concerned denies neither history nor the sociopolitical context of our cultural past. On the contrary. But, from the outset, Schlanger is not concerned with the changing status of the classics in our memory as the consequence of a general law. To foreground a causal relation allows one to judge, to categorize, that is to say, to forget the singular, practical effects. Let us dwell for a moment on the child Diderot imagining what Nero might really have thought when the last words of his mother, Agrippina, were reported to him. I am not sure that this momentary thought leaves us altogether unscathed. As Schlanger reminds us, critical commentary, which today seems to us so natural, creates distance. "Flaubert or Zola can be brought into the classroom if the assignment is not to rewrite a love scene but to analyze it" ("How Old Is Our Cultural Past?" 20). The momentary presence of the child Diderot among us has, I believe, practical effects. He disturbs the tranquillity of the sociopolitical analyst. After all, the sociopolitical analyst occupies one of the positions defined by the "critical commentary." How could he or she avoid the temptation to judge his or her "distanced" practice as "normal"? Direct sociopolitical questions assume that the critical practices of the present are more "normal" than those of the past. They assume a link between the scholarly, academic rehabilitation of the novel and the triumph of a liberty that was not accessible to our predecessors. They assume, further, an essential progressivist conquest, whatever precautions we take with the term "progress."

The abstraction that Judith Schlanger invites us to consider is not antihistorical. Rather, its first effect is to historicize the present. It allows the idea of change to escape the staging of a progress that leads up to us, without, however—and this is the most important point—leading us to an exhausting "deconstruction" of progress, the critique of a critique, a mourning indefinitely reworked, a placing under suspicion that obsessively denies a possible link between suspicion and progress. Schlanger's abstraction has something to do with humor, with the possibility of living our present not as that which must be the end, the ne plus ultra, but as that which will pass. That which will pass not in the sense in which it would be insignificant—the position of irony—but in the sense of a past that is not finished, that has not been and cannot be passed beyond, because it may always rise again, "fascinating and new." Since Schlanger has given existence to the child Diderot imagining Nero thinking of Agrippina, I find myself aware of the possibility of other pasts—as well as of other presents. And what if the memory of this child should one day belong to a past that will exceed and perplex the recollection of today's children, learning to appreciate Flaubert's genius in the sociopolitical context of his age? The abstraction that Schlanger proposes has the effect of "dechronologizing" history, of transforming history as we narrate it, as it imposes itself on us as that which must be narrated. The effect of the narration is to tell us about ourselves while it recounts the past.

But, then, should we not be concerned that Schlanger's abstraction may effectively transform history—this memory which today is ours—into pure arbitrariness, into a mere fabrication that will pass like all the rest? Again, we confront irony, which is the typical position of one who apparently despairs—"If God does not exist, everything is permitted"—in order better to affirm behind the scenes that, in the end, the ultimate position of lucidity has been attained. Ne plus ultra.

Yet again, the practical effects of Schlanger's abstraction respond to this despair. For to define memory in terms of production in the present upsets only those who remain haunted in their very despair by the ideal of a "true" memory, of a present that would acquire by right the power to judge once and for all its past. To define memory by the method of "focusing" that invents the image or by the "status" that distributes judgments does not mean that invention and distribution are arbitrary. Schlanger has always emphasized that one does not invent pertinent and interesting ideas at will. Our method of producing the past is certainly self-interested. It is nonetheless interesting. It is a work, our work, with its risks, problems, and adventures. For the past to be lived as a work does not as such liberate us from it as if by magic, nor does it take away interest in this past.

Perhaps it may even be that when the past is lived as a work it becomes enriched by other risks, problems, and adventures. The question is: What risks and new interests does Schlanger's abstraction open for us? How does it sensitize us to our interests of the present? A new present that will bear its new truth of the past, certainly—but otherwise, that will re-create what it understands by truth, certainly—but otherwise. Those are the practical effects of what I have called humor: to know, and to explore the effects of knowing that, by definition, the power of judging granted us by the newness that history creates in and through us is nothing more than one of the effects of this newness. Perhaps Schlanger's abstraction proposes a new power of judging—a humorous power of judging that would free relativism from pejorative connotation. Perhaps there is another present, fascinating and new, and through Schlanger's abstraction it is already here.

To explore somewhat more precisely the effects of this humor of the present, I have chosen a field in which the existence of a dynamic between the present and memory has already been elucidated, a field with which I am also most familiar—the sciences. More precisely—because the distinction seems to me necessary—it is the field of those sciences that do not have to consider that the subject of their analysis can interpret or anticipate or mislead their questions, in the way a human being, a text, or a rat can.

The history of science is well known for its difficulty. I shall take a single but telling example. Few writers on science are as attentive to its history as Stephen Jay Gould. Let us look at Gould's review of Martin Rudwick's book *The Great Devonian Controversy*.[1] Gould combines a profound respect for Rudwick's work with a "structural" criticism. Rudwick, within the domain of the history of science, has submitted himself to the imperative that is supposed to define the very craft of the historian: not to read the events of the past in the light of later ones. For Gould, if the principle is undeniably legitimate, its practical result is, as it happens, disastrous. The narrative constructed in this way is in fact comprehensible only to those who are already familiar with the history of geological dating in the nineteenth century and know how the subsequent history has placed a coherent interpretation on the data that divided the protagonists in the "Devonian controversy."

The narrative strategy adopted by Rudwick is faithful to history. It reproduces in the reader's mind the dense confusion of facts, clues, and arguments that produced the codification of the history of the earth. But was it necessary to reproduce this confusion in the reader's mind? Should one subject the reader to such an ordeal? Surely, remarks Gould, "mystery writers don't tell the end at the beginning, but even their most complex stories are orders of magnitude simpler than the Devonian controversy" (*Urchin*, 90). Let us underline this remarkable point: no "purely human" story would have the density and complexity of the entangled multiple stories that combined ambitions, arguments, interpretations, clues, and geological strata.

Gould joins a second, "conceptual," criticism to the first. The history narrated by Rudwick does not end like a detective story with "everything...cleared up." Rudwick resists the temptation to stage the truth of the earth as a reconciliation between the protagonists. He chooses, rather, to recount the resolution of the controversy as a purely social construction, as a successful negotiation between contending positions. Here, too, Rudwick is faithful to the imperative that defines the contemporary requirements of the history of science. The earth is not entitled to bring about an agreement among the protagonists in a controversy, for it is closure of the controversy, the production of agreement, that determines what the earth has to say to geologists and how it says it. But, remarks Gould, the narrative method chosen by Rudwick frustrates the reader. It prohibits him or her from articulating what he or she cannot help surmising: if the principles of dating that emerged from the controversy are those we still use today, they are not *only* a social construction and the result of a negotiation.

Rudwick—and with him all those who recognize in his book the great merit of having restored the history of the dating of the earth to a human history "like the others"—might say, "Very well. Let the reader be frustrated. Let him or her be confused. The reader is seeking irrepressibly to judge yesterday's history by today's truth and to give scientific truth a status that transcends human beings and societies." Confronted with this verdict, Gould has the notable courage to defend the thankless position of "I agree, but . . ." If we remember the great Devonian controversy, it is *nevertheless* because we are now able to understand it. If Rudwick can tell the story so expertly, it is *nevertheless* because even if the discipline of the historian imposes a certain silence on him, he now knows why such-and-such a protagonist was able in good faith to maintain such-and-such a position. It is *nevertheless* because—as important as was the role played in this story by human beings, their ideas and passions, and by institutions and their power relations—the earth itself, indeed, the "earth in-itself" played an irreducible role.

How can Gould, or I, dare to give to the "earth in-itself" the right to intervene in the narration? How could it when its right to speech depends on the intermediary role of its different, contending representatives? When the earth can become the subject of consensual representation only through the closure of the controversy? This is indeed the truth in the name of which we have undertaken to rewrite the past of our sciences. This is the truth that Gould reproaches Rudwick for having followed too seriously, without humor.

If we look closely, however, the "earth in-itself" has already appeared implicitly in Rudwick's narrative: through the complexity of the controversy, the density of which is incommensurable with the purely human intrigues that we can imagine, in the passion itself of the protagonists, each attached to criteria that contradict those of the others but which they all knew would have to be reconciled, without knowing how. Even if the earth has no power independent of its representatives, it does have the power to tie up the controversy and to impede its representatives from coexisting in indifference. This could have been its only power. Controversies exist that have not been resolved. In our case, *it happens that* the "earth in-itself" intervened by yet another means. The Devonian controversy, like plate tectonics, according to Gould, constitutes a "sweet" victory in geological knowledge. The analyst will protest: victory is proclaimed by the victors and belongs only to them. Speaking for Gould, I retort, No, the victory belongs to the *event*! The event is that which nothing can guarantee, but without the *fact* of which geology as we know it and as we speak of it would not exist. The event mixes up the narrative categories, for it has rendered the present-day geologists capable of actually judging their past, and with a generosity, a coherence, and a richness such that, one would like to think, those who have been "vanquished" would be the first to accept.

Why does Rudwick feel the need to hide the fact that the Devonian controversy belongs to a "beautiful story"? Rudwick feels this need because he is afraid that if he does present this history as a "beautiful story,"* it will revert to the classical schema whereby the position of the protagonists is judged from the beginning in the name of the truth of the earth. To establish the seriousness of his profession, the historian has to establish a critical distance from the belief systems of those he is describing. The "earth in-itself" is not an object of possible knowledge. It is not entitled to figure as an actor in a story in which the only legitimate actors are human beings and institutions and in which the only possible denouement pertains therefore to the order of negotiation and construction. The truth of the earth is that which men have constructed. As a subject, the earth does not have the right to bring them into agreement.

Perhaps the earth does not have the right to do this, but, we can say with Gould, we have to recognize that *in practice* the earth has done it. If the Devonian controversy figures in the memory of geologists as a "beautiful story," it is very much because no method could either guarantee or legitimate *de jure* what happened *de facto*.

For the historian, irony is the resource that establishes the stability of his or her critical distance from what is being described. But the historian who proposes for instance a new reading of the French Revolution—freer, he or she hopes, in relation to the dominant categories of the present—will always find allies, others who take an interest in the new present that allows this new reading of the past. The history of science is a difficult genre not only because it presumes, like every other historical practice, to escape the authority of the present that dictates what must be thought of the past but also because escaping the authority of the present risks producing not liberation but frustration, as if it did not allow new words and new focuses but did disallow and censure the old ones. Rud-

---

*Stengers's term is "une belle histoire": a story with a harmonious and coherent resolution of elements that appear to be conflicted and incommensurable at the outset.—Eds.

wick, as a historian, indeed had to re-create the undecidable *de jure* in the place where the decision had been made *de facto*, but he really did much more. To demonstrate the power of the historian's categories over those of the actors whom he or she studies, he has excluded the words that distinguish in the life of the sciences a "beautiful story" from a human, all too human, history like the others. To that end, he had to do violence to the very thing in this history that was most dear to geologists. The frustration of the reader is, I believe, the symptom of this violence.

How, then, to narrate the history of geology? The singularity of the history of science—what makes the work of the historian difficult—is that a question of this type, properly speaking, is constitutive of a scientist's work. And this is not in the usual sense in which, for example, the memory of the Romans is an irreducible element in the French Revolution, but rather in the sense in which what is actively sought is *the production of a "beautiful" story*.

A "beautiful" scientific history is a story that succeeds in mixing up the categories that are required by a purely human history, undecidable history, "true" fiction pitted against "true" fiction. It is a story that gives way to the *event*, distributing a "before" and an "after" that will transform the narrative. It marks the fact that a nonhuman *tertium quid* has made some of those who claimed to represent it capable of a new relationship to the past. The task and the possibility of differentiating and marking, which Horace entrusted to time in a century that allowed for the recognition of the *vetus atque probus,* are what organize here and now the relations between scientists among themselves and with their subject matter. *How can we invent the means to confer on this "subject matter" the capacity of making a difference among us and of making history with us?*

Clearly, Thomas Kuhn located the particular relationship between scientific practices and the question of history when he showed that every "paradigm shift" brings with it a new narration of the past. The history of science as it is recounted by scientists is a systematically false history, but the possibility of this falsification is not, as such, arbitrary. It is a work all but disinterested, but also, let us say with Judith Schlanger, a rare and interesting one. It follows an event, the production of a present that, not *de jure* but *de facto*, has actually redistributed the judgments on the past. *The falsification that characterizes the story of science, as told by scientists, marks the fact that a "beautiful story" has found the means of being told.* Does this mean that historians ought to bow to the authority of the categories of history narrated by scientists? That they ought to repeat their "good" stories without standing back and taking critical distance? Not at all! The question, for me, is how to get out of the relations of force: how to escape the confrontation between the categories that make up the historian's craft and power, and those of an activity one of whose constitutive passions is to "date" the past, to close the stories that historians would like to leave indefinitely open, because human history is always, by right, open. Surely, it is here that we return to the theme of humor as I have defined it. Humor alone is capable of escaping from the space defined by the confrontation of forces. What practical effects could humor about the past have on the present that scientists and historians share?

The geological history of the earth can be made the object of a system of dating. Today this is a fact. It is a fact that defines not only the present of geologists, but a present shared by a complex network of specialists, researchers, and amateurs—a network that would not have existed without this fact. Moreover, history itself is, to a certain degree, part of this network. When it studies prehistoric times, does not history need techniques of dating that initially had to be tried out on the long past of the earth? Humor is therefore the capacity of knowing gaily that history has produced a present from which the historian is not free to abstract him- or herself because the history of the dating of the earth is a "beautiful story," that is, a story productive of the fact of the possibility of dating. Like the others, he or she is the inheritor of this possibility that distinguishes our common present from the "Devonian controversy" past. The fact of which we are all to some degree inheritors is that human history has found a way of making history with an "earth about 4.6 billion years old," and not only, for example, with an earth that is the locus of the seasonal rhythms. The fact is that human history has succeeded in implicating *this* 4.6 billion-year-old earth in the multiple and complex network of its historical narratives. But this fact, of which we are all in one way or another inheritors, does not dictate of itself how it ought to be narrated. There lies the freedom of the craft of history. For the possibility of dating may be the end of a particular story, that of the Devonian controversy; it is also productive of a new historical space.

There is a very good Jewish story about three rabbis who are debating a point of biblical interpretation. One of them, in order to clinch his argument, invokes the Most High. A thunderbolt resounds in answer. The other two exclaim, "The argument is not admissible. God gave this text to human beings to discuss; he has nothing more to do with the discussion of its meaning."

The event creates a difference between before and after. But what is this difference? On what, where, and how does this distinction bear? The event does not tell us. A great many actors who have all, in one way or another, been produced by the event will undertake to deduce lessons from it; they will produce new stories, some of which will be beautiful, others much less so. Like the others, the historian is produced by the event. Like the others, with other interests and other means, he or she seeks to make of it history.

Could the humor of the historian make the present of the scientists capable of being different from the one we know? Do scientists *need*, as Thomas Kuhn has affirmed, to believe that the event authorizes and guarantees a conquest that always furthers and expands a paradigmatic meaning? Certain scientists think so and characterize the history of science as a dangerous discipline capable of undermining the confidence requisite for the researcher. To return to the expression introduced by Judith Schlanger, memory, which allows us to wonder or marvel, to reintroduce the world between one "us" and another "us,"[2] would be dangerous not only for the ordering of the sciences but also for their innovative power. The reader may guess my position regarding such an argument. Whatever the answer, however, it is remarkable that the debate about the relationship of the sciences to their pasts is situated on terrain similar, I believe, to that of Schlanger's abstraction. This is where "truth" questions itself less as a matter of "right" than as a matter of practical effects.

NOTES

1. Martin J. S Rudwick, *The Great Devonian Controversy: The Shaping of Scientific Knowledge Among Gentlemanly Specialists* (Chicago University of Chicago Press, 1985) For Gould's review, see Stephen J. Gould, "The Power of Narrative," in *An Urchin in the Storm* (London Penguin Books, 1990), 75–92.

2 Judith Schlanger, *Penser la bouche pleine* (Paris. Fayard, 1983)

4

Naming the Landscape: Leisure Travel and the Demise of the Salon

NANCY AUSTIN

INTRODUCTION

From 1667, the date of the first state-sponsored exhibition of paintings known as the Salon, until the late nineteenth century, French artists depended for exposure, commissions, and patrons on the institution of the Salon with its explicit hierarchical standards of artistic merit, which placed history painting at the top and landscape painting at the bottom.[1] The hegemony of the Salons was contested by privately initiated or publicly sponsored exhibitions in 1855, 1863, and 1867.[2] Building on these precedents, a group of artists organized in 1874 what became known as the first Impressionist exhibition.

One of these artists was the French painter Claude Monet, who is often presented as the paradigmatic modern artist, a pioneering genius whose formal inventiveness established a new canon that could only be exhibited outside the gatekeeping institution of the Salon. I argue here that Monet's landscape painting reflected a familiar image of France much appreciated by a bourgeois generation raised with the possibility of leisure travel newly made convenient by the railroads. The subjects of Monet's landscapes in the 1860s and 1870s are conventional when compared to the illustrations used to promote leisure travel in popular magazines and guidebooks from the 1850s onward.

Monet's decision to seek an audience outside the institution of the Salon should be seen in this context. Within the discipline of art history the history of modernism still tends to be written as the story of internal formal developments pushed forward by men of genius. This kind of history ignores how popular culture or events usually considered external to the history of art prepared ideological changes that were then incorporated into high culture and later presented as being self-generated by an artistic avant-garde. Monet's decision to exhibit outside the Salon demonstrates the influence of external processes on the history of art and is one moment in that history in which a changing view of nature occurred first in the popular domain before being exploited by high culture.

This is demonstrated further by my research, which indicates that although landscape painting never comprised more than one-third of all paintings exhibited at the Salon from 1852 to 1888, after the 1850s the way landscapes were named shifted from the general to the specific, for example, from *Sunset* to such typically named landscapes as *A Stream in the Forest of Mans* (which is in the province of Seine-et-Marne). In addition, there was a trend toward portraying sites now identified as being within France. The most popular sites change over time and follow the development of the French railroad lines. Between 1845 and 1860 railroads penetrated most of France, making the entire national landscape available as a leisure travel destination. Ironically, this emphasis on the specific and on regional differences occurred as these very qualities were being obliterated.[3]

The primary characteristic of cultural production in the nineteenth century is not landscape painting's displacement of history painting as the premier genre of art, but the increasingly dominant conception of art as a distinctive commodity marketed more efficiently by an entrepreneur than by the state.

THE DEMISE OF THE SALON

In 1852, at the beginning of the Second Empire, the Salon was unquestionably accepted as the most important institution governing the production, marketing, and consumption of art in France. Auctions had been controlled since the Revolution (Green, *Spectacle*, 32 and note 26). Independent exhibitions rarely occurred in France although they were familiar in England where there was no comparable state support (J. Whiteley, "Exhibitions," 69–78). Until the 1850s, dealers in France were artisans who made and sold picture frames as well as luxury goods, a category that included landscape paintings (Green, *Spectacle*, 29–34). By the end of the century, the Salon had been supplanted by the new figure of the contemporary picture dealer and the independent exhibition. Historians have explained the demise of the Salon in various ways.

According to John Rewald's respected *History of Impressionism*, the "new phase in the history of art inaugurated by the impressionist exhibition of 1874" was the culmination of twenty years of "slow and consistent evolution."[4] The Impressionists' iconoclasm and independence "brought them into repeated conflicts with the reactionary jury of the Salon, to the extent that to show their works outside of the official exhibitions seemed to be the only means left them to approach the general public" (Rewald, *History*, 8).

To correct this prevalent view of the renegade artist combating an unyielding Salon, recent historians have begun to research the persistent viability of the Salon into the 1890s and to demonstrate the marketing acumen of many nineteenth-century artists, including the Impressionists.[5] Jon Whiteley concludes, "The Salon was monopolistic, not because it was the centre of a closed shop system, but because artists were loathe to relinquish it.... [T]he Salons, funded by the state and internationally renowned for the standards which it set, gave an outlet to the artists that ensured their patronage, independence and status in a way that neither the dealers nor the independent shows could match successfully before the 1880's" ("Exhibitions," 78). Patricia Mainardi's studies have pointed out the contradictory functions of the Second Empire Salons as either *exhibitions* of pictures for sale, where, as a form of entertainment, admission could be charged, or free, didactic, government-sponsored *expositions* of pictures to see.[6] Various attempts by the state to segregate the dual meanings were not successful (Mainardi, "Double Exhibition").

Nicholas Green's premise that art is not an ahistorical, "ontologically constant" category led him to posit "circuits of production and consumption" in nineteenth-century France that are "multidirectional, with the recognition that points of distribution and consumption may be equally [as] important as the moment of production in the projection of cultural meanings."[7] The following study of leisure travel and landscape painting at the Salon examines some of the ways the production, marketing, and consumption of visual representations of the French landscape in the second half of the nineteenth century were interconnected practices; these findings reinforce the tenuousness of any conception of art as evolving hermetically.

NAMING THE LANDSCAPE AT THE SALON, 1852–1888

With a few exceptions, the official Salons were held for six weeks every spring in Paris on the Champs-Elysées at the Palais de l'Industrie.[8] The Salons were large exhibitions of paintings—the focus here—as well as prints and drawings, sculpture, and architecture. The Salon catalog (titled *Explication des ouvrages de Peinture, Sculpture, Gravure, Lithographie et Architecture des Artistes Vivants*) listed all works exhibited. Each entry included the artist's name, nationality, master painters the artist had studied with, the title of the work, and occasionally a descriptive or literary passage. Broad categorical changes in the Salon painting subject matter chosen by French artists can be determined from the titles.

From 1852 to 1888 landscape painting consistently comprised between one-quarter and one-third of all Salon painting. According to Cynthia White and Harrison White, between 1737 and 1857 landscape painting accounted for between one-fifth and one-third of paintings sold at Paris auctions; it seems that the taste and market for landscape painting remained quite constant over this period (White and White, *Canvases*, 34).

As a genre, landscape painting at the Salon was not static from 1852 to 1888. The perceived subject matter of landscape painting by French artists exhibited at the Salons changed significantly during this period. A new identification with the French landscape arose. The percentage of landscapes by French artists that specified a French locale increased significantly after the 1850s; how landscapes were named shifted from the general to the specific:[9] for example, as indicated earlier, from *Sunset: Landscape* or *Quiet: Landscape*—paintings by Jean Corot from the Salon of 1852—to such typically named landscapes from the Salon of 1859 as *Sunset: View from Canon Rock (Forest of Fontainebleau, Valley of Cernay (Seine-et-Oise)—Autumn*, and *Return from Oyster Fishing During Spring Tide Cancale (Ille-et-Vilaine)* from the Salon of 1874.[10]

Naming the landscape thus became an integral aspect of the painting. This articulation of difference—by insisting that this was a view of here and not anywhere else—is evident despite the generic similarity of many of the landscapes.[11] Whether or not figures are included in the composition, naming the landscape indicates a new gesture toward emphasizing the setting and reporting on the present. For example, Jules Breton's popular painting from the 1859 Salon, now known as *The Return of the Gleaners*, was actually titled *The Return of the Gleaners (Artois)*. The naming of non-French sites changed too. Italy was consistently the most common foreign landscape subject, but within Italy there was a shift from views of Rome in 1852 to Venice in 1888.

Additionally, tabulating the sites named in the titles of Salon landscape paintings disclosed that certain locations were painted more often than others and that the most frequently chosen sites fluctuated in popularity. These fluctuations followed the development of the French railroad lines and the promotion of leisure travel to these destinations. Salon landscape painting, however, was comparatively slow in picking up these trends in leisure travel. For example, the rail line between Paris and Strasbourg opened in 1852. The landscape of Champagne and Alsace-Lorraine was named as the subject in one painting in the 1852 Salon; in 1859 there were fourteen landscapes that specified sites in Champagne or Alsace-Lorraine.

During the second half of the nineteenth century, the image of the French landscape presented at the Salon by French artists was intimately tied to depictions of four regions: the Île-de-France, Normandy, Brittany, and Provence; a little over half of the locations specified were in, or of, these historic provinces (see Fig. 1).[12]

Further, there are trends within each of these provinces. Table 1 summarizes for select years the specific locales that were the setting for at least 5 percent of the paintings for any one historic province and which additionally were depicted by at least four different artists. For example, the most often cited location in the Île-de-France is, consistently, the Forest of Fontainebleau. This is not the case with Normandy or Provence; by the end of the 1850s, it is the regions themselves that are named, followed by specific coastal resort towns or historic cities. It is not until after 1870, when Brittany became easily accessible by rail, that a group of Salon landscape paintings named specific locations within that province.

Gustave Courbet is often portrayed as the radical artist of the 1850s because of his commitment to portraying the landscape around his native Ornans in the Franche-Comté. Actually, Courbet's interest in the landscape of this region is not unique. The 1852 Salon included Courbet's *Landscape: Shores of the Loue (Doubs)*, as well as Claude-Jules

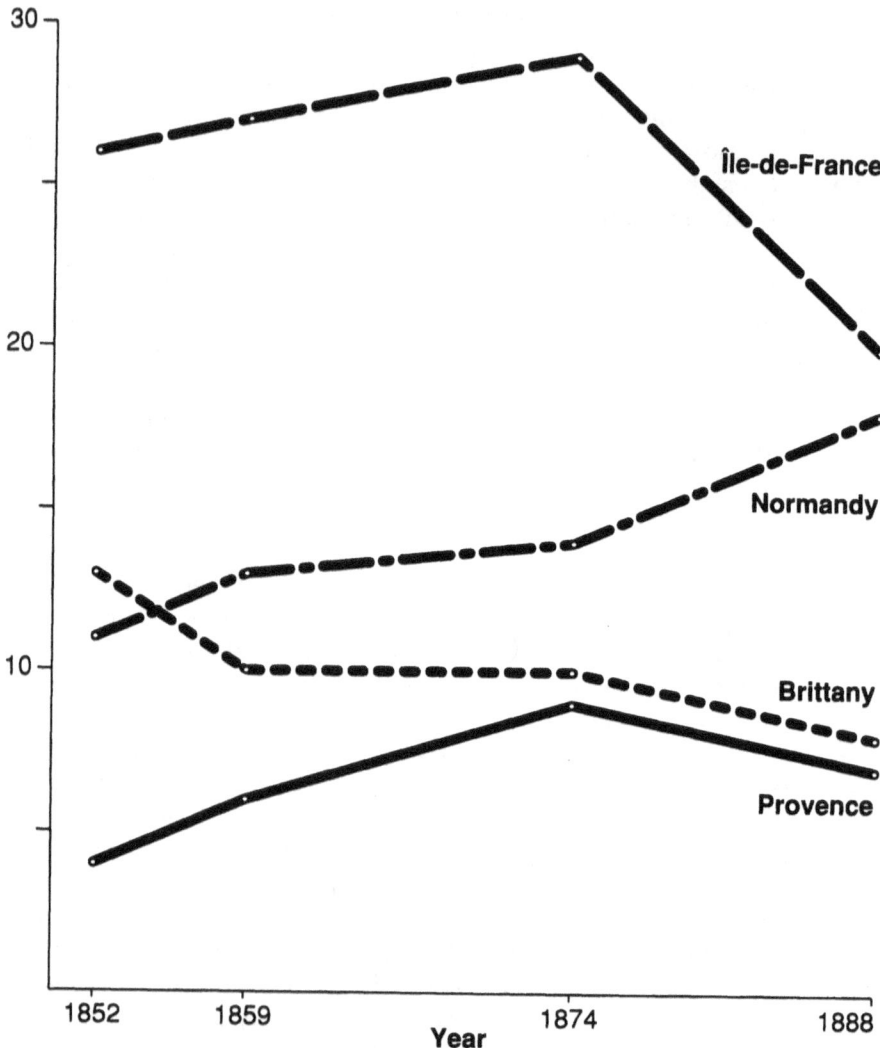

Fig. 1. Percentage of Salon landscapes by French artists that specified a site in, or of, the historic provinces of the Île-de-France, Normandy, Brittany, and Provence.

Table 1 Specific locales that were the setting for at least 5 percent of the paintings of a historic province and which were chosen by at least four artists in selected years, 1852–1888

	Île-de-France	Normandy	Brittany	Provence
1852	Forest of Fontainebleau	[none]	Brittany	[none]
1859	Forest of Fontainebleau	Normandy Honfleur Trouville	Brittany	Marseille Provence
1874	Forest of Fontainebleau	Normandy Trouville	Cancale	Provence
1888	Forest of Fontainebleau	Normandy Rouen	Brittany	Marseille Provence Toulon

Grenier's *Shores of the Doubs, Sunset* and *View in the Franche-Comté, Evening*. Grenier had been exhibiting landscapes of the Franche-Comté since his debut in the 1847 Salon and continued to do so until 1881.[13] By the 1859 Salon, three other artists from the Franche-Comté were exhibiting landscapes naming that region, as was one Parisian artist.[14]

Certainly the monumental scale of Courbet's paintings distinguishes his work from that of Grenier, but the rejection of Courbet's *Burial at Ornans* from the 1855 Exposition Universelle juried exhibition—which provoked him into taking the unusual step of setting up a private exhibition of his own painting, and charging admission—is not so much an indication of the unresponsiveness of the Salon as it is a foreshadowing of the new role of the entrepreneur dealer in France, even if in this instance the dealer is the artist. Other artists had successfully charged admission to private exhibitions in England, but not in France (J. Whiteley, "Exhibitions," 69–78). Courbet's 1855 exhibition was not a success, but it led to his more successful, second independent exhibition a dozen years later. The marketing of Courbet as a distinctive landscape painter of the Franche-Comté did not result in major sales of those paintings until 1875. From the mid-1860s into the early 1870s, the Courbet paintings of Trouville and other Normandy sites were the ones that sold, a trend predicted in the Salons since the late 1850s.[15] Although Courbet once proposed to "transform the waiting rooms of railway stations ... into 'temples of art' by depicting on their walls the accomplishments of the départements of France," it was Courbet's solo exhibition of 1855 that more accurately foretold where the consumption of art would occur in the century that followed (Nochlin, *Realism,* 179–81).

THE RAILROAD AND THE FRENCH LANDSCAPE

The railroad's penetration of the French countryside in the decade of the 1850s made leisure travel rapid and economical. The number of places one could conveniently travel to increased from very few to essentially anywhere in France. In the 1850s, more than 300 million travelers rode the railroads in France.

The first French rail lines from metropolitan Paris to the Forest of Fontainebleau were inaugurated in 1849.[16] The connection from Paris to Rouen opened in 1843, and the extension from Rouen to Le Havre on the Atlantic coast was completed in 1847. It was not until 1852 that the concession to build a rail link to Brittany was granted. The route from Paris via Lyon to Marseilles, complicated by the mountainous terrain, did not open until 1855 (Bois, *Les Chemins,* 13, 16, 21, 79).

In 1852 one could take a train to the Forest of Fontainebleau close to Paris, or to Normandy, but not to Brittany or Provence (Fig. 2). The tier system of fares was intended to make train travel affordable; in the mid-1850s, second- and third-class passage to the Forest of Fontainebleau was less than the daily wage of a Parisian printer or roofer, and the trip from Paris to Normandy was a week's wage.[17] Prior to this time one could have taken a trip to the Atlantic coast of France, for example, to the resort areas around the commercial shipbuilding center and port of Le Havre in Normandy, or to Brittany further away to the southwest; however, the 228-kilometer trip from Paris to Le Havre would have taken two to three days by horse-driven coach. After the 1850s, the same trip to Le Havre could be made in five hours on the express train; one could breakfast in Paris and dine in Le Havre (Joanne, *Itinéraire,* 78). In 1852, five years after the line opened, 629,000 people made this trip (Bois, *Les Chemins,* 17).

The railroad lines penetrated Brittany about a decade later than Normandy (Fig. 3). The final link in the train line from Paris to Saint-Malo near Mont-Saint-Michel and the bathing resort of Cancale was inaugurated in June 1864. The more direct route from Paris via Versailles to Granville was not completed until July 1870. Until the mid-1860s the

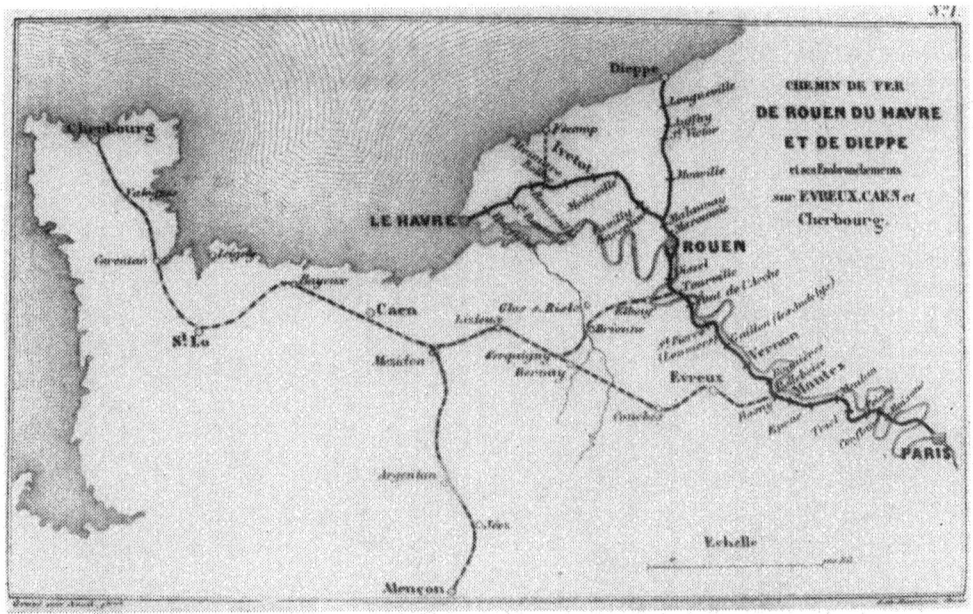

Fig. 2. Train routes completed, 1853 (from Victor Bois, *Les Chemins de Fer Français*, Paris, 1853).

best one could do was take the five-hour express train to Le Havre and then travel by boat to Morlaix or Brest, a twenty-hour voyage, longer than the trip from Le Havre to England.

Leisure travel and tourism were not invented with the advent of the railroad.[18] What is distinctive is the railroad's dramatic collapsing of distance compared to other means of transportation and the marketing of this new experience to a vast population that was already experiencing a change in the relationship between work and leisure.[19] While a tourist in 1838 confided to his diary, "left Wednesday night from London in order to be in Paris before Saturday evening...," another tourist in 1859 could report, "We left the London Station at half-past eight on Monday morning, and arrived at the Hôtel du Louvre in Paris a little before twelve at night—the distance being about three hundred and twenty miles, the fare something less than sixteen dollars, first class."[20]

Landscape paintings that specify a site are but one manifestation of the widespread pursuit of pleasure in the landscape, a pursuit which acceler-

Fig. 3. Train routes completed, 1864 (from Adolphe Joanne, *Itinéraire de la France: Normandie*, Paris, 1864).

ated after the 1850s. One could argue that the new vogue for painting *en plein air* (out of doors) treated the landscape as a found panorama—that spectacle popular in the first half of the century where customers entered a circular rotunda to view all around them a vast painted landscape of a particular site.[21] In this sense, there is not such a gap between Jacques-Louis David advising his students to visit the panoramas and paint the landscapes there, and the later Second Empire painters who traveled by train to reach their landscape-painting sites.[22] As Boime has pointed out, the social practices of artists and tourists alike were influenced by the earlier nineteenth-century industrialists and entrepreneurs who had reshaped the physical landscape by the construction of railroads and resorts and built the industries that provided new means of advertising and introduced new types of spectacles.[23]

MARKETING THE LANDSCAPE

Railroads facilitated the expansion of domestic leisure travel in the 1850s; an appetite for the French landscape was created in part by the articles and imagery in popular magazines and guidebooks. These sources, with their widely distributed popular images, can be seen as an early example of low art assimilated a decade later by high art.[24]

L'Illustration was a popular illustrated news weekly that began publication in 1843 (Fig. 4).[25] In 1852 the majority of *L'Illustration*'s travel articles were for destinations beyond France. It was during the 1850s and 1860s that *L'Illustration*'s reportage turned increasingly toward leisure travel within France. During these years *L'Illustration* promptly and prominently reported almost every new train line that opened. The articles featured a map of where the new train lines would take the traveler and illustrated the local scenery one could experience (see, for example, Fig. 5). Images of the Normandy coast appeared in the pages of *L'Illustration* many times in many different contexts. An 1859 *L'Illustration* book review on the second edition of *Sur la jetée du Havre et ses environs* is essentially an extended travel article with illustrations of

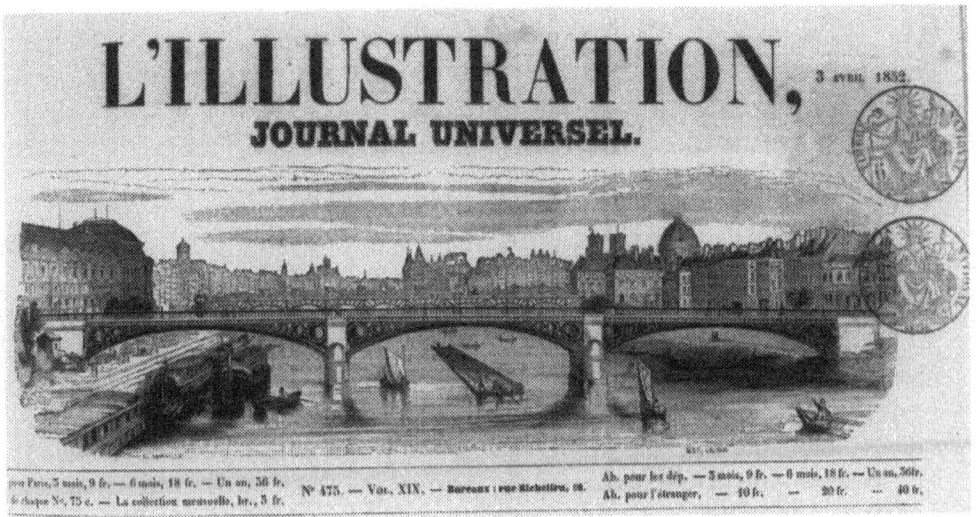

Fig. 4   The masthead of *L'Illustration*, 1852.

Fig. 5. Opening of the railroad to Dieppe via Argenteuil, 1862 (from *L'Illustration*, vol 39, 1862)

Normandy's specific landscape, including the famous rock formations at Etretat, later painted by Gustave Courbet and Claude Monet, among many others. By the mid-1860s, *L'Illustration* carried a regular series on excursions one could take near the Normandy coast. These articles included train maps, landscape vignettes, and images of leisure (Fig. 6).

New guidebooks augmented the travel articles found in magazines like *L'Illustration*. One early guide to the Normandy coast, *Guides*

Fig. 6.   Regatta at Le Havre, 1864 (from *L'Illustration*, vol. 44, 1864).

Itinéraires de Paris au Havre, was put out by the railroad company. By the mid-1860s, Adolphe Joanne's popular in-depth series of guidebooks were available for almost every area of France. The 1866 guide to Normandy alone described more than one hundred trips one could take between Paris and the Normandy coast. The 1862 Joanne guide to the region between Lyon and Marseille describes the landscape at each of the fifty-three train stations one would pass on that journey. It was not necessary to go far to experience the countryside. The environs of Paris abounded with leisure destinations for a Sunday picnic, according to guidebooks on metropolitan Paris and illustrated articles in *L'Illustration* (Fig. 7).

The visibility of the French landscape in *L'Illustration*'s pages extended to the coverage of the yearly Salon. During the 1850s, *L'Illustration*'s breadth of coverage of the Salons increased substantially; by 1859 Salon paintings from the six-week Salon were illustrated almost weekly for four months. The prominence given the Salons continued throughout the 1860s and 1870s. In 1852, the Salon painting *L'Illustration* reproduced depicted a picturesque Italianate village setting (Fig. 8). In 1859, the focus was on landscape paintings of particular places within France. This naming of the landscape is insisted on, even when it would not seem that this high degree of specificity informed the visual image.

Fig. 7. Parisians' Sunday Picnic, 1862 (from *L'Illustration*, vol. 40, 1862).

The painting's realism resides as much in its linguistic meaning as in its formal properties (Figs. 9–11).[26] Many of the compositions are organized around a flat landscape and stream that recedes into the horizon. The distant view is interrupted in the midground plane by a stand of trees. Small-scale figures are visible. It is the same pleasant view of the distant countryside one would see from the window of a passing train; the eye is drawn to the midground at the expense of the foreground. Trees are cropped at the edges of the picture plane. Moreover, what is depicted is not just any landscape, but the border of a particular river in a particular place in France.

Green argues that the development of a Parisian-based "metropolitan gaze" led the city dweller to "consume the picturesque" and become absorbed in nature in a new way (Green, "Circuits," 29–34, and *Spectacle*). He recognized that the regional specificity of early nineteenth-

Fig. 8. *L'Illustration*'s coverage of the Salon of 1852 (from *L'Illustration*, vol. 19, 1852).

century picturesque travel prints "cut against the grain of metropolitanism," but concluded that by the early 1840s such general landscape titles as *Cows by a Pool* and *Sunset behind the Trees* were evidence that landscape's appeal was "less to particular places than to the audience's involvement with *natura naturans*" (*Spectacle*, 43). The findings presented here suggest Green's conclusions should be modified.

Fig. 9. From the Salon of 1858: *Les bords d'un ruisseau à Ecouen*, by Lambinet (from *L'Illustration*, vol. 33, 1859). (photo: The Boston Athenæum)

Consider, for example, the 1862 *L'Illustration* article on the opening of a new train line to Dieppe via Argenteuil (see Fig. 5). In the field of the *L'Illustration* page, such icons of the industrial revolution as the railroad and the illustrated popular magazine mingle. Words and images direct the new experience of modernity. In the middle image the railroad bridge steps across the landscape. On the bottom, framed by the imagined train window, is the landscape vignette one would pass on the train as it races from point A to point B, where one would debark and promenade as in the top image. Easel painters participated in this new experience. The railroad, along with other technical innovations like portable tubes of paint, allowed artists to exploit a new means in the production of easel painting. In a sense then, a specific title is proof of having undertaken this journey. Naming the landscape is an act of possession and an essential aspect of the painting's modernism, distinct from formal, compositional issues.

Fig. 10. From the Salon of 1859: *Les graves au bord de la mer, à Villerville (Calvados)*, by Daubigny (from *L'Illustration*, vol. 33, 1859). (photo: The Boston Athenæum)

CLAUDE MONET

L'Illustration's small black-and-white printed images of the French landscape defined a culturally resonant subject matter. Monet participated in celebrating this subject matter, but in oil paintings (Figs. 12 and 13). Rather than see Monet as a radical modern painter at cross-purposes with the society he marginally courted, his cultural production should be contextualized within a broader study of the relationship between art, modernism, and changing institutions of culture.

Monet's choice of subjects in the 1860s and 1870s is the same as that chosen to promote leisure travel in popular magazines such as *L'Illustration*, or in guidebooks. For example, Monet often painted the rural villages and roads of Normandy and the popular Atlantic coastal resort towns and tourist sites such as the Le Havre jetty and the famous rock formations at Etretat, all familiar types of imagery from guidebooks and

Fig. 11. From the Salon of 1859: *Le Château de Puyréaux sur la Charente*, by André (from *L'Illustration*, vol. 33, 1859). (photo: The Boston Athenæum)

L'Illustration's vignettes of Normandy. Monet's *Déjeuner sur l'herbe* follows not only the artistic tradition of the *fête champêtre* but also the popular weeklies' illustrations of everyday life in the 1850s and 1860s. His frequent inclusion of a railroad bridge in a landscape setting composition of the 1870s is hardly unusual; from the 1850s on, *L'Illustration* proudly included images of bridges in the reports on the developing train lines.[27] The landscape imagery in *L'Illustration* seems more descriptively picturesque when compared to Monet's paintings. Monet's innovations are in form, surface composition, and color, but not subject matter.

Monet began painting in the late 1850s with his mentor, Eugène Boudin. In 1858 Boudin and Monet both painted the landscape of Rouelles. Two of Boudin's paintings, entitled *Landscape (Valley of Rouelles)* and Monet's first major oil painting entitled *Vue prise à Rouelles*, were exhibited at the Exposition Municipale de la Ville du Havre in 1858.[28] The following year, 1859, Boudin had a painting ac-

Fig. 12. Claude Monet, *The Port of Honfleur*, 1866 (whereabouts unknown; courtesy Document Archives Durand-Ruel).

cepted for the Salon and Monet went to Paris to see the Salon himself for the first time; by 1865 Monet's own landscape paintings had been accepted at the Salon.

Monet exhibited at the Salons of 1865, 1866, and 1868. His subject matter—*Mouth of the Seine, Honfleur; Point of Hève at Low Tide; Forest of Fontainebleau*; and *Ships Leaving from the Jetty at Le Havre*—, was not exceptional in the mid-1860s. The Salons had been exhibiting paintings like this for more than a decade. Monet, a young man in his mid-twenties, had achieved some recognition and success. Like every Impressionist except Cézanne, Monet had work accepted at the Salon in the mid- to late 1860s (White and White, *Canvases,* 142–44).

Historians often focus on Monet's failures at the Salon. For example, Monet's *The Port of Honfleur* was rejected at the Salon of 1867 and *The Jetty at Le Havre* from the Salon of 1868; however, he was able to exhibit both paintings at the Exposition Maritime Internationale at Le Havre in

Fig. 13. Claude Monet, *The Railroad Bridge at Argenteuil*, 1873 (private collection; photograph courtesy Christie's, London).

1868 where he was awarded a silver medal (Wildenstein, *Catalogue* w77; Rewald, *History,* 184). That same year Monet sold a painting of his that had been exhibited at the Salon of 1866 to the editor of the magazine *L'Artiste* (Rewald, *History,* 184–85).[29]

Before the first Impressionist exhibition of 1874, Monet's paintings had been exhibited by dealers in Paris and London and bought privately (Wildenstein, *Catalogue* w77, w164–65).[30] While Monet was living in London in 1870–72 to evade the Franco-Prussian War, he painted landscapes of the fashionable parks of London, which the dealer Paul Durand-Ruel bought on speculation, paying double the price Monet's work usually sold for (White and White, *Canvases,* 124–25). By the end of 1873, Durand-Ruel had spent over seventy thousand francs buying up the paintings of Monet and Pissarro.[31] In January 1874, three months before the opening of the first Impressionist exhibition, works by Monet, Pissarro, Sisley, and Degas sold at an Hôtel Drouot auction brought unprecedented high prices (Moffett, *New Painting,* 105). Stories about Monet's struggles for money should be balanced against the record of his actual income from sales and an allowance still sent by his father, as the work of White and White has begun to document. They write, "Monet was the first of the younger Impressionists to succeed financially.... At auction and exhibition, his prices were generally the highest. He was a better businessman than the others, could shrewdly appraise the market, and was capable of refusing an offer from a dealer if he thought it too low.... The expenses incurred by a middle-class level of living were coupled with irregularity of income. Monet saw himself as poverty stricken, as indeed he was for short periods. But a middle-class standard was never abandoned" (*Canvases,* 138–39).

Monet contributed to the first Impressionist exhibition, which was held in April 1874; seven Impressionist exhibitions took place in the following decade. Each featured paintings of well-known leisure travel subjects (see especially Moffett, *New Painting*). Stylistically influenced by the emphatic design qualities of Japanese prints, the media of the photograph, and new ideas about light and color, Monet must nonetheless have felt confident that his paintings would find an audience. Monet's series paintings of the 1880s can be seen as a continuation of a very long involvement with tourism and leisure travel.

CONCLUSIONS

Art historians who believe that art evolves through internally driven formal inventions minimize the influence of external processes on that evolution. For example, Kermit Champa argues:

> What reputation [Monet] had gained in recent years had come from work he had shown outside the Salon. Thus, with a complete awareness of possible consequences, Monet began to consider abandoning the traditional paths of success at the Salon once and for all. It would be difficult to overemphasize the revolutionary nature of such a move on Monet's part.... The radical form of development that Monet's art was taking virtually necessitated an assault on the political institutions of art.... Official institutions could no longer contain the threat that Monet represented.... Once the Salon jury had forced (or left) Monet to go it alone, the breach between academic and avant-garde painting in

France was complete. The avant-garde proceeded to develop along lines which it defined for itself.³²

An alternate interpretation would be that the Impressionists were painters selling a view of nature first popularized by leisure travel over twenty years earlier and who were now awakened to a changing market by the prices paid at successful auctions and by speculating dealers. At the

Fig. 14. Masthead of *L'Illustration*, 1888. (photo: The Boston Athenæum)

independent exhibitions, the artists were addressing that portion of the Salon audience that seriously wanted to buy easel paintings. The main difference was the unimpeded development of private-enterprise marketing strategies appropriate to selling art as a new kind of luxury good.

An evolutionary history of nineteenth-century painting displaces earlier paintings with the formal achievements of the Impressionists; one canon is replaced by another. The continuity of a narrative of art history is assured. Yet, to maintain that there is one canon or one culture is a political assertion. There is no such thing as one culture; there are, rather, different cultures, each of which is a construction of practices. In the 1850s, new means of leisure travel opened up new ways of experiencing nature that were reinforced in various ways in the rest of culture during the 1860s and 1870s. By the late 1880s, this constellation of mutually reinforcing practices had split apart (Fig. 14). The marketing and consumption of representations of the French landscape after midcentury are details that can help focus cultural production in the nineteenth century as a whole.[33]

NOTES

1. The body of art-historical literature on cultural institutions such as the Salon is slowly growing. Important recent work includes Albert Boime, *The Academy and French Painting in the Nineteenth Century* (London: Phaidon, 1971), and "America's Purchasing Power and the Evolution of European Art in the Late Nineteenth Century," in *Saloni, Gallerie, Musei e loro Influenza sullo Sviluppo dell'arte dei secoli XIX e XX*, ed. Francis Haskell (Bologna· C.I.H.A , 1979), 123–39; Jon Whiteley, "Exhibitions of Contemporary Painting in London and Paris 1760–1860," in Haskell, ed., *Saloni*, see esp. Haskell's introduction and 69–87; Cynthia A. White and Harrison C. White, *Canvases and Careers: Institutional Change in the French Painting World* (New York. John Wiley & Sons, 1965); Nicholas Green, *The Spectacle of Nature: Landscape and Bourgeois Culture in Nineteenth-Century France* (New York. Manchester University Press, 1990), the special issue of *Art Journal* 48 (Spring 1989) devoted to nineteenth-century French art institutions and edited by Patricia Mainardi; William Hauptman, "Juries, Protests and Counter-Exhibitions Before 1850," *Art Bulletin* 67 (March 1985): 95–109, Linda Whiteley, "Art et Commerce d'Art en France avant l'Epoque Impressioniste," *Romantisme* 4 (1983): 65–75, Mainardi's two recent books, *Art and Politics of the Second Empire· The Universal Expositions of 1855 and 1867* (New Haven. Yale University Press, 1987) and *The End of the Salon Art and the State in the Early Third Republic* (New York: Cambridge University Press, 1993)

2 World's Fairs were held in Paris in 1855 and 1867 Independent exhibitions organized by artists were mounted at these times by Gustave Courbet, and in 1867 by Edouard Manet In 1867 planning was begun for what became the first Impressionist exhibition, held in 1874 In 1863, the Salon jury rejected three-fifths of the submitted works, the state agreed to hold an exhibition of rejected works The Salon des Refusés was immensely successful, drawing crowds of three to four thousand on Sundays. See Albert Boime, "The Salon des Refusés and the

Evolution of Modern Art," *Art Quarterly* 32 (Winter 1969): 411–26, and Charles Moffett, *The New Painting· Impressionism, 1874–1886* (San Francisco The Fine Arts Museum of San Francisco, 1986), 94.

3. I conducted the initial archival research for this chapter in 1979 at the Boston Public Library for a graduate seminar on Monet. That research formed the basis of my 1982 M A. thesis I would like to thank Susan Walther Danly for helpful discussions during that period of my research, and Kermit Champa for initially suggesting the topic. In the intervening decade, the historiography of art has changed the implications of my initial findings This paper reflects those changes The work of Richard Brettell and Scott Schaefer in the 1984 Los Angeles County Museum of Art exhibition catalogue, *A Day in the Country*—particularly the articles, "Rivers, Roads, and Trains" and "The Impressionist Landscape and the Image of France"—overlap somewhat with the material presented here

4. John Rewald, *The History of Impressionism*, 4th rev. ed. (New York Museum of Modern Art, 1973), 8.

5. See Lois Fink, *American Art at the Nineteenth-Century Paris Salons* (New York: Cambridge University Press, 1990), and Pierre Vaisse, "Salons, Expositions et Sociétés d'Artistes en France 1871–1914," in Haskell, ed., *Saloni,* 141–55

6. Patricia Mainardi, "The Double Exhibition in Nineteenth-Century France," *Art Journal* 48 (Spring 1989)· 23–28, and "Nineteenth-Century Art Institutions, Editor's Statement," ibid., 7–8 See also J. Whiteley, "Exhibitions," 69 nn. 1–5.

7. Nicholas Green, "Circuits of Production, Circuits of Consumption The Case of Mid-Nineteenth-Century French Art Dealing," *Art Journal* 48 (Spring 1989): 59

8. The Salons of 1850–51 and 1852 were held at the Palais-Royal, in 1853 it was held at the Menus-Plaisir After that date the Salons moved to the Palais de l'Industrie, which was built for the 1855 Exposition Universelle Salons were held biannually from 1853 to 1863, after which they occurred annually for the rest of the century No Salon was held in 1871 because of the political situation. For more information, see P. Mainardi, *Salon,* 18–19

9 These conclusions are based on a study of more than 8,700 Salon titles. Computers would greatly assist future research aimed at determining broad changes in the Salons. The method used here is as follows All landscapes were noted. Vague titles were checked whenever possible in contemporary magazine illustrations of the Salons Then, each Salon landscape painting by a Frenchman that specified a site in France was listed The site was located geographically within one of the ninety departments of France using the United States Board on Geographic Names, *France: Official Standard Names*, Gazetteer no. 83 (Washington, D.C.: GPO, 1964). Contemporary guidebooks were consulted for sites still unlocated; frequently these turned out to be sites within popular places such as the Forest of Fontainebleau. Very few sites could not be located The sites were then grouped by department into the historic provinces For example, Normandy is made up of the five departments· Calvados, Eure, Manche, Orne, and Seine-Maritime.

10 Salon of 1859, no 26 by Théodore Aligny, Salon of 1874, no 811 by Albert Girard and no 721 by François Feyen-Perrin

11. See, for example, Figures 9–11 and the discussion on page 48.

12 To some extent this is a continuation of earlier trends in picturesque genre painting. See Linda Nochlin, *Realism* (New York Penguin Books, 1971), 88; and Green, *Spectacle.*

13. Claude-Jules Grenier (1817–83) See Ulrich Thieme and Frederik C Willis, *Allgemeines Lexikon der Bildenden Kunstler*, vol 14 (Leipzig: E A. Seeman, 1921), and Paul Brune, *Dictionnaire des Artistes et Ouvriers d'Art de la Franche-Comté* (Paris: Bibliothèque d'art et d'archéologie, 1912) Grenier was born in Baumes-les-Dames (Doubs) and studied in Paris at the École des Beaux-Arts and with Alexandre-Gabriel Descamps and Eugène Delacroix Many of his works were watercolors and pastels

14 Those born in Besançon were Victor Jeanneney, Antonin Fanart, and François-Camille Marquiset. Jacques Louvrier de Lajolais was born in Paris.

15. Hippolyte Mireur, *Dictionnaire des ventes d'art faites en France et a l'Etranger pendant les XVIIIème et XIXème siècles* (Paris: Maison d'édition d'oeuvres artistiques, 1911), 2 283–84.

16 Victor Bois, *Les Chemins de Fer Française* (Paris, 1853), 130. For general information, see Kimon Doukas, *The French Railroads and the State*, Studies in History, Economics and Public Law 517 (New York: Columbia University Press, 1945); François Legueu, *La S N.C.F. de la diligence à la BB* (Paris: Plon, 1962); and Patty Lurie, *A Guide to the Impressionist Landscape* (Boston: Little, Brown, 1990).

17 White and White, *Canvases*, 130, Adolphe Joanne, *Itinéraire Générale de la France (Normandie)* (Paris, 1866), 569.

18. Richard Brettell, in "The Impressionist Landscape and the Image of France" (*A Day in the Country*, 27–49) notes that no major history of tourism in France has been written despite available material. For general information, see Dean MacCannell, *The Tourist: A New Theory of the Leisure Class* (New York: Schocken Books, 1976); Robert W. McIntosh and Charles R. Goeldner, *Tourism: Principles, Practices, Philosophies* (4th ed., New York: John Wiley, 1984); A. Burkart and S. Medlik, *Tourism, Past, Present and Future* (London: Heinemann, 1974); James Bozard, *The Beaten Track: European Tourism, Literature, and the Ways to "Culture," 1800–1918* (Oxford: Clarendon Press, 1993).

19 See also Theodor Adorno, "The Culture Industry: Enlightenment as Mass Deception," in *Dialectic of Enlightenment*, ed Max Horkheimer and Theodor Adorno (New York: Herder & Herder, 1972); Fernand Braudel and Ernest Labrousse, eds., *Histoire économique et sociale de la France*, vol 4 (Paris: Presses Universitaires de France, 1979), Eugen Weber, *Peasants into Frenchmen* (Stanford: Stanford University Press, 1976); and Bonnie Grad, *Visions of City and Country* (Worcester, Mass · Worcester Art Museum, 1982)

20 George P. Putnam, *The Tourist in Europe* (New York: Wiley and Putnam, 1838), 176, and Hiram Fuller, *Sparks from a Locomotive* (New York: Derby and Jackson, 1859), 202

21. For more information on panoramas and other spectacles of the period, see J Whiteley, "Exhibitions," 74–75 and nn. 96–106, and Richard Altick, *The Shows of London* (Cambridge: Harvard University Press, 1978)

22 On David's advice to his students, see J. I. Hittorf, "Sur l'origin des panoramas," *Revue Générale d'Architecture et Traveaux Publiques*, vol 2 (Paris, 1841)· 227, quoted in Stephan Oettermann, *Das Panorama* (Frankfurt am Main: Syndikat, 1980), 286 n 33. On panoramic travel, see Wolfgang Schivelbusch, *The Railway Journey· The Industrialization of Time and Space in the Nineteenth Century* (Berkeley and Los Angeles: University of California Press, 1986)

23 Boime, *Academy*, 182; Palmade, 110–15.

24 Rather than continue in the direction of the recent Museum of Modern Art exhibition, *High and Low: Modern Art and Popular Culture* (1990–91), and document the low-art sources of high art, thus always returning to the privileged high-art object, the history of art would benefit from further research on the commonalities that join easel painting and aspects of popular culture such as journalism, tourism, and shopping. Until his death, Nicholas Green had been pursuing the way many of these practices were joined around notions of pleasure "Visual representations need to be seen as part of an interlocking set of histories which involve multiple relations and dependencies across a range of social fields and practices The production of pleasures and desires, the creation of new knowledges and subjects, can be intimately bound up with the functioning of power This point is particularly important for work on those fields which are unified around notions of pleasure, art, literature, etc." (Nicholas Green and Frank Mort, "Visual Representation and Cultural Politics," *Block* 7 [1982]: 59–68) Also see

John House, "Review of *The Spectacle of Nature* by Nicholas Green," *Burlington Magazine* 132 (November 1990): 801–2

25. For comments on *L'Illustration* and other journals that discussed culture, see Green and Mort, "Visual Representation," 59–66.

26. Nochlin's excellent study, *Realism*, contextualizes the images discussed, but only to reinforce their status as genuine works of art.

27. For example, *L'Illustration* 34 (1859): 320 and 63 (1874): 324. For a discussion of the railroad bridge at Argenteuil, see Paul H. Tucker, "Monet and the Bourgeois Dream: Argenteuil and the Modern Landscape," in *Modernism and Modernity*, ed. Benjamin Buchloh (Halifax: Press of the Nova Scotia College of Art and Design, 1983), 21–41.

28. Daniel Wildenstein. *Claude Monet: Biographie et Catalogue Raisonné*, Vol. I: *1840–1881* (Lausanne and Paris: La Bibliothèque des arts, 1979), w1 and p. 5.

29. Arsène Houssaye bought Monet's *Woman in Green [Camille]* for eight hundred francs. A Parisian laborer typically earned five francs per day.

30. M. Hagerman and Louis Latouche included Monet's work in their special exhibitions at the 1867 World's Fair. See Moffett, *New Painting*, 94.

31. Moffett, *New Painting*, 106. See also Ralph E. Shikes and Paula Harper, *Pissarro, His Life and Work* (New York: Horizon Press, 1980), 105.

32. Kermit Champa, *Studies in Early Impressionism* (New Haven: Yale University Press, 1973).

33. I would like to thank my colleague Mario Moussa for many fruitful discussions on the politics of cultural hegemony.

5

Beauty, Language, and Re-Presentation: Notes Toward a Critique of Aesthetics—With Special Reference to Architecture

KARSTEN HARRIES

For many years I taught a course on the meaning of modern art. Teaching this course, I came to question more and more the aesthetic approach that, I would claim, ever since Alberti, but especially since the early eighteenth century, has helped shape the development of art. Just such questioning led me to become interested in architecture: architecture, an essentially impure art, invites us to question the presupposed understanding of purity and thus the aesthetic approach. Calling into question the aesthetic approach, it also calls into question the traditional understanding of beauty. The following remarks accept that invitation.

What do I mean here by the aesthetic approach, more specifically by the aesthetic approach to architecture? Let me begin with that often-cited remark with which Nikolaus Pevsner introduces his *Outline of European Architecture*: "A bicycle shed is a building; Lincoln Cathedral is a piece of architecture."[1] To be sure, like a bicycle shed, Lincoln Cathedral is also a building. Whatever else he may be doing, the architect builds, but he does something more. How then is this "more" to be understood? Pevsner's answer is expected: what distinguishes works of architecture from mere buildings is that they are "designed with a view to aesthetic appeal" (*Outline*, 23).

But what constitutes "aesthetic appeal"? Erwin Panofsky's answer is representative. According to him, we experience an object aesthetically when "we just look at it (or listen to it) without relating it, intellectually or emotionally, to anything outside of itself.... Only he who simply and wholly abandons himself to the object of his perception will experience it aesthetically."[2] Aesthetic beholding may be defined in terms of such absorption in the beheld presence. No longer do our usual cares and concerns dominate our sight; because questions of utility no longer matter, we are free to attend to what lies before our eyes, free to let it be what it is. Note also that, if the aesthetic object should not refer to anything outside itself, its point cannot be to signify; its success has nothing to do with what makes for a successful representation, allegory, or symbol. So understood, the aesthetic object should "not mean, but be."

Textiles and pottery produced by different cultures can teach us that craftsmen have always been concerned with more than is demanded by considerations of utility and meaning, concerned with creating pleasing configurations of shape and color. But generally this would seem to have been only a secondary concern, subordinated to some primary concern or other, for example, to the desire to make an urn, a festive garment, or a sacred image. Thus the primary concern of those who crafted some gothic or baroque altarpiece was not to create an aesthetic object: serving religion, art here addresses our deepest concerns. The altar's beauty *serves* this attempt. The beauty of architecture has much to tell us about the nature of this service and about its relationship to beauty.

That the aesthetic approach to art, which insists that art be for art's or for beauty's sake and makes self-sufficient presence constitutive of both, cannot be considered the norm by which the production of what we generally call art has been or should be judged is suggested by Panofsky when he points out that Poussin's assertion that "la fin de l'art est la délectation," was revolutionary in its time (*Meaning*, 10). The key to this revolution is provided by what I have called the aesthetic approach to art.

To claim this is to insist also that the aesthetic approach belongs to the modern period. As is well known, we owe both, the term "aesthetics" and the establishment of aesthetics as one of the main branches of philosophy, to Alexander Gottlieb Baumgarten's dissertation of 1735, in which he hoped to show how, within the framework furnished by the philosophy of Descartes, room could be made for the study of taste and art, more especially of poetry. The fact that philosophical aesthetics is an offspring of rationalism and thus part of the Enlightenment's somewhat questionable legacy points to its place in the social-historical context.

Especially revealing is a simile Baumgarten offers his reader: a successful poem is said to be like a world, where, following Leibniz, Baumgarten takes the world to be a perfectly ordered cosmos.[3] In this best of all possible worlds, nothing is missing, nothing superfluous; everything is as it should be. Perfection means such completeness. The work of art, Baumgarten asserts, should be a similarly perfect, self-sufficient whole.

To speak here of *perfection* is to insist on the self-sufficient presence of the beautiful. To the extent that the artist's goal is beauty, his concern will not be to create a work that refers those who enjoy it beyond itself, say, by expressing some edifying thought or by representing some cherished object or person. To praise such a work for being true or to condemn it for being false is to miss what matters: that it absorbs all our attention. Presenting itself to us as being just as it should be, a beautiful work of art should deliver us from the sense of arbitrariness and contingency that pervades our everyday life and forces us to struggle with many possibilities of existence. Absorbed in the work of art we no longer face different possibilities. Thus absorbed we no longer are burdened by an open future. In time, aesthetic experience lifts the burden of time, allowing us to exist, if only for a time, sub specie aeternitatis, in a seemingly timeless present.

That architecture has difficulty rising to such self-sufficient perfection should be evident: architecture will not be divorced from everyday concerns. As Kant observes, not beauty, but "the suitability of a product for a certain use is the essential thing in an *architectural work*."[4] To be sure, it is possible to consider and even to build works of architecture as aesthetic objects, as is demonstrated, for example, by Alexander Tzonis and Liane Lefaivre's discussion of classical architecture. Invoking the authority of Aristotle, they too insist that the work of architecture, like every work of art, "is a world within the world, 'complete,' 'integral,' 'whole,' a world where there is no contradiction."[5] Given this conception of the work of architecture as another world, all "outside conditions" must be considered "significant obstacles." By its very nature, the aesthetic approach to architecture is opposed to every contextualism. "In ancient Greece, temples" thus "turned a cold shoulder to every structure that happened to be next to them, even if this other structure was another temple" (Tzonis and Lefaivre, *Classical Architecture*, 243). I do not want to raise here the question of the adequacy of this characterization. But the basic point must be affirmed and could be illustrated with modern examples: *to the extent* that the aesthetic approach as I have described it governs building, works of architecture must *turn a cold shoulder*, not only to their neighbors, but to a world that would constrain them with its demands and necessities.

Of course the world will not be denied. It provides the given, the inevitable point of departure. But if the status of the work of art as a self-sufficient whole is to be preserved, it may do no more than that. Given the aesthetic approach, Paul Valéry's definition of poetry as *"an effort by one man* to create an artificial and ideal order of a material of vulgar origin,"[6] the material in this case being ordinary language, holds of every work of art. Quite in the spirit of Valéry, Tzonis and Lefaivre thus proclaim that "the *poetic* identity of a building depends not on its stability, on its function, or on the efficiency of the means of its production, but on the way in which all the above have been limited, bent, and subordinated by purely formal requirements" (Tzonis and Lefaivre, *Classical Architecture*, 276).

But rarely, if ever, will architecture be permitted to turn a cold shoulder to the world: it has to be both beautiful and practical; indeed, considerations of utility will almost always take precedence over purely aesthetic concerns. But to the extent that this is the case, beauty in architecture can appear only as an addition to what necessity dictates. This is to say also that from the aesthetic point of view, the architect inevitably has to compromise the purity of his artistic vision. So understood, architecture is an essentially impure, unchaste art. Nonaesthetic constraints continually threaten its aesthetic respectability. Never will its shoulder be cold enough, its presence unsullied by the meanings of the world. Buildings have to be more than objects for aesthetic contemplation. On the aesthetic approach, the beauty of architecture has to appear as an extra, as something added on to what necessity dictates, as decoration in a broad sense. The tensions that result from this mingling of pragmatic and aesthetic concerns all but rule out aesthetic completeness.

Developing some of the implications of Pevsner's distinction between architecture and mere building, I have argued that on the presupposed aesthetic approach, beautiful presence has to be wrested again and again from a world that is too much with the architect. The beauty of architecture has to appear as something added on to what the necessities of building dictate. The aesthetic approach forces us thus to understand the work of architecture as essentially a *decorated shed*.

The term is of course not my own, but belongs to the authors of *Learning from Las Vegas*, Robert Venturi, Denise Scott Brown, and Steven Izenour. Given the aesthetic approach, their call for an architecture of decorated sheds is anything but controversial. It simply admonishes us to recognize and affirm the inevitable compromises that beauty must make with necessity. From the aesthetic point of view, architecture can claim the dignity of the other arts only to the extent that it liberates itself from the requirements of building and becomes a strange kind of abstract mega-sculpture. From the point of view of function, the aesthetic component that is to transform functional buildings into art, into works of architecture, cannot but seem superfluous and arbitrary. That is true not only of applied decoration but equally of forms and proportions that answer only to an aesthetic concern. The historicizing, eclectic architecture of the late nineteenth century has provided modernists with an obvious paradigm.

But did Venturi and his associates really call for a return to the half-hearted historicism of the nineteenth century with its borrowed decoration? Were they really committed to what I have called the aesthetic approach? Did they not rather call it into question? What they deplored was, after all, not so much the modernist turn away from decoration and ornament, as the way "modern architects abandoned a tradition of iconology in which painting, sculpture, and graphics were combined with architecture."[7]

We meet here not so much with a demand for decoration, as with a repudiation of what is experienced as the muteness of modern architecture, with a longing for architecture as text, for buildings that carry messages, that can be read. If *Learning from Las Vegas* calls for decoration, it calls not for decoration that offers no more than an aesthetic supplement but for decoration that allows buildings to speak. Such decoration can no longer be understood as just a beautiful presence, for all speech owes its meaning to what remains absent.

The authors of *Learning from Las Vegas* hoped to make architects more self-conscious about how they use signs and symbols. Evident is the longing for an architecture that can be read, for buildings that invite us to understand them in the image of texts. Much architecture of the past invites such reading. Think of a gothic or a baroque church: such a church is much more than just a decorated shed, that is, a functional building to which an aesthetic component had been added. Beyond and even before its aesthetic function, decoration here has a quasi-linguistic function. The decorative elements carry a message, communicate meaning. Like most postmodern architects, Venturi would reclaim for architecture this obscured textual dimension. Architecture is to rediscover its voice. By its insistence on the self-sufficient, absorbing presence of the beautiful, the aesthetic approach had to muffle this voice; it had to render beauty mute.

Learning From Las Vegas would return to architecture its voice. For this reason it calls on us to learn from Levittown and Las Vegas: "Like the archetypal grain elevators some generations ago, the Flamingo sign will be the model to shock our sensibility towards a new architecture.... This architecture of styles and signs" is said to be "antispatial" (Venturi, Brown, and Izenour, *Learning,* 161). "Communication dominates space as an element in the architecture and in the landscape" (8).

If modernist architecture let space triumph over communication, *Learning from Las Vegas* would invert that triumph by celebrating "the dominance of signs over space" (9). Meaning is to triumph over what lacks meaning, spirit over body.

With this turn to the word we are close to an artist like Marcel Duchamp, the prototypical postmodern artist. Here is how Duchamp understood what distinguished his work from all modernist art:

> I wanted to get away from the physical aspect of painting. I was much more interested in recreating ideas in painting. For me the title was very important. I was interested in making painting serve my purposes, and in getting away from the physicality of painting. For me Courbet had introduced the physical emphasis in the nineteenth century. I was interested in ideas—not merely in visual products. I wanted to put painting once again at the service of the mind. And my painting was, of course, at once regarded as "intellectual," "literary" painting.[8]

Duchamp went on to assert that "until the last hundred years all painting had been literary or religious," that is to say, had been at the service of words, most often of the Word. I would have said, since the rise of the aesthetic approach and its substitution of the pursuit of presence for the pursuit of absent meaning. From this perspective modern art's turn from the literary to the visual appears as a curious deflection from the mainstream of art.

In this light *Learning from Las Vegas*, with its call for a literary architecture, appears as an attempt to return architecture to its mainstream. Duchamp's emphasis on titles has its counterpart in Venturi's emphasis on signs; Duchamp's turn away from the physical side of painting toward ideas, in Venturi's turn away from buildings as first of all articulations of space toward an "architecture of communication."

I would like to agree with this call for "an impure architecture of communication" (Venturi, Brown, and Izenour, *Learning,* 18), and the implied turn away from the elusive pursuit of aesthetic presence. Still I wonder, what language is architecture to speak? We are told to look to the typical American main street with its "false fronts, disengaged and turned perpendicular to the highway as big, high signs" (18), asked to explore the often ugly, but symbol-laden suburban edges of our cities, with their magic miles of shopping centers, gas stations, and fast-food restaurants, invited to give Los Angeles and Las Vegas a chance to fire our imagination. But what really is the lesson to be learned from this architecture of "signs of persuasion that shout their gorgeous cacophony but hide their restraining order" (77)?

Learning from Las Vegas has given particularly striking expression to the linguistic turn that has helped shape recent architectural theory and practice. The same concern to restore to architecture its lost or perhaps just disregarded voice shows itself in the vogue enjoyed by talk about semiotic and structuralist approaches to architecture, about architecture's semantics and syntactics. The fact that for two or three decades now architecture and architectural theory have been so fascinated by language and linguistics invites questioning and reflection. As Manfredo Tafuri points out, "the emergence, within architectural criticism, of the language problem" answers, not just to a sense of crisis in architecture, but to a widespread conviction that this is a language crisis.[9] Is it? In just what sense can we speak of a *language* crisis in architecture? Such talk presupposes that we can meaningfully attribute a language to architecture. But what do we mean when we claim that architecture possesses a language?

We should be on guard before the linguistic turn taken by architectural theory. As Roger Scruton insists, often it has offered little more than a jargon that obscures more than it reveals. And yet I cannot follow Scruton when, invoking the authority of Frege, he insists that the syntax of language derives from its relation to truth and concludes that for this reason "the whole 'science' of semiology is founded upon a mistake."[10] This presupposes an overly reductive understanding of language even in its literal, perhaps we should say, its proper sense, an understanding that could not begin to do justice to the language of poetry. If the language analogy has something to offer to architectural theory, it would seem to be the discourse of poetry to which we should look, rather than the discourse of science with its true or false assertions.

We may consider any communication relying on some code "language." An expressive sigh, for example, or a style of painting is language in this sense: relying on a code, they communicate a particular way of standing in the world and of seeing—a particular ethos. Sign and signified here can be given a quite specific meaning. In this sense architecture, too, belongs to language, not because it makes assertions, nor because its "saying" can be translated without significant loss into spoken or written words, but because of its style and of particular configurations of elements within that style. Scruton has done us a service by showing that talk about the language of architecture is often careless and misleading. But need it be? Has Umberto Eco, for one, not shown us that there is good reason to speak of the language of architecture, that it is worthwhile to attempt to understand that language, that is, to develop a semiotics of architecture? Such attempts seem especially important, given the language crisis of modern architecture.

Still, when one applies Eco's semiotic approach to architecture, the results are disappointing. All too often the discussion remains so general that instead of illuminating what one might call the language of architecture, it rather obstructs what is specifically architectural. Take Eco's version of the often-told story of the first human shelter:

> Still "all wonder and ferocity" (to use Vico's phrase), driven by cold and rain and following the example of some animal or obeying an impulse in which instinct and reasoning are mixed in a confused way, this hypothetical Stone Age man takes shelter in a recess, in some hole on the side of a mountain, in a cave. Sheltered from the wind and rain, he examines the cave that shelters him, by daylight or by the light of a fire.... He notes the amplitude of the vault, and understands this as the limit of an outside space, which is (with its wind and rain) *cut off,* and as the *beginning of an inside space,* which is likely to evoke in him some unclear nostalgia for the womb, imbue him with feelings of protection, and appear still imprecise and ambiguous to him, seen under a play of shadow and light. Once the storm is over, he might leave the cave and reconsider it from the outside.... Thus an "idea of the cave" takes shape, which is useful at least as a mnemonic device, enabling him to think of the cave later on as a possible objective in case of rain; but it also enables him to recog-

nize in another cave the same *possibility of shelter* found in the first one. At the second cave he tries, the idea of *that* cave is soon replaced by the idea of cave *tout court*—a *model*, a *type*, something that does not exist concretely but on the basis of which he can recognize a certain context of phenomena as "cave."[11]

Particular caves now have come to denote "cave" or, more generally, the idea of shelter, and to connote feelings of protection. But this language of denotation and connotation does little to illuminate what is specifically architectural: in this sense anything at all may be said to denote and to connote. A particular rose, for example, is seen *as* a rose. In this sense it denotes "rose." But "rose" also carries a host of connotations. How then does talk of denotation and connotation help us to understand the distinctive language of architecture?

Suppose we insist, mindful of the suggestion that to build is necessarily also to communicate, that a building is a human creation that to function must signify how it is to be used: to function successfully as a door, that door must signify "door." But this still does not distinguish buildings or their parts from tools or machines. Hammers, telephones, and cars also signify what they are. And inevitably they not only denote but carry a host of connotations, and often the connotations will concern the producer, who wishes to sell his product, more than the denotation will, which are more easily taken for granted. Buildings, too, can be discussed in this way as complicated tools or machines, but such an approach fails to do justice to the distinctive way in which they speak to us. Nor do we make up for this failure when we consider the specific functions buildings serve and inquire into the requirements of human dwelling. Such inquiry threatens to lose sight of the distinctive voice of, say, a particular house or a factory: these buildings speak to us as they do by the inevitably particular way they bound space.[12]

Works of architecture speak to us as all buildings do, and yet Pevsner insists on a difference: architecture must be thought both in relation to and in opposition to all merely functional building. The same goes for its "language." But how then is that language to be understood? Eco points out that buildings denote the building type they exemplify. Works of architecture, I want to propose—very tentatively, only as a kind of trial balloon and quite aware of how preposterous such a proposal is likely to seem—do not just denote the kind of building they are; they *represent* buildings and building types. *Architecture is an art of representation.*[13]

Some buildings represent in the most obvious sense, for example, seafood restaurants shaped like lobster traps, cheese stores shaped like wheels of Swiss cheese, rock shops that look like rocks. But the very fact that in such cases a building's representational character cannot be overlooked, although it may amuse us, also prevents us from taking the structure seriously as a work of architecture. My attempt to saddle architecture with the idea of representation may thus seem much less promising than Venturi's call for an architecture of signs. If the latter invites an architecture of billboards with appended sheds, the turn to representation threatens to elevate the Long Island Duckling to the status of the Parthenon of a new architecture.

Such elevation is hardly my intention. I am fully aware that the lessons the Long Island Duckling holds are for the most part negative: lessons about what to avoid. But if so, what do I mean by "representation"? To develop my suggestion I could turn once more to examples of architecture that historicize so much that they are very often quite literally representational. Or I could turn to the gothic cathedral, which was built to represent the Heavenly Jerusalem. Instead I would like to take a look at Marc-Antoine Laugier's *Essay on Architecture*, a key text of eighteenth-century architectural theory.

According to Laugier, what lifts architecture beyond mere building would seem to be its power of representation: architecture should represent the primitive hut, an ideal building, supported not by the authority of the Bible, like the Heavenly Jerusalem, but, or so Laugier thought, by reason and nature. What Laugier has to say about the architecture of his own time suggests indeed the need for a double representation: since the Greek temple is thought to have provided the paradigm of representational architecture, architecture today would do well to represent it and thus to return to the *archē* of building.

To speak of its *archē*, architecture has to make conspicuous the usually taken for granted and hardly noticed natural elements of building. Greek temple architecture is supposed to have accomplished this by translating wooden vertical supports into columns of stone, the supported horizontal members into entablatures, the inclined members that carry the roof into pediments. Such translation re-presents the translated element, which translated draws our attention to its presence. Re-presentation makes visible.

It is easy to show that what Laugier took to be the authority of reason and nature owed all too much to the prejudices of the culture to which he belonged. But this should not lead us to dismiss the view that *building becomes architecture when it re-presents itself by turning to the architecture of the past in order to represent an imagined, ideal architecture that answers to dreams of genuine building and dwelling*. It would be foolish to look for this ideal building in history or in some timeless Platonic heaven. A necessarily precarious construction of the imagination, it can be expected to change with changing hopes and expectations.

In the eighteenth century, Laugier was not alone in his understanding of the representational character of architecture. Such a view seemed an almost inevitable extension of the then widely taken for granted representational character of all art. For a more explicit statement we can turn to Laugier's contemporary, Francesco Milizia. According to Milizia, architecture "is an art of imitation, as are all the other arts. The only distinction is that some of them have a natural model on which the system of imitation may be based. Such a model architecture lacks, but she has an alternative one offered to her by the natural industry of men when they built their first dwellings."[14] *Architecture represents building.*

That architecture in its highest sense is an art of representation was also Goethe's view. Goethe distinguishes three stages of the art of building. The first and most basic does not really deserve to be called "art," for here building only serves the human need for comfort. Building becomes an art only when it is also concerned with creating objects that present themselves to the eye as a harmonious whole.[15] So far Goethe only restates the familiar understanding of the work of architecture as a functional shed transformed by aesthetic considerations. But such a view does not satisfy him. Architecture of the highest rank requires something else: a turn to poetry, to fiction, and that means also to representation:

> Architecture is no art of representation, but an art for itself. But at its highest stage it cannot do without representation. For the sake of illusion, it translates the properties of one material into another, as, e.g., wooden construction is imitated by all the columnar orders. It translates the properties of one building unto another, as it combines, e.g. columns and pilasters with walls. It does this to become varied and rich. And as it is hard for the artist always to feel whether he is doing the right thing, so it is hard for the knowledgeable critic to judge whether he has done the right thing. (Goethe, "Baukunst," 671)[16]

Only a few years after Goethe, the philosopher Schelling insisted that only representation allows us to understand the character of architecture. For, as Kant observed, by its very nature architecture serves needs that have nothing to do with what beauty requires. If it is to raise itself to the level of art, architecture therefore has to distance itself from functional building, even as it must remain such building:

> As long as architecture serves mere need and is only useful, it is *only* this and cannot be beautiful at the same time. This it can become only when it becomes independent of such need. But since it cannot become absolutely independent, since finally, by its nature, it again and again borders on this need, it becomes beautiful only when it becomes at the same time independent of *itself*, becomes, so to speak, the *potentiation* and the free representation *of itself*.[17]

Hermann Bauer suggests that this understanding of architecture as an art of representation offers us a key to the architectural sensibility of the late eighteenth and early nineteenth century, to its love of the picturesque and of Palladian architecture (Bauer, *Rocaille*, 72). And no doubt it does. But is the significance of such insistence on the representational character of architecture thus limited? Could it be that, as Schelling suggests, it is precisely its self-reference that gives architecture its distinctive voice and raises it above mere building? To deserve to be called a work of architecture, a house may not just be a house; nor does it help to point out, with Eco, that to function successfully as a house, a building must denote the house type. To deserve to be called a work of architecture the house must represent a house, and by so doing, re-present itself as a house, Goethe might say, create the fiction of a house. The same can be said of a church, a museum, a city hall, a railroad station. Representing other architecture, the work of architecture re-presents itself in the image of an ideal, thus creating a fiction about itself. By its choice of what to represent and of the form of representation, it communicates a particular understanding of what is taken to matter in architecture and signifies a particular ideal of building and thus of dwelling.

The architectural theory of the Enlightenment found in the Greek temple's translation of an originary wooden edifice into a structure of stone the most obvious illustration of the essence of architecture as an art of representation. Consider once more the translation of wooden posts into columns of gleaming marble. Representation here means translation into a different medium. As a result of such translation, a particular building element is rendered conspicuous and that precisely is the point: representing a vertical support, the column re-presents itself in such a way that as we attend to it, we attend also to its ideal essence. From the point of view of function, such re-presentation is of course an unnecessary frill; the wooden post's translation into a gleaming column appears as unnecessary as all decoration.

Such association of re-presentation and decoration invites a reconsideration of the function of ornament. Should ornament perhaps serve so to re-present the ornament-bearer that it presents itself to us as a fiction of itself? Ruskin's attempt to locate what distinguishes architecture from mere building in the addition of ornament becomes more plausible when we understand ornament as having a re-presentational function.

Let me turn to a different example. Buildings serve dwelling. It is thus hardly surprising that, at least since Carlo Lodoli, architectural theorists have appealed to function when they wanted to challenge inherited paradigms. Taken literally, Lodoli's commandment, "In architecture only that shall show that has a definite function, and derives from the strictest necessity,"[18] appears to leave no room for ornament, nor for representation in architecture, nor indeed for any understanding of architecture as something different from mere building. The architectural manifestos of the twentieth century demonstrate the continued life of Lodoli's commandment. A rigorous functionalist has to reject all attempts to have a building re-present its functionality. He has to be critical of the many buildings designed to have the look of being functional, often at considerable cost, that is to say, at the price of true functionality. We can thus distinguish *rigorous functionalism* from what we can call *rhetorical functionalism*. The latter aims not so much at functional building as at a building's self–re-presentation as a functional building. Think of the Seagram Building or the Centre Pompidou. Rhetorical functionalism seeks to give buildings the look of being functional; it connotes an embrace of the economic imperative that has helped shape the modern world, acceptance of all the advantages of science and technology. Rhetorical functionalism communicates a modernist ethos, calls us to a particular way of dwelling. We may well want to question this call, wonder whether it does not do violence to the requirements of genuine dwelling, even as it claims to do justice to the shape of modernity. All I want to insist on here, however, is that what makes such buildings works of architecture is the addition of features, of ornament in an extended sense, that lets them become representations of an architectural ideal.

An analogous point must be made concerning Lodoli's other commandment, that "architecture must conform to the nature of materials" (Algarotti, "Saggio," 97). There is a sense in which the necessities of building enforce such conforming: every craftsman must understand the nature of his materials if his work is to succeed, if knives are to cut or walls to support vaults. But just as regard for function does not mean that an attempt has been made to display that function and to make it conspicuous, so regard for materials does not mean that an attempt has been made to call the nature of the material of which an object has been made to our attention. Quite the opposite. When tools work well, we often forget what they are made of. We really look at such objects of daily use only when something goes wrong: we lose a heel of a shoe or tear our pants. Suddenly the familiar and usually overlooked becomes conspicuous and all too visible. The same may be said of buildings: after the unfamiliarity of a newly painted wall has worn off, the broken yellow we have chosen may only call itself to our attention when suddenly made to glow by the late afternoon sun or when it blisters or peels.

But do not buildings that deserve to be called works of architecture invite us to attend to materials in a very different way? Heidegger thus says of a Greek temple that it "does not cause the material to disappear, but rather causes it to come forth for the very first time and to come into the Open of the work's world. The rock comes to bear and rest and so first becomes rock; metals come to glitter and shimmer, colors to glow."[19] We can distinguish buildings that merely presuppose a regard for the properties of materials from architecture that re-presents these materials and thereby reveals their properties: the heaviness of stone, the glitter of metals, the glow of colors. Re-presenting its materials, the work of architecture reveals its being. Such revelation presupposes that materials are worked in a way that invites us to step back from our usual involvement with things. Representation here means quite literally re-presentation: the builders of the Parthenon took up, worked, and re-presented the marble from Mount Pentelicus.

I do not want to insist on what is often called truth to materials, only on the rhetorical function of their re-presentation. Re-presentation lets materials speak. The importance of that function becomes apparent when we consider the variety of materials, for example, materials made available only by modern technology, such as steel, concrete, plastics, and tinted glass, as opposed to more traditional materials such as granite, brick, and wood. Different materials are differently affected by the passage of time and speak of different attitudes to time and thus of different ideals of building and dwelling.

My point here is not to argue for or against the choice of particular materials, only to suggest that the re-presentation of materials is part of the language of architecture. It helps the architect to communicate an often quite specific ideal of building and dwelling.

I began with the suggestion that architecture—precisely because, on the aesthetic approach, it has to be considered an essentially impure art—

invites us to question that approach. And inviting us to question the aesthetic approach, it also invites us to question the often taken for granted understanding of beauty as self-sufficient, absorbing presence. But has this discussion of architecture provided a pointer to guide such questioning? Does beauty have a re-presentational function?

To Pevsner's remark that what distinguishes architecture from mere building is that "it is designed with a view to aesthetic appeal" I have opposed the suggestion that a building becomes a work of architecture when designed as an idealizing self–re-presentation. But how deep is this opposition? Could it be that aesthetic appeal and self–re-presentation belong together? Does beauty help to re-present the beautiful just as an ornament helps to re-present the ornament-bearer? Consider in this connection the familiar concept of aesthetic distance: to understand the aesthetic object as thus distanced is to suggest that the aesthetic object presents itself to us as if in a frame. Beauty frames.[20] Thus "framed" the beautiful re-presents itself, becomes present once more. Think of a strikingly well dressed person, or of a gold bracelet circling an arm. Fashion offers countless opportunities to explore the re-presentational power of beauty.

An obvious way of transforming something familiar and therefore all too readily overlooked into an aesthetic object is quite literally to re-present it by displacing or translating it as we do when we carry it into a new environment, or place it on a pedestal, or put it into a frame. Duchamp demonstrated the revelatory power of such re-presentation with his ready-mades. Although such an approach can all too easily become automatic, I would grant that such re-presentation of the familiar seizes an essential aspect of all art. What is usually called representation in art can also be considered a kind of re-presentation, where what representation re-presents is not the material thing itself, but only its appearance. Representation here does not preserve the material identity of the represented; it means translation not just into a different environment but into a different medium, where such translation may itself be a re-presentation that celebrates the material employed. Consider Turner's *Steamer in a Snowstorm*: it is a re-presentation of paint which reveals its medium's stubborn materiality. The appeal of this work is bound up with the rift it opens up between representation and re-presentation, between absence and presence, a rift that is also collusion: the storm is not only represented, but re-presented, that is, reenacted.

Or think of the Parthenon frieze as both a representation of the Panathenaic Festival procession and a re-presentation of Pentelic marble. As this last example hints, architecture, especially, lives in such tensions. This is recognized by the Enlightenment's understanding of the work of architecture as both a representation of some precursor structure and a self-representation. Here, too, representation intertwines with re-presentation, absent meaning with material presencing. The temple's columns represent wooden posts while at the same time they re-present the marble. Representing posts, the columns also re-present themselves *as* posts, as vertical supports weighed down by the lintel's horizontal, now transformed into an entablature. The Doric column's fluting may seem mere decoration, but it, too, has a re-presentational function, re-asserting the column's verticality.

All this suggests that the added aesthetic component that according to Pevsner transforms buildings into works of architecture is not adequately understood as an aesthetic complement. That goes especially for architectural ornament. In *The Critique of Judgment* Kant offers us ornament as an example of a free beauty, a rather surprising choice—is not ornament essentially dependent, created to serve the ornament-bearer? How are we to reconcile such service with the self-sufficient presence demanded of the beautiful? The re-presentational function of ornament calls for a thoughtful consideration, not just of Kant's particular example, but of the presupposed understanding of beauty. Could it be that we arrive at a reduced and therefore inadequate understanding of beauty when we place one-sided emphasis on its absorbing presence? Could it be that, like ornament, beauty, too, must be sought in the interplay of presence and re-presentation? Think of the beauty of a person.

NOTES

1. Nikolaus Pevsner, *An Outline of European Architecture* (Harmondsworth, U.K.: Penguin, 1958), 23.

2. Erwin Panofsky, *Meaning in the Visual Arts* (Garden City, N.J.: Doubleday, 1955), 11.

3. Alexander Gottlieb Baumgarten, *Reflections on Poetry,* trans. Karl Aschenbrenner and William B. Holther (Berkeley and Los Angeles: University of California Press, 1954), 63.

4. Immanuel Kant, *Critique of Judgment,* trans. J. H. Bernard (New York: Hafner, 1951), 166.

5. Alexander Tzonis and Liane Lefaivre, *Classical Architecture: The Poetics of Order* (Cambridge: MIT Press, 1986), 9.

6. Paul Valéry, *The Art of Poetry,* trans Denise Folliot (New York: Vintage, 1961), 192.

7. Robert Venturi, Denise Scott Brown, and Steven Izenour, *Learning from Las Vegas: The Forgotten Symbolism of Architectural Form,* rev ed (Cambridge: MIT Press, 1977), 7.

8. Marcel Duchamp, "Painting... at the service of the mind," in *Theories of Modern Art: A Source Book by Artists and Critics,* ed. Herschel B Chipp (Berkeley and Los Angeles University of California Press, 1969), 393–94 See also Karsten Harries, "The Painter and the Word," *Bennington Review* 13 (June 1982): 19–25.

9. Manfredo Tafuri, *Theories and History of Architecture*, trans. Giorgio Verrecchia (New York: Harper & Row, 1980), 274.

10. Roger Scruton, *The Aesthetics of Architecture* (Princeton: Princeton University Press, 1979), 165.

11. Umberto Eco, "Function and Sign: Semiotics of Architecture," *Via* 2 (1973): 131.

12 See also Karsten Harries, "The Voices of Space," *Center: A Journal for Architecture in America* 4 (1988): 34–49

13. See also Karsten Harries, "On Truth and Lie in Architecture," *Via* 7 (1984). 47–57, and "Representation and Re-Presentation in Architecture," *Via* 9 (1988): 13–24

14. Francesco Milizia, *Memorie degli architetti antichi e moderni*, 3d ed., vol. 1 (Parma, 1781); cited in Joseph Rykwert, *On Adam's House in Paradise* (New York: The Museum of Modern Art, 1972), 67.

15. Johann Wolfgang von Goethe, "Baukunst," in *Gesamtausgabe*, ed. Wolfgang Freiherr von Lohneysen (Stuttgart: Cotta, 1961), 670.

16. See also Hermann Bauer, *Rocaille. Zur Herkunft und Zum Wesen eines Ornament-Motivs* (Berlin: de Gruyter, 1962), 71

17. Friedrich Wilhelm Joseph von Schelling, *Philosophie der Kunst*, vol. 5 of *Sämtliche Werke* (Stuttgart. Cotta, 1859), 578 See also Bauer, *Rocaille*, 71

18 Francesco Conte Algarotti, "Saggio sopra l'architettura," in *Opere*, vol 2 (Leghorn, 1764); cited in Emile Kaufmann, *Architecture in the Ages of Reason: Baroque and Post-Baroque in England, Italy, and France* (New York: Dover, 1968), 96

19. Martin Heidegger, "The Origin of the Work of Art," in *Poetry, Language, Thought*, trans. Albert Hofstadter (New York: Harper & Row, 1971), 46.

20. Karsten Harries, *The Broken Frame: Three Lectures* (Washington, D C.. Catholic University Press, 1989), 85

6

Making Space:
For a Poetry of Architecture

MARY ANN CAWS

> How can I understand something moving
> if not *against* something?
> —Gertrude Stein

RESPONDING IN KIND

Let me start with my favorite title, taken from John Ruskin, that seer of so many things. *The Poetry of Architecture*, he called a very early book—and that is the notion I want, at least implicitly, to address. What is the poetic when it merges with or re-presents the architectural? How do poetry and architecture mix? How does building in one realm interpret itself in another?

Or, more broadly, how does reading relate to two fields, the verbal and the visual? Can I take the apposition (and then the opposition) of stasis and motility, as it can be related to the built and what is in the act of being built, as essential here? This impulse is, I believe, not simply oxymoronic but lyric in the true sense of the term. It provides the impulse for some of the best recent philosophical writing and to wider considerations of the spatial contrasted with the linear, of the relation or the telling of our relation to space, line, and the mind imagining them, building through and on them.[1] What is our approach to the building-text constructed as a representation of itself? Surely how we each answer has import for our textual as well as for our architectural or architextural studies.[2]

READING WHAT WE BUILD

> A longing for architecture as text, for buildings that carry messages that can be read.
> —Robert Venturi, Denise Scott Brown, and Steven Izenour,
> *Learning from Las Vegas*

The first question that leaps to my mind when I read about aesthetic appeal concerns the issue of self-representation. This leaping is aggravated, or at least intensified, when I have to confront, even at second hand, Erwin Panofsky. Like the Virginia Woolf of feminist critics, he is the mentor/cult figure of even amateur art historians. Take Panofsky's own bizarre abandon in such a sentence as the one concerning our aesthetic experience of an object: "Only he who simply and wholly abandons himself to the object of his perception will experience it aesthetically."[3] I am being called on to get absorbed in something as if it were a matter of, well, love. Now I am on my guard. I have always liked the idea—and the actualization—of the suspension bridge and rather tend to think of my attitude, in aesthetics and perhaps beyond it, as deeply suspensional. I even go so far as to equate it with my most ingrown professional attachment, that of the lyric behavior that defined surrealism as a movement in the twenties and thirties. That movement has—I openly admit it—modeled my mind. André Breton, its leader, demanded we give up the distinction between the seeing eye and the object it sees: okay, I did. I gave up a lot.

So I am jumpy now about giving myself, even with a special sense of *abandon*, over to some constructional experience. Deconstruction at least permitted my essential nervousness a play and a space to play in, *without* self-abandon.

But are we not falling into a trap of abandon when we end up with personhood substituting for buildinghood? We are ascribing self-representation to our own building and our building-up: "What distinguishes works of architecture from mere buildings is that they are 'designed with a view to aesthetic appeal.' "[4]

My mind wanders: "Mere buildings"... I think of Arthur Danto's discourse on the topic of "mere real things."[5] That in its turn sends me straight back to old dear Henry James and his own splendid ironization of "The Real Thing," that story in which the real persons are too real to model themselves convincingly, in which their own representation is only possible by an other. No self-representation without imitation, it goes, more or less. So much for the instinctive reading process, but I remain mired in my meditation about the personalization of object presentation means. Sure, I am all for Venturi's "architecture of communication." I love to read buildings and everything else and to listen while Manfredo Tafuri speaks of a *language crisis* in modern architecture,[6] to say nothing of Umberto Eco on language too. Yet abandon still bothers me: whatever happened to agency? I am tired of smittenness; perhaps I want my subject back.

Now in this fiction that buildings as creative works create about themselves, I am asked to participate. I *like* participation: don't get me wrong. I am just wary of abandon. Buildings call us, and this we all admit, to a certain way of dwelling—is it a one-way experience, or are we to assume they care how we dwell? Do they have an ego? a super-ego? If we are going to communicate, it takes more than one.

As a child, I was haunted by what I remember as walls looking at the people dining within them in one of Scott's novels, *Quentin Durward*, I seem to recall; I never dared, grown-up, to look again within those pages. When I was in college, encountering all those Baudelairean trees observing us while we were trying to take a plain ordinary stroll in a plain forest, those pieces of nature insisting on corresponding with us got on my nerves. My classmates in college were all entranced with the notion of *correspondances* French-style: drawing out the *ances* so elegantly you would think Charles Baudelaire had gone to Haverford, taking a course or two in French at Bryn Mawr just like me. If I was going to get stared at every time I took a walk, "Oooh, *correspondances*!" was something I never ever wanted anything of. It's enough to have all those "oeil-de-boeuf" dormer windows staring at you in Paris streets without it getting to the nice plain American countryside. Down with personhood in buildings, I thought. In nature, too.

But Heidegger is different, all right: I am much more comfortable with how he sees various building materials coming forth so bravely to represent themselves, thrusting "into the Open of the work's world."[7] They were material only and now they become a material work. I like the plot of that one: it's upbeat, and it doesn't stare at you. Harries insists, as does Heidegger, on the rhetorical function of materials re-presenting themselves, speaking out as themselves afresh. Like Ruskin, without the inflammatory diction of his spellbinding rhetoric of which I have been so enamored for so long. Let me then simply eschew the personhood of the building, at least for the length of this response, and respond just to the latter notion, that of the re-presentation afresh of materials as themselves functioning for the outer gaze and the projected inward dwelling, the indwelling that most concerns us.

MAKING ROOM

I am assuming that we take architecture to be a dialogue between mind and space, in the medium of building material like that response André Breton encountered so frequently, "a response in the exterior world to a question you didn't know you had." A representation itself of thinking as of dwelling, of a problem and a specific solution whose double fascination goes past that specificity to speak of the meeting of the world and the human brain.

And so I want to point out three differing examples of constructors whose work I admire for their strongly personalized space-making, their poetic involvement with dwelling and seeing and being in space. They may seem to have nothing to do with each other, these artists: one concerned with history and politics in poetry and with a garden to learn them in; the second, with holding on to past vision, with nostalgia in a tiny space; and the third, with largeness and openness, with how art opens on the world. And yet, I think, they all teach about dwelling; they certainly all teach about mind and its encounter with building.

The first is the Scottish genius of a conceptual poet and gardener, Ian Hamilton Finlay, agoraphobic and unwilling to leave his rugged territory called Little Sparta at the edge of Edinburgh where poetry indwells in inscriptions and the fog clings to the land. Where action consists of writing and building and having built, not on simple sentiment, but on the strength of thought and architectural tradition—there is even a goose hut built on the Abbé Laugier's principles. Where conversation, even of buildings, is sparse, and counts all the more. Where you cannot visit and return unchanged. Here writing nestles amid some leaves, on some stones, angled, small, and all the more explosive in intention. It is a garden of philosophy, dedicated to the French Revolution in general and to Saint-Just in particular. Yet it has that kind of gentleness that knows how to share the land with violence. It is a garden of the heart and mind; by its tiny pond and on its hills under what is often an angry Scottish sky, you suspect that if the soul were to conceive of itself, to re-present itself these days, it would be in a place like this where the exterior speaks of the interior.

The second artist, Joseph Cornell, was concerned, like Mallarmé, with a Theatre of the Mind: how to build it and read it. He presents an architecture of the box as a model of the mind. Matta convinced him that he was framing experience as would an architect, and so he was.

In this constructed space, there develops a philosophy of inwardness and holding. These boxes are, in a sense, his three-dimensional diaries.[8] Here inside, there is room not just for his imaginings but ours also. Time passing is inscribed in his fountain boxes as in his films, as sand pours into a broken glass like a baroque *vanitas*, one more *memento mori* that ironically makes us feel more alive, where the interior speaks—as surely as Proust from his cork-lined room—to and of the exterior world.

The third constructor is an artist of action painting whose constructions make the grand gesture believable, who has known how to restore warmth to painting and let us live there. All the light of coasts Western and Eastern are here, all the primitive saturations of color found their forms in Robert Motherwell, in his series called *The Opens*; they are what I want to close with. You take a canvas leaning against a larger canvas, draw its outline, see how like a door it opens on what is behind it, joining inside and outside space. And then you upend it, suspend it from the ceiling, and now it is a window, giving out on the world. A door-window—a *porte-fenêtre*—opening like an architectural conception embodied in a canvas. Here is the conversation between interior and exterior, re-presenting all the possibilities, visual, conceptual, and vital, that we might have thought we had lost.

I am speaking, then, not about the beauty of any person, but rather a world that the personal makes possible and visible. That we can finally live in. This beauty of building, this *poetry of architecture*, is translatable into every language, instantly visible in what it offers, and knowing what it is to offer that.

The three architects of the mind I wanted to re-present here have known how to mingle building and poetry. Their seemingly opposed responses, small and immense, to the philosophy of dwelling, contribute to the conversation about what we are, I think, trying to build and rebuild, here and elsewhere, in our ongoing, impassioned work:

> I touch only the heart of things
> I hold the thread. . . .[9]

NOTES

1. On how the theories of Peter Eisenman and Jacques Derrida work together, see, for example, "Architecture and Conversation: Derrida, Bernard Tschumi, and Peter Eisenman," in my *Art of Interference: Stressed Readings in Visual and Verbal Texts* (Princeton: Princeton University Press, 1989)

2. In my *Metapoetics of the Passage: Architextures in Surrealism and After* (Hanover: University Press of New England, 1981), I try to develop the notion of an "architexture," a conversation about buildings-in-text to dwell in

3. Erwin Panofsky, *Meaning in the Visual Arts* (Garden City, N.J.: Doubleday, 1955), 11.

4. Karsten Harries, "Beauty, Language, and Re-Presentation," 62 Harries is speaking here of Nikolaus Pevsner's *Outline of European Architecture* (Harmondsworth: Penguin, 1958), 23.

5. In his *Transfiguration of the Commonplace* (Cambridge: Harvard University Press, 1981), 1–32.

6. Manfredo Tafuri, *Theories and History of Architecture*, trans. Giorgio Verrecchia (New York: Harper & Row, 1980), 174

7. Martin Heidegger, "The Origin of the Work of Art," in *Poetry, Language, Thought*, trans. Albert Hofstadter (New York: Harper & Row, 1971), 46.

8. As for his written diaries, they are excerpted in large doses in my *Joseph Cornell's Theater of the Mind: Selected Diaries, Letters, and Files* (New York and London: Thames & Hudson, 1994).

9. André Breton, "Vigilance," in *Poems of André Breton*, ed. and trans. Jean-Pierre Chauvin and Mary Ann Caws (Austin: University of Texas Press, 1986), 79

7

Intentionality Without Interiority: Wittgenstein and the Dynamics of Subjective Agency

CHARLES ALTIERI

> You care also to know who you are.
> Nothing so much as view but more than noise,
> For the hum pertains to you, fanning the interior
> And entering here through the window screen.
> —Ann Lauterbach, "Holding Air"

I hope to use Wittgenstein to elaborate a way of thinking about subjective agency that I think is sufficiently in tune with prevailing attitudes to gain a hearing and sufficiently different from them to be worth the trouble to attempt getting it right. Let me go straight to what I take these prevailing attitudes to be. If we take the basic issue to be how we explain the sense that subjectivity actually has force as agency, we find, in literary criticism at least, a narrow range of options. Its theoretical stances seem to be shaped primarily by poststructuralist principles calling our attention to how our notions of subjectivity depend on imaginary constructs subjecting us to the very systems of representation that we want subjective agency to control. Our hopes for an inner sanctuary from the marketplace in fact deepen our dependency on those ideological and personal relationships promising us images for an ego that in fact is nothing but a lack tormenting us with its insubstantiality.

So the case went for at least a decade. Now the picture is changing because "sophisticated" criticism has grown dissatisfied with accounts of slippage and ideological recontainment. The age seems to demand versions of the subject that can carry effective notions of agency so that we can speak theoretically of how individuals can generate resistance to the prevailing social order and sustain the moral and political values necessary to correlate our heightened senses of heterogeneity with the possibility of forming communities with which we can fully identify. But in order to satisfy these demands we resort to the same overall philosophical frameworks that displaced the subject and are much stronger at tracking error than in guiding judgment in practical matters.

Consider what seem the available theoretical options for developing an account of subjective agency. We could accept Lacan's emphasis on the role that the imaginary serves in shaping subjects as subjected to certain roles and structures, but then the best we could do is hope that his vague category of the real will serve progressive political interests because it is the register of those contradictions basic to social life as currently constituted. Or we could satisfy ourselves with Derrida's and Nancy's claims for shifting from traditional ideas of the self-reflexive, self-determining subject to some version of the notion of agency as singularity. For Derrida this singularity becomes the signatures we leave as traces embodied in the working style as it plays on the margins developed by constantly undoing the authority of prevailing categories, since in this way we both define differences and open ourselves to irreducible alterities and heterogeneities in social life. And for Nancy singularity places within what we had treated as the subject its own dependencies on the otherness allowing it to imagine its own distinctive place in society: singularity is the exposition of individual being which exposes its finitude by marking its spacing at the conjunction of various social textures, each weaving an intricate interplay of what we can take as psychic process, what we must grant to factors fundamentally outside the agent's control.[1] Finally, disgusted with all this we might be tempted to Richard Rorty's confidence that we have no need for a theory of the subject so long as we are clear on our interests in irony and in solidarity.

But none of these stances provide adequate conceptual means for accomplishing the ethical and political work we desire from them. In practical terms they cannot attribute to subjects the powers of articulate self-expression or judgment necessary for ordinary social relations, much less for deep interpersonal ones, and they cannot ground the kind of long-term commitments that I have argued elsewhere are necessary for cogent views of identity and responsibility. And in theoretical terms they remain trapped within systems that rely on quite limited and limiting binary oppositions between what can be represented, and hence subjected, and what escapes representation, only to be imagined as lack or alterity. In practice and in theory poststructuralism proves far better at locating alterity and heterogeneity than at defining what we can make of those conditions as we attempt to take responsibility for our own lives and imagine how these lives can take on significant social commitments. So I hope here to offer an overall stance on questions of subjective agency that takes a quite different departure, shaping its psychology on logical and grammatical features of what seems basic to the very possibility of attributing contents to first-person states. Taking up this perspective still allows us to use the strategies basic to poststructural critiques of empiricist confidence in third-person languages on the one hand and, on the other, of romantic and existential efforts to postulate deep inner selves with the powers we desire, could we only free that inwardness from the profound alienation it suffers before the social orders imposed upon it. Yet this perspective does not require such severe resistance to traditional notions of personal expressivity, judgment, and responsibility because it need not take its terms from the system of binary oppositions that still trap poststructural theory within the ontologies that it hopes to undermine and transform.

My vehicle for this alternative approach will be Wittgenstein's somewhat cryptic and underthematized comments on intentionality, since I find there at once a delicate psychology and a powerful means of securing public evidence for one's claims about agency. Wittgenstein can lead us to see how much of what we take as inner life can be read in what lies outside us, in how we use the grammar of the language, without our having to insist that because we see these factors within the language we are subjected by them. Subjective agency becomes less a matter of what we attribute to inner life than of what we display as particular modes of using those public resources to establish specific variants and secure distinct social bonds. Therefore, it may become possible finally to establish an alternative to Cartesian thinking without simply reducing subjectivity to behaviorist or social-constructivist analyses.

Let me try two ways of stating the general difference Wittgenstein can make in our thinking about subjective agency. The first, which I develop elsewhere, focuses on a basic contrast showing how much more radical

Wittgenstein is than Derrida, at least on the topic of how we might think about subjectivity. Derrida's Cartesian roots are nowhere more evident than in his treatment of intentionality. For Derrida we can only conceive intentionality as a process condemned to fighting against itself because as soon as the agent realizes an intention, the agent's difference is subsumed within the realization.[2] Fulfilled intentions are facts in the world, not states of a subject. Once desire is realized it becomes a fact in the world, an impersonal matter of public knowledge, no longer engaging and directing a singular investment. But the realization of desires frustrates or displaces intentionality only if one assumes that intentionality is primarily a structure in which agents bind desire to specific goals, which then do put intention in effect outside the subject and demand an unworking of realizations. We might also imagine, however, a Spinozan perspective in which what matters most for the subject is not the fate of specific objects of desire but the agent's sense that he or she can continue to form intentions about what is realized and about the interests that make certain realizations desired. Then the crucial issue for subjectivity is no longer the necessary struggle against determining itself but the possibility of understanding what provides transitions among intentions and dictates the subject's sense of directed agency. It is precisely this shift which enables us to explain why in most cases we do not actually feel any loss when intentions are realized; instead we feel the need to adapt to the situation thus produced. And that is why when certain realizations prove disturbing we cannot simply change objects but must reconsider the filiations and commitments shaping how and what we desire.

If there is an intentionality that cannot be represented in terms of specific intentional objects, there emerges an obvious question that leads to the second, even more general way I want to cast the basic difference Wittgenstein can make in our thinking about subjectivity. How do we speak about what we cannot imagine representing in any adequate way? Or, to put the same question in grammatical terms, what are the consequences in our practices for the fact that any strong sense of subjective agency necessarily cannot be represented as an object of knowledge? What we "know" must be available in principle for all subjects, or at least must be available for confirmation by other subjects. What we know must be describable, yet any strong notion of subjective agency requires positing a mode of being in the world that cannot be so described because it must be experienced from a particular point of view. Most philosophers who take us as the subject of the subject are sensitive to these issues, but only Wittgenstein seems to grasp its most fundamental implication—that we cannot hope to rely in such discourse even on oppositional structures when the terms of those oppositional structures are set by our models of knowledge. That is, we cannot follow most analytical philosophy in deciding that, because the subjective cannot be an object of knowledge, it can be banished to the netherworld of propositional attitudes that can be prised off the assertive core of an utterance. Nor can we take the opposite tack, which I see as basic to poststructuralism (and, in a more positive form, to romanticism) of taking subjective agency as lack or as a working that has the force it does precisely because it undoes or complicates all our positive categories. Whether this marginality be dismissed or idealized, it leaves the domain of subjectivity without any distinctive claims on us that we can articulate without falling back into the binary opposition between what can be represented and what cannot. Despite its endemic suspiciousness about its heritage, poststructuralist theory remains bound to a set of oppositions whose inevitability it does not question.

Wittgenstein, however, tries to locate subjective agency in relation to a much more fluid, less metaphysical structure of differences. Suppose for example that we developed some of our thinking about the first person in relation to its productive differences from second-person discourses. Or, more generally, suppose we could recognize what Michel Ter Hark's brilliant book on Wittgenstein calls an "asymmetrical logic" between first- and third-person procedures.[3] Then we can hope to find alternative ways of making attributions about subjectivity—not simply as the other of representation but as a set of functions whose workings we can explore by testing for the powers that our languages give to subject positions and by providing phenomenological analyses of what takes place as agents identify with those powers. Then we have new reasons for appreciating Wittgenstein's efforts to avoid the methods of analytical philosophy while addressing its fundamental concerns, and then we have means of exploring aspects of how we experience subjectivity that may in fact prove shared or shareable despite the heterogeneous social conditions we occupy. Then we may even be able to understand what is involved in seeking agreements in domains where we cannot rely on the prevailing apparatuses for the production of "knowledge."

Recent work in linguistics helps clarify how we can develop the significance of this postulated asymmetry distinguishing a domain of first-person concerns from any simple binary opposition to third-person procedures. John Lyons offers a suggestive example developing a contrast between sentences such as "I remember myself switching off the light" and "I remember switching off the light."[4] In the first case intentionality is not a significant semantic factor because there is a clear referring term that can be processed by anyone familiar with the language and situation. When the "I" functions deictically, we can treat subjective agency in terms of propositional attitudes and can parse statements in accord with third-person principles. But the second case introduces what might be called an "experiential" rather than a "descriptive" version of the same sentence: "I remember switching off the light." Here the memory is not of a fact. Nor is it quite of a "sensation" or a "feeling," since these terms still try to fix the force of the "I" in terms of properties we can treat as simply accompanying the descriptive components of the sentence. We go less wrong if we speak of the memory as a one-place complex or state that does not separate into an "I" observing something outside it, but that instead simply presents the "I" as at once the force that does the remembering and the object that memory restores to the person's attention.

These subtle differences take on a fuller substance in another of Lyons's examples, this one focused on the difference between deictic and modal uses of the "I" ("Deixis and Subjectivity," 103–6). If I use the verb "express" in a transitive, nonreflexive sense, especially in past-tense situations, I can once again locate an object that in principle can be understood independently of any distinctive first-person elements. One could say, "I expressed rage," or "I finally get to express my personality." But "express" can also have "self-reflexive properties that cannot be reduced . . . to the assertion of a set of propositions" or recuperated within a "neutral metalanguage with an objective, or transcendent, point of reference" (104). The crucial operator here is the relation of agency to the progressive present tense (analogous to the imperfect tense). Suppose someone says, "I am expressing my rage: do not ask me to describe it," then the relation to the rage has significant parallels to a statement like "I am expressing my personality." It makes less sense to look beyond the object to something independent that the agent tries to define than to take the expression itself as actually shaping the object of attention. The expression at once exemplifies the relevant state and tries to provide some aspects of context that will clarify why this distinctive manifestation matters to the agent: the activity carries the meaning of what is expressed. So if we want to characterize what the agent is trying to put before us, we must not project some independent object or condition that he or she is attempting to describe. Instead the condition consists primarily in what the activity displays.

Therefore such expressions are neither objects for knowledge nor marks of lacks that haunt or unwork our descriptive categories. They are simply elements that require an entirely different model of what language carries and how we go about making assessments of what such sentences propose. The relevant questions are not whether we can have determinate knowledge about such meanings but how we can position ourselves so as to appreciate what the statement involves and how it might engage us in some corresponding activity. Speaking only of the ontology involved, we might say that we encounter a situation where we see clearly what is limited about Descartes's "I think therefore I am." This equation confuses a substantial present tense allowing clear identity statements for entities (it is I who think) with the progressive present (I am thinking), then tries to draw a conclusion that relies on the second to demonstrate the first—that is, that there is a stable identity in the thinking. But in fact the "I think" only makes sense as a progressive present, and thus warrants only the conclusion "As I think, that I am." We cannot make any more stable representations, of thinking nor need we, since thinking focuses attention instead on the particular activities within which we use thinking for specific effects.

There is obviously much more to be said about the linguistic distinctions indicating different aspects of subjective agency. But for my generalizing purposes Lyons's work must serve to set a stage on which to explore more directly psychological features of agency. So I turn to a recent argument by Richard Moran that seeks to construct for this distinctive first-person activity a conceptual model that can accommodate the remark of Wittgenstein most evocatively establishing what this asymmetry involves: "If there were a verb meaning 'to believe falsely,' it would not have any significant first person present indicative."[5] We certainly can say that "I have false beliefs," but that is a statement about the beliefs, whereas Wittgenstein wants us to see that the agent cannot take the believing to be false. One judges beliefs as false because one has a second-order positive belief. Moran then shows that cases like this warrant recognizing that "it is not the case that every relation in which I stand towards another person is a relation in which I can stand towards myself."[6] And that in turn means that there can be constitutive features distinctive to the role that first persons play in the processes of assenting and dissenting. We can engage in those processes without on every level appealing to criteria or yielding to concerns for what can be known. For the first person not only makes reflections but also generates decisions that shape how those reflections are framed. But in saying this we must be careful to insist that although the decisions in question do not depend on specific acts of reasoning, they may well stem from a history of reflections within a project or discipline.

To demonstrate this, Moran asks us to examine how we can and cannot exercise self-control over our own mental states. Notice the fundamental differences between deciding whether or not to believe another person and returning to Wittgenstein's question of whether or not one believes oneself. In the first case we rely on criteria, on what we know about the person or about the assertion. In the second case we simply do not examine ourselves in that way. One cannot but believe oneself because in effect the believing simply is the orientation of the person. Where could one stand in order to doubt one's belief? Clearly the doubting would be in relation to another condition of believing. Similarly, in the first person we cannot "choose to hope" or "want to expect." And it is highly unlikely that we can treat ourselves unjustly or knowingly deceive ourselves.

Why not? What is it about propositional attitudes or about our orientation toward justice and resistance to deceit that brings such differences about? And why, the reader of Lyons might ask, does it become appropriate to speak about a progressive-present-tense use of an expression to characterize those activities which cannot be subsumed under third-person reasonings. For Moran, possible answers lie in turning to "the complexity of abilities involved in the ordinary faculty of self-awareness" (7). Self-awareness cannot be equated with self-knowledge. We can be self-aware as we engage in the progressive present, but knowledge requires a different relationship to time, one in which we can maintain the distance necessary to set a representation in a propositional relation to the world it claims to describe. In the decision mode, however, agency consists in a specific orientation, or tilt, that gives reasons their valences and acts their purposes. Thus we cannot distrust our believing or choose to hope because there is no room between the agent and the orientation for doubts to enter or for truth criteria to be applied. We do not make ourselves believe or hope; we find ourselves already in the process of believing or hoping. There is no self-consciousness independent of this sense of being always already in some disposition, of having already taken a path in relation to the world.

Even if we grant Moran's analysis of self-awareness, and if we are careful to distinguish active self-awareness, which orients belief, from a self-awareness that simply locates the agent through deictics, we still must ask how we can make such states objects of reflection, so that we begin to build on them corollary claims about the needs, interest, and powers characteristic of subjective agency. How can we engage in discourse about materials that cannot be represented so as to constitute asymmetrical knowledge claims? For this level of the issues we must turn directly to Wittgenstein, still the only thinker fully aware of the methodological challenges that this asymmetry involves and, correspondingly, of the enormous differences in how we conceive persons and values that might follow from shifting our methodological focus. Specifically, I argue that Wittgenstein's notion of aspect blindness offers us concrete ways of exploring and testing claims about the powers of agency without relying on argument or description. And on that basis he allows us to appreciate what is involved in expressing the force we find in these processes of orientation, to see how expressive acts become sources of value, and to adapt ourselves to the kinds of criteria we can apply when these expressive acts lead us into arenas where we cannot use our models for "knowledge."

Let me start with Wittgenstein at his most subtle, where the challenge to description manages to suggest an alternative ontology for imagining what is involved in the dynamics of subjective expression: "We say 'The expression in his voice was genuine.' If it was spurious we think as it were of another one behind it. *This* is the face he shows the world, inwardly he has another one. But this does not mean that when his expression is *genuine* he has two the same." (*PI*, 606). If we assume a symmetry between first- and third-person perspectives, it follows that any representation of the self should be tested against what we can determine as facts about the self. The representations refer either to states of the body or to some version of an inner life. And then we find ourselves forced to think within a set of persistent and misleading binary oppositions. The inner is contrasted to the outer, the private to the public, sensations to representations, and propositional attitudes to verifiable assertions. Consequently, we find ourselves populating that inner life while lamenting the gulf that keeps us wondering whether the signs we must read are genuine or deceptive. And phenomena such as choice or self-reference or expressivity seem difficult to discuss: having no clear place within the prevailing oppositions, they seem, as Wittgenstein said of sensations, "not a something, but not a nothing either" (*PI*, 304). But notice what happens in Wittgenstein's statement. When we do see an expression as fitting its agent, we do not take it as representing some other expression identical to it, and we do not imagine a gulf between inner and outer life.

What then do we imagine taking the place of the old model? One cannot simply replace it with another single structure without restoring a comparable version of the old binaries.[7] One can, though, begin to imagine what it might be like to treat subjective agency differently by asking how we might preserve this sense of immanence or continuity between the agent and the agent's expressions so that we might make predictions about the agent based not on what might be within but on the specific modes of appearance that the agent projects as bearing on the attribution of distinctive or singular identities. This new model will deal not with substances but with processes—processes exhibiting the agent's states as aspects of practices or ways of engaging in certain situations and processes at times requiring an observer to participate in some activity rather than to stand outside it as interpreter and judge.

If we can examine that model without being too quick to insist on arguments or even to leap on the mistakes of those still trying to explore where Wittgenstein might lead, we can hope to grasp on more intimate terms how our identities are figured within the ways we carry on our activities and how different agents can conform to one another's expressions even when they cannot make propositions about them. Let us then elaborate three basic themes that emerge through this Wittgensteinian approach to subjective agency. First I focus on Wittgenstein's notion of aspect blindness—in part because of its methodological importance for showing without analytically describing those areas of experience where we need to attribute distinctive force to subjective intentionality and in part because this technique enables us to locate subtle yet elemental features of experience ignored by philosophy that works directly with general arguments. Second, I elaborate the conditions that the play on aspects reveals by drawing contrasts between Wittgenstein and Husserl on intentionality, contrasts that enable us to see how we might preserve a strong sense of subjective agency without postulating internal objects and a hidden interior life that negotiates these objects. Finally I sketch some of the implications of Wittgenstein's distinction between "truth" and "truthfulness" in order to indicate the ethical corollaries that emerge from his work on expressive aspects of subjective agency.

Wittgenstein's notion of aspect blindness provides a brilliant means of gaining access to fundamental aspects of intentionality without positing any inherent foundational principles: we find out what is essential to us by projecting what we might lose if we could not rely on certain specific powers. And in the case of aspect blindness, the very process of testing gives us access to how much is involved in our abilities to manipulate aspects. The means of testing becomes itself important testimony to the complex capacities characterizing intentional agency. By projecting aspect blindness we imagine how we would have to live if certain possible alignments of the psyche were lacking. For example, one who is aspect-blind cannot handle the most fundamental imaginative practices that most of us take for granted. His or her world would remain completely coherent as a set of ideas and representations, but there would be no "will," no contingent first-person functions framing and varying and personalizing the world as we find it given to us:[8]

> One might say of someone that he was blind to the expression of a face. Would his eyesight on this account be defective? ... If you feel the seriousness of a tune, what are you perceiving? Nothing that could be conveyed by reproducing what you heard. I can imagine some arbitrary cipher ... to be a strictly correct letter of some foreign alphabet. Or again to be a faultily written one. ... And I can see it in various aspects according to the fiction I surround it with. And here there is a close kinship with experiencing the meaning of a word. (*PI*, 210)

This passage is intricately constructed to move from the eye to the ear to the experience of meaning—its aim to set the physical medium by which we perceive in tension with some other active force that enables faces to have expressions, sounds tunes, and texts meanings. That is, once we ask about aspects, we open the possibility for a world in which perceptions and paths change while the describable facts remain the same (*PI*, 196). Wittgenstein manages in a thoroughly concrete way to call our attention to how much of our lives requires adjusting not for changes in facts but for changes in attitude, or, more precisely, for changes in the position that subjects come to occupy and that color what will count as facts. Such experiments then show how much of what we take to be objective about the world is neither simply given nor quite constructed. We are not dealing with facts apart from the frameworks, or with frames that are somehow imposed by will. Consider for example trying to recall a face or make elements of a scene cohere as "this" specific situation. As we are searching, not even God could see in our minds what we seek (*PI*, 217), because there is no fact of the matter, there is only the effort to find a perspective or angle from which we can go on. Eye, ear, and mind have the powers they have because they live a life of possibilities and projections. Where the God's eye idealized in the *Tractatus* can only see, the human eye can explore aspects that bring to bear different fictions and compose elaborate comparisons or complex scenarios. This eye must renounce the possibility of aligning with a single scheme of facts as if there were a givenness to the world independent of our projections. But it gains the possibility of linking eye to an "I" constantly reworking and refiguring what in any situation we need to take as given, what fluid.

Husserl too dreamed of a model of subjective agency that could be contoured to that givenness without being overwhelmed by it. Rather than setting world against will, a phenomenological approach to intentionality might locate will as an aspect of the world, as if we became aware of ourselves through the forms that the world in fact takes for us. But for Wittgenstein the notion of specific intentional forms proved dangerous precisely because these forms so contain desires that they blind us to aspects of intentional activity that are more contingent and perhaps more profoundly indicative of the full subtle powers of subjective agency. Where Husserl stresses the forms that align mind and world, Wittgenstein focuses on the actual processes of framing. So in Wittgenstein intentionality consists in the ways that agents shape routes within the world and thus provide the bases for defining convictions, expressing priorities, and ultimately accepting responsibility for the routes chosen. Hence Wittgenstein's analyses of mental life can be far less static. Instead of attending to how situations unfold their essential structure, he can stress the directional force that intentionality disposes. Agents can be primarily doers rather than knowers. Subjects are less concerned with how the world appears than with how human consciousness animates and frames those appearances. "The eye's plain version" becomes a secondary mode of apprehension, fit for the gathering of information but completely inadequate for how agents invest in what they see or project. (One might say that Wittgenstein wants an intentionality for Cézanne's eye rather than for Corot's.)

Both these differences from Husserl and the stakes involved become clear if we take as our case of aspect blindness the inability to distinguish between making copies of what we see and making models of how we engage aspects of what we see:

> If I know the schematic cube has various aspects and I want to find out what someone else sees, I can get him to make a model of what he sees, in addition to a copy, or to point to such a model; even though *he* has no idea of my purpose in demanding two accounts. But when we have a changing aspect the case is altered. Now the only possible expression of our experience is what before perhaps seemed, or even was, a useless specification once we

had the copy. And this by itself wrecks the comparison of 'organization' with color and shape in visual impressions. (*PI,* 196)

When we deal with aspects, with the capacity to see an image as a duck or as a rabbit, we deal with a situation where there can be "the expression of a *new* perception and at the same time of the perceptions being unchanged" (*PI,* 196). And that in turn entails having a sense of subjective agency that can at once be part of the world that seems stable and a source for what tilts that world in various directions. We must be able to imagine forces within that agency which can simultaneously understand everything that the copy offers and compose models giving distinctive emphasis to certain aspects that in the copy simply coexist with others.

Kant's "Transcendental Dialectic" showed that even for a copy we need to posit activity by a subject; Wittgenstein then asks us to reflect on what additional powers we must acknowledge in order to understand how and why we make models as well as copies. For copies the subject can be a transpersonal one. There must be a subject position, but the subject position is one that is shared by any agent who knows how to make or use the copy. And if we understand the copy, we necessarily have the power to occupy that subject position. But understanding the model does not carry the same possibilities. When I am given a model (in the sense that Wittgenstein uses here), I am not given a place for me to stand but an index of where someone else stands so that I can appreciate the particular tilt being given to what the copy represents. The model is of a situation constructed from a specific point of view in order to make visible the aspect from which it derives its relation to other contexts and concerns shaping the agent's stance.

Once we allow a distinctive role for producing models, philosophy faces the problem of having to account for a force that is aspect-provoking as well as aspect-seeing while explaining how that tilt does not distort the agent's capacity also to make and understand copies. The aspect-establishing agent does not simply bring to bear a point of view; instead he or she enacts possibilities within what remains an utterly public world, with each aspect in principle also shareable once we are given the model. So we need a version of the intentional subject who moves fluidly between how agents differ and how they share worlds. Yet we cannot attribute these differences to any interiority on the part of the agent, at least not any interiority for which we claim causal powers. For if we attribute the modeling to such interior forces we would have trouble explaining how the intentional activity takes on such fluid and apparently immediate shifting of perspectives. And we would be led back into the infinite regress that haunts all third-person principles used to account for basic agent decisions or progressive-present-tense judgments: we have to explain what causes this cause rather than some other cause being effective in determining what aspect we take up. In order to grant a subject's directional force without incurring that endless regress, we need a principle of agency that can manifest its singular position simply as that feature which allows the copy to function as a model.[9]

Wittgenstein offers two basic ways of understanding how intentional activity can establish these principles. The first defines a process of decision that extends Moran's account. We do not need to ground intentionality in any inner process in order to see how it mobilizes distinctive aspects of singular agency. We need only imagine ourselves capable of orienting ourselves to specific processes and paying attention to our place within them: "What is the natural expression of an intention? Look at a cat when it stalks a bird; or a beast when it wants to escape" (*PI,* 647). Oddly, it is by eliminating all humanistic assumptions that Wittgenstein can capture an immediacy for which there is no available third-person account. The orientation is too spontaneous and fluid to allow any notion of internal causality that presents the agent as somehow interpreting its own sensations and desires, as if it could reason about the directions it sets itself to take. Yet it is clear that agents can reason from within the direction chosen or can engage in reflective practices that do deliberate about future directions. So Wittgenstein needs to supplement that immediacy with a second feature of intentionality exploring the relational principles basic to the making of models: "Why do I want to tell him about an intention too, as well as telling him what I did? Not because the intention was also something which was going on at that time. But because I want to tell him something about *myself,* which goes beyond what happened at that time" (*PI,* 659). In one important respect, then, it is a mistake to treat intentions as discrete states with independent causal properties. Phenomenologically we attribute contents to intentions not as specific isolated states but as aspects of ongoing processes, for example, in the case of the stalking cat. There intentionality is part of the process of stalking, not a separate directional procedure. Were the cat to discuss that intention, it would have simply to describe the deed and add contextualizing or evaluating factors. Explanation would consist not in a causal link between aspects of the event but in a characterization enabling us to get a fuller sense of the roles that the agent's investments played in giving a specific cast to what emerges.

Examples like that of the cat suggest that if we want to understand subjective agency in actions it often proves less accurate to speak of an "intention to" do something than of an "intention in" an action that gives it a distinctive character. In the first case the intention is something separate that we think we can identify and whose causal force we can trace. But if we conceive the intentionality as evident within the activity, we treat it as an aspect of the action itself—not a cause but as what Kant called a purposive process. In such cases the purposiveness consists in a sense of the actor as locating within this action correlated states and concerns—both as qualities of attention within the action and as means of opening paths leading to subsequent possibilities. Thus for Wittgenstein intending is "as little an experience" as meaning because neither has experiential content (*PI*, 217). If meaning and intending were to have experiential content, we would be able to separate each from the content of the meaning or the specific focus of the intention. And then we would need intentions to intend, meanings to mean, and we would have to read the content of meaning and intending as modified by whatever the distinctive content of the experience of meaning and intending were. So it seems far more reasonable to view both meaning and intending as means of framing content and of directing attention in certain ways. Both these aspects of intending take place as conditions, not as actual experiences (unless we equate "intending" with "trying," a quite different grammatical phenomenology). Consequently, if we desire more information about intentional states, we are better off turning from description to speculation on how this action connects to the agent's overall traits and concerns.

But even if "one compares 'meaning him' with 'aiming at him' " (*PI*, 689), one needs still to explain in what the aim consists. If we require models rather than copies, what indicates that need, and how do we locate the power in the agent to establish what the model leads us to postulate? Finally, what version of agency can explain how the perception at once remains unchanged and yet takes on a different aspect: why is it that I at once share a world of cogent meanings, become transparent to others, and still retain the power to so charge the world with individual investments that others will ask us to bring other contexts to bear so that they can appreciate what our stakes are in given actions and views. Wittgenstein does not propose abstract psychological answers to these questions. Instead he asks us to understand subjective agency in terms of the powers agents come to exercise through the full grammatical force of three elementary linguistic operators, the deictics "now" and "this," and the multifaceted "as." The two deictics afford the most elemental means of establishing personal investments and defining singular orientations, whereas the "as" (which I discuss elsewhere)[10] goes a long way toward clarifying what we do when we attribute identities to the ways in which the "now" and the "this" are handled. Taken together, these three principles of agency grounded in grammar provide a model of subjective investment that is at once highly particular and abstractly elemental or formal and hence open to being shared as a principle even though its manifestations differ. Wittgenstein, in short, makes philosophy a modernist art.

"Now" and "this" define the temporal and spatial coordinates by which subjective desires modify the world and make the third-person perspective an inadequate interpretive stance. The third-person stance can analyze whatever stance the agent takes, but it cannot define the stance or the projections that accompany such framing. And these indexical operators offer the clearest, most elemental forms for those aspects of decision which establish orientations and link the present to possible futures and plausible pasts. It is the grammar of these deictics then that dramatizes both dimensions of aspect seeing that we have been considering. Because the "now" and the "this" are in one sense only shifters, only transparent operators that bring no specific content, we understand why the perception need not be changed by the perspective that realizes it. There are cognitive intentions that define a knowing subject and do not impose opaque perspectives. But because these operators also make present the concerns of what we might call a willing subject who sets cognitions in relation to a background involving practices, other contexts, and projected future states, they lead beyond simple shifters. Here the deictic does not simply serve as a placeholder. It also can carry a promissory quality that we can best grasp by attending to how understanding its force may require a model and not just a copy. A pure shifter would function the same way for anyone; the intentional "now" and "this" suggest a direction within the shifter that invites our seeking a better grasp of the perspective thereby brought to bear.

Making this distinctive force clear seems to me the most important feature of Wittgenstein's concern for the duck-rabbit experiment and more generally for the entire phenomenon of aspect seeing. Traditionally, critics have concentrated on the features of metaphor that emerge in Wittgenstein's discussion. But we also need to ask why Wittgenstein found metaphor so central to his work as a psychologist. Are there any distinctive attributes of speech situations in which metaphor plays a pronounced role? Wittgenstein addresses that question, in effect, by reminding us of what happens when there is no sense of seeing something as something else: an agent viewing the duck-rabbit would see one of these images and rest content with that. But the situation changes drastically when the agents realize that there could be more than one image. Then something like choice occurs although we must be careful to temper any humanistic understanding about what choice involves, because it seems as if it were in large part the modification in the object that brought the subject to the specific assertion, "Now I see it like this," "now it is a duck" or a rabbit, or even, "now it is a duck-rabbit."[11]

In each of these utterances the agent is not only reporting a perception, he or she is also recognizing his or her own framing participation in what is seen. Once I say "now" I see it this way, I also make possible a clearer sense of what it is about me that warrants such a frame or that might want to explain how I might take responsibility for it (*PI*, 195–96). So although the substratum of such experiences is "mastery of technique" (*PI*, 208), the mastery itself leads beyond the technique to a sense of how one's own power manages a fit with the world so that will and imagination (*PI*, 207) prove nonetheless anchored within what can yield descriptions and organize practices. And then we begin to see how it is possible to imagine desire and value moving within those social practices without displacing them into private factors that have no articulate expression. The "now" and the "this" mark workings of desire that need not lead back to isolated or negating subjectivity: "I have a theme played to me several times and each time in a slower tempo. In the end I say, " '*Now* it's right,' or '*Now* at last it's a march,' '*Now* at last it's a dance.' The same tone of voice expresses the dawning of an aspect" (*PI*, 206). So "now" contains a then; having located a place for one's own desires one knows how to go on in a way that can be shared with others.

There is a strong temptation to confine one's reflections on aspect blindness to such moments of recognition. These moments are enough to challenge prevailing accounts of the mind and to indicate the ineradicable decision making that first-person orientations provide. And Wittgenstein is certainly reticent with respect to more substantive claims about human agency that might follow from his analyses—which should come as no surprise, given the speculative excesses in German philosophy from Fichte to Spengler. But reticence is not silence. I think there are materials in his *Philosophical Investigations* that invite our shifting the focus from how agency is manifest in specific intentional moments to how that agency calls attention to itself as an active force expressing emotions and determining values. Such materials then make it possible to move from the agent's relation to a public grammar to the agent's interests in manipulating that grammar in the service of personal expression. The route to a model of expressive agency begins with the capacity of the "now" and the "this" to clarify and recast concerns for the relation between will and happiness that had obsessed Wittgenstein since the *Tractatus*. Then the distinction between models and copies affords one important way of treating this will as an expressive force. And finally Wittgenstein's resistance to traditional philosophical argument leads him to a distinction between "truth" and "truthfulness" enabling us to link expression to his theme of confession and hence to clarify our possible stakes in the entire enterprise of worrying about intentionality as the basis for philosophical psychology.

Wittgenstein opens the question of how will is connected to intentionality late in the first part of the *Philosophical Investigations*; then he returns to it as part of the thematics of "fit" and adaption involved in his discussions of coming to hear a tune or recognize a face. For the grammar of "now" and "this" proves capable not only of specifying an agent's orientation but also of actually affirming the path indicated. "Now" is a discovery term, marking the dawning of an aspect, but it is also a commissive, in the sense that it enables the agent to identify with a specific alignment of its being: "Now, at last, it's right." But to understand the full drama of that sense of rightness we must begin with the essentially transcendental attitude toward the will that Wittgenstein maintained in his *Notebooks, 1914–16*, then his *Tractatus*. Where his *Philosophical Investigations* distinguish sharply between first- and third-person stances, his earlier writings developed similar values by drawing their line between the claims of the world—the domain of empirical knowledge, in which propositions could be asserted—and the claims of a will transcendental to those propositions but fundamental for there being anything beyond fact in our experiences:

> 6.41 The sense of the world must lie outside the world. In the world everything is as it is, and everything happens as it does happen: *in* it no value exists—and if it did, it would have no value.
> If there is any value that does have value, it must lie outside the whole sphere of what happens and is the case. For all that happens and is the case is accidental.
> What makes it non-accidental cannot lie *within* the world, since if it did it would itself be accidental. . . .
> 6.42 And so it is impossible for there to be propositions of ethics.[12]

Because knowledge must be "in the world," there cannot be a "knowing subject." The subject is the condition of will at the margin of the world that registers and responds to the "miracle" that what exists does exist (*Notebooks, 1914–16,* 86). And since value resides at that margin, "What is good and evil is essentially the 'I,' not the world" (80). Therefore happiness and unhappiness are conditions depending entirely on the agent's will—with "will" to be understood not as a specific reasoned assertion but as an atmosphere giving color and value to a world of facts.

Wittgenstein's early position is by no means naive. It has no need to treat will as a separate empirical faculty that would require us to populate mental life with ghostly dramas. Instead the will is a function of certain relationships between agent and world, not a separable process with a content that can be isolated as an object of attention. Consequently the agent can avoid the problem of needing a will to will in order to get this faculty started in the first place. And he can separate knowing from the effects of will, so that will does not create the shape of facts but only establishes the registers in which facts are experienced. In fact, for early Wittgenstein the only stable means of happiness is to align subjectivity completely with the necessities that the world presents. Paradoxically, one becomes completely independent of the world by entirely accepting the givenness of things as they are and "renouncing any influence on happenings" (*Notebooks, 1914–16,* 73). By renouncing power over the world, one can focus entirely on the clarity and purpose one can give one's own life.

Here, though, we encounter one of the deep problems in psychology that require the new beginning the *Philosophical Investigations* establishes. As Michael Hodges points out, one cannot build a willing subject on the model of the transcendental knowing subject, nor give it that kind of freedom from contingency. Where the knowing subject shrinks to an extensionless point, with the eye folded within one's knowledge claim, the willing subject must remain particular, bound to one life for whose particularity it is responsible. Happiness is not shareable as truth is, and failures to attain happiness are not general failures but a specific situation with consequences only the concretely positioned agent must undergo (Hodges, *Transcendence and Wittgenstein's Tractatus,* 92, 107–53, 175–77).

Wittgenstein's later concern for the affective intensity indexicals can bring to bear provides him a powerful way of addressing these problems. The "now" and the "this" still frame facts without changing their cognitive status, but now this version of willing does not require any sense that will too is a transcendental relation that can occupy an independent totalizing perspective. Willing becomes simply a specific way in which the "now" frames a situation or process so as to carry the agent's full sense of finding a fit for the concerns it brings to bear.[13] The will constitutes values not by constructing fictions but in the form of certain qualities of concern and commitment within the agent's actions and reactions as if the indexical and present-progressive features of the "now" and the "this" make it possible to show how these concerns need not take the form of discursive reasons.

Where reasons have been, there the dramatic force of specific qualities of engagement can be. And where will had to frame an entire world to compose happiness and unhappiness, will now engages "things as they are" in terms of the full intricacy of qualitative equivalence sustained by that "as." For the grammar of "as" allows a rich interplay between indexical self-reference and complex equivalence terms by which we can give substance to the self-reference. Consider how we might see the will brought to bear in an agent's representing an act as bearing certain properties so that the representation serves both to specify his investments and to dramatize the force they have within the particular set of possible options. Insofar as we attribute this bringing to bear on properties to an intentional agent, we can correlate the domains of epistemology and axiology and then show how in each domain we can appreciate activities and investments that cannot be grasped from a third-person perspective. Thus when I present myself as a scholar, I immediately place my activities in a domain of values that does not alter facts or require any separate will to scholarship. Yet there emerges a clear focus for my investments and a public theater for assessing how my actions in fact satisfy what I want to invest them with.

This Wittgensteinian view of the will is difficult to state in general terms, but that is largely because it fits so well into a mode of thinking that replaces general forces by attention to degrees of intensity and aspects of engagement made possible within its paths. As with notions of meaning and intending, willing is a phenomenon best understood in relation to act-and-state terms like "aiming," "attending," and "trying," rather than in terms of discrete states to be experienced in themselves. Wittgenstein captures all these distinctions by condensing a cloud of philosophy into this drop of grammar: "I can always will inasmuch as I can never try to will" (*PI,* 619). The very idea of trying to will reflects the basic problems with the inherited models he is trying to displace. As soon as I try to will, I abstract the "I" from any "now" and "this" distinct from the agent's own self-reflection so there is no ongoing process within which the will takes hold and finds an activity that makes it exactly what one wants will to direct toward the world. Therefore, any working notion of will must assimilate it within the trying, rather than making it the object of trying.

It is instructive in this regard to notice the basic differences between our grammars for talking about wishing and about willing. I can try to change my wishes since wishes are objects that the mind produces and controls. With the will, on the other hand, there is strong temptation to speak with Nietzsche of the mind serving the will rather than controlling it. But for Wittgenstein we need not make the point so melodramatically. It suffices to locate will within the acts of mind rather than within or beyond reflexive consciousness, so that there need be no abstract dichotomies nor any dependence on mysterious inner principles. And we see how willing is continuous with the most elemental individuating impulses that tie the "now" and the "this" to what Wittgenstein's great precursor Spinoza projected as a *conatus* fundamental to all desiring agency and capable ultimately of a reflective grasp of its own relation to what calls it into being.

There remains the question of why philosophers could have held the idea that we try to will or why at least they have not managed to escape it. I think the persistence of that notion stems from the need that divides Spinoza's *Ethics* into two very different books, one devoted to the immanence of the *conatus*, the other to developing a reflective rationalism whereby the *conatus* can grasp its relation to the whole. We must account for both the immediate framing qualities of the will and a second-order capacity to take as its object not only particular conditions but its own basic orientations. In other words, wills invest in particular goods, and they can make reflection on their own conditions a basic factor in determining happiness and unhappiness.

At this point our earlier discussion of models comes back into focus. If we imagine combining the marks of will with the effort to cast actions as models, that is, as defining purposes and inviting relations to other aspects of the agent's behavior, we can go on to give an account of what we do when we take responsibility for or, better, *in* certain expressions of ourselves. And that in turn provides a basis for understanding how we can envision the "I" as a bearer of value because of the identities it seeks for these expressive activities. My ultimate concern in developing notions of expression is ethical. I want to show how an expressivist ethic goes a long way toward reconciling agent-centered concerns with modes of assessment that depend on third-person perspectives that can be elaborated in terms of the community to which the agent appeals as the arbiters for the identities sought.[14] And I think this approach enables us to keep identity issues central without insisting that agents unify all the disparate aspects of their lives. Bids for identity require our unifying only those aspects of our lives which are contained within the identity sought. My identity as a teacher does not entail my offering an audience any information about what I do in other contexts, but my identity as a friend might require much more general accountings of my actions and concerns. Because this topic is so broad, I concentrate on only those aspects of expressive behavior that get clarified by Wittgenstein's treatment of intentionality.

Returning to aspect blindness will provide a powerful measure of what Wittgenstein's treatment of indexicals offers for reflecting on how agents can be said to offer expressions that establish identity claims. Consider closely the textual movement by which Wittgenstein's "now" and "this" expand into second-order affirmations (*PI,* 213–15). At first Wittgenstein reflects simply on how we experience a sense of "now" as we register a sudden awareness of how the elements of a piece of music fit together. This new grasp of relations is akin to "experiencing the meaning of a word" and to registering the force that meanings have to redirect our orientations. Then Wittgenstein makes an important transition from questions of meaning to reflections on agency by asking repeatedly what a person would be missing were he blind to this fit. There is no better example for the contrast between these two states than the experience within works of art of elements taking on the force of the word becoming "completely filled with its meaning." A poem, for example, allows one not to have to stop with the individual meanings of the words. The poem allows us to view the play of aspects as if it were organized by some more encompassing fit that we measure in terms of whether or not the sentences take on a particular "ring." So now the "now" is taken beyond the punctual moment of discovery to a glimpse of how those moments are embedded in larger, shareable structures of expectations, "almost as if this word were a picture of the whole thing."

Wittgenstein's passage then shifts to an odd narrative of taking a walk and imagining that the city lay on his right even though he had no conscious reason to think it. So it seems as if this experience of fit cannot be determined by sense experience even though the sense of coherence it produces is inseparable from feeling one has found a path through some aspect of the material world. On that basis he returns one last time to analogies with works of art since there is no richer vehicle for feeling these sensuous elements entering expressive syntheses and hence establishing identities as overall configurations: "I feel as if I knew 'the city lay over there.... I feel as if the name 'Schubert' fitted Schubert's works and Schubert's face" (*PI*, 215).

Let us use this recognizing fit as homecoming to establish an analogy for the two basic value dimensions that allow the "now" to take on expressive force for subjective agency. One is entirely punctual, the sense of empowerment and invested attention that characterize having found a path that leads one out of confusion. The second takes exactly the same form, but functions entirely on a self-reflexive, second-order reading of the shape that one's overall desires have come to take, so that one can claim that they too seem to fit as if one had experienced a homecoming. The relation of the desiring subject to the multiple paths that the world offers becomes for reflection a mode of being within which one feels one knows one's way, almost as if in the process of telling more about oneself one could make one's own name fit one's life.

But we need another level of analysis before we can get a full picture of expressive activity. This example from Wittgenstein explains why people take such pleasure in Schubert but not the satisfaction that Schubert could take in his own creative activity. For that we must shift from the "now" and "this" of locating oneself within the world to the kind of "now" and "this" that defines particular tilts we can attribute to distinctive persons. Unless we make that shift we confine ourselves to a thematics of fit that grounds the will at the cost of subordinating the full potential agency of the one willing—a common feature of what Henry Staten calls conservative Wittgensteinian thinking.[15] We can at least indicate an alternative direction in Wittgenstein's *Investigations* by shifting to the role played in that text by the concept of confession, for his concern for this phenomenon organizes a complex field of distinctions necessary to connect expression to responsibility to the entire process of pursuing and assessing identities.

Once again all ladders start in the need to finesse third-person processes, this time in Wittgenstein's quest for alternatives to two basic features of Frege's and Russell's emphases on descriptions and truth-functional analyses. Wittgenstein wanted a form of meaning that was too immediate to involve the kind of judgment that governed empiricist thinking, and he wanted a version of psychological activity that was not directly bound either to the analysis of sensations or to the representation of private interior processes. Thus he developed a reading of expressive acts that emphasized their functioning as what his commentators call "avowals" rather than as any mode of representation, either of ideas or of inner states:

> How does a human being learn the meaning of the names of sensations? of the word 'pain' for example. Here is one possibility: . . . A child has hurt himself and he cries; and then adults talk to him and teach him exclamations and, later, sentences. They teach the child new pain behaviour.
> —"So you are saying that the word 'pain' really means crying?"
> —On the contrary: the verbal expression of pain replaces crying and does not describe it. For how can I go so far as to try to use language to get between pain and its expression? (*PI*, 244, 245)

This is perhaps the richest concrete practical rendering we have of the difference it can make to use notions of one-place predicates developed largely in relation to Kantian aesthetics. Such one-place expressions are not amalgams of specific assertions, each with a referent, as would be the case if we imagined the expression as a picture of a situation. Instead the expression functions in the same way that a work of art does: rather than offering a picture of some real Hamlet, Shakespeare's play offers a "Hamlet-picture," a specific intransitive configuration that we use not to represent a person but to orient others toward one possible configuration of details that can itself function as a label. In the case of expressions of pain, this means that we do better not to treat the statement as a description of pain, but instead take it as a means of pointing to how the agent is presenting his relation to the grammar that word invokes.[16] Similarly, statements of hoping and fearing are not descriptions of inner states but positionings of the agent to demonstrate the stakes that are involved in various propositions. In such cases we cannot separate the articulation from the agent, and we therefore must shift attention from what we can observe to what we can infer about the state that the speaker seems to be in.

We cannot respond to such expressions by testing their truth values in terms of some independent analytic procedure. Instead, response is a matter of adjustment, of positioning ourselves so that we can perform certain actions or ask questions that invite clarifications. Avowals shift semantic force from a relation of word to world to a relation of word to the agent's activity within a world. And that shift has two important consequences. Speculatively, it allows us to make sense of claims like Kant's that there are legislative aspects of intentional framings that actually arrange parts of the world and shape future interactions without the reasoning or formal models required by third-person language-games. Avowals are usually quite simple, as in the case of expressing pain. But the model of semantic force and of the way an audience is invited to respond can extend to far more complex cases. What matters is that we have to grant principles of organization internal to the utterance or utterance situation that are not shaped by truth-values but by the urgencies of a productive energy, which we then respond to by projecting contexts for those energies and in some way attuning ourselves to how the expressor reacts to our interpretations.

The second consequence is practical. This different semantics requires changing our expectations concerning the kind of knowledge we can expect about subjective agency and the discursive norms we can employ in making judgments. If we need to understand agents, the criteria we use for assessing interpretations will involve a good deal of "imponderable evidence" (cf. especially *PI,* 228), organized less by the canons of argument than by types and dense examples drawn from cultural backgrounds. We see then how the arts matter for a culture as repositories of those examples and the discourse they generate, but we also see that in principle there is nothing distinctive about the arts because all cultural memory functions in analogous ways. Even more important, we recognize why in discussing subjective agency the only constants we can project must be highly abstract. As soon as we try to construct ideas about distinctive traits characterizing actual agents, we find ourselves having to rely on specific cultural images while at the same time adapting ourselves to the legislative capacities enabling agents to develop different permutations of their heritages.[17] And that means it is a mistake to take the "I" as resistant to the symbolic order. The tension between the subject and the symbolic order derives primarily from the fact that the two occupy different structural levels. Considered formally, the "I" is a relational principle that has no specific cultural content; rather than being set against the symbolic, it depends on the symbolic for expressing its own intensities or aligning itself with the texture of social relations that language affords.

Confession proves the most comprehensive and most important mode of expression for Wittgenstein because this comprises what we might consider second-order avowals. As we should expect from Wittgenstein's bashfulness and distaste for melodrama, his own comments on confession lack any explicit autobiographical content, but they do nonetheless make quite clear how different a discursive universe we enter when we focus on avowals:

> The criteria for the truth of the *confession* that I thought such-and-such are not the criteria for a true *description* of a process.

> And the importance of the true confession does not reside in its being a correct and certain report of a process. It resides rather in the special consequences which can be drawn from a confession whose truth is guaranteed by the special criteria of *truthfulness*. (*PI,* 222)

Concerns for truth remain, but subordinated now to what he calls criteria for truthfulness, criteria which I take to involve the ways we can connect the agent's own investments and expressive desires to the descriptions that he or she might offer. That is, confessions extend the semantics and the ontology of avowals because we expect the same attention to the agent's working within a world, and we rely on what will allow us to take the statements as fundamentally one-place predicates. Obviously, any elaborate confession will involve propositions about what happened. But we respond to it as a confession only when we shift registers so that the important concerns are for truthfulness rather than for truth. We care more about the effort at truth than we do for specific accuracy in particular cases (although consistent efforts at accuracy are part of truthfulness). At stake, after all, is not only what happened but what identities and identifications one can claim by virtue of how those happenings become the material for the agent's expressive activity.

We make judgments about the confession exactly as we do judgments about expressions: we try to see how they connect to other features of a life by displaying the agent's own emphases and by inviting us to take certain attitudes toward the agent. But confession also requires a second-order version of those processes because the response desired is not only to some specific expressive act but to what might characterize the person making a series of expressions. Confessions define wills in the very process of coming to terms with what might constitute third-person descriptions. If we try to assess such expressions in terms of impersonal criteria, we are likely to impose categories precisely where the agent seeks to define an individual relation to facts. Therefore it becomes crucial that an audience align itself provisionally with the particularizing features of the utterance since that is the only way that one can assess truthfulness or give the mode of affirmation that the agent desires. Then one might bring to bear more general criteria of assessment, but always at the risk of losing the agent's distinctive investments. For example, imagine what we would lose if we approached works like Joyce's *Portrait of the Artist* and Proust's *Remembrance of Things Past* without focusing on their efforts to establish the rhythms and intricacies of a distinct sensibility that none of our interpretive categories can capture.[18]

An embarrassing range of questions still haunts my arguments, even if one accepts the basic claims I have been making. What is at stake in actually accomplishing a confession? Why does truthfulness matter so much, given the emphasis in Wittgenstein on the public nature of language and the immanent pragmatic exchanges that characterize our response to expressive acts? And why at my conclusion do I come this close to the old language of being faithful to some inner core? A rough answer to all three questions is simply that one can risk echoing traditional values because in fact Wittgenstein provides a path for understanding our desires for expressive identities that breaks substantially from those traditional notions of authenticity, while attempting to preserve a sense of demands on the self that I think becomes even more important in our simulacral culture.

The core of these differences lies in the comments by Wittgenstein on genuineness with which we began our consideration of his approach to subjective agency. Because we can speak of avowals rather than descriptions, we can make attributions of genuineness that do not require our representing some deep inner core of the self. Confessions describe by correlating truths with the activity of defining one's own concern for truthfulness. So they offer what ultimately become elaborate one-place predicates intended to sustain claims to possess an identity in relation to some specific set of expectations. By showing how the will can be immanent to a process of expressive activity, Wittgenstein makes questions of identity inseparable from the very processes by which we take responsibility for certain tasks or projections. And, more important, he shows us why it might matter to us that we both do the task well and understand as well as we can who we become in such activity. We "know" now all too well that there is probably no external authority that can define such responsibilities or impose demands that we will feel we must honor. Wittgenstein shows how we can live without that knowledge, since genuineness is simply the substance that we establish in terms of how we wield the "now" and the "this." That, I suggest, is a minimalist version of modern heroism that must, and can, suffice for our continuing to take seriously the ethical weight we can place upon the pursuit of personal identities, and for our appreciating the social relations we enter because of that pursuit.

NOTES

1. In chapter 7 of my *Canons and Consequences* (Evanston: Northwestern University Press, 1990), I address these problems in Lacanian and Derridean theory. But although I address Derrida on singularity, I do not there take on how Jean Luc Nancy's recent writings try to extend that notion so that it also ties individuals to communities. For his work, see especially his *Inoperative Community*, trans. Peter Connor (Minneapolis: University of Minnesota Press, 1991), and both his own essay and the others collected in Jean Luc Nancy et al., eds., *Who Comes After the Subject?* (New York: Routledge, 1991). Here I will not directly address Nancy since my concern is simply to develop an alternative way of thinking about the subject, but I do spend considerable time on the limits of his perspective in a so far unpublished essay, "Monuments Operative and Inoperative; or, What the Vietnam Veterans Memorial Has to Teach Us."

2. I develop this argument in "Temporality and the Necessity for Dialectic: The Missing Dimension of Contemporary Theory," *New Literary History* 23 (1992): 143–54.

3. Michel Ter Hark, *Beyond the Inner and the Outer: Wittgenstein's Philosophy of Psychology* (Dordrecht: Kluwer Academic Publishers, 1990), 81. Ter Hark goes on to claim that "as a result Wittgenstein will dispense with the phrase 'direct, inner evidence' in his analysis of the third person." It is also important to note how effective Ter Hark is in criticizing others, such as Daniel Dennet, who develop versions of intentionality not sensitive to this asymmetry. In that same spirit I suggest that, despite his staunch defenses of what distinguishes human beings from computers, John Searle, in his *Intentionality* (Cambridge: Cambridge University Press, 1983) seems to me to overgeneralize when he claims there is no parallel between intentionality and intensionality. He is probably right in relation to belief sentences, since in principle the believing can also be made the object of propositions. Just as we test claims about the world, we can test claims about what is believed about the world. But it is by no means so clear that we can perform the same analyses of experiential statements such as "I remember turning off the light," or of self-referring belief sentences such as "I believe that this action is a perfect reflection of me." In the first case (to be developed below) there is no object, no "me" turning off the light but only a first-person state. And in the second case we cannot separate a meaning of "me" from the contents of the belief. Here Jacques Lacan's *Four Fundamental Concepts of Psychoanalysis* (trans. Alan Sheridan [New York: Norton, 1977]) is very interesting for his spelling out various permutations of the difference between "I see myself running and "I see myself seeing myself."

4. Lyons, "Deixis and Subjectivity: Loquor ergo Sum," in *Speech, Place and Action*, ed. R. J. Jarvella and W. Klein (London: John Wiley & Sons, 1982), 117–18. I take some freedom with Lyons's claims as I transfer them from his linguistic account to this more general argument, but I hope I do not distort their force, in part because if he is right there are strong grounds for insisting that narrative analyses also cannot suffice in our accounting for subjectivity because the "experiential" features can only be displayed, not thematized. Narrative cannot account for what frames it or what lives within it beyond what can be made the object of descriptions.

For a linguistic account that can handle the complex uses of "as" that we need for the anti-Cartesian ontology that Lyons argues for, see Joseph Edmonds, "The Prepositional Copula *as*," *Linguistic Analysis* 13, no. 2 (1984): 127–44. And for a superb linguistic analysis of issues involving intentionality, see George M. Wilson, *The Intentionality of Human Action*, rev ed. (Palo Alto: Stanford University Press, 1989). I must confess that I am afraid to say anything about this book because I am not sure I understand its full force.

5. Ludwig Wittgenstein, *Philosophical Investigations*, trans. G.E.M Anscombe (New York: Macmillan, 1968), 190. Henceforth *PI* when cited parenthetically in the text.

6. I quote from page 5 of Moran's dissertation, "Attitudes Towards the Self" (Cornell University, 1989). The core of the argument I rely on has been published in Richard Moran, "Making Up Your Mind: Self-Interpretation and Self-Constitution," *Ratio*, n.s., 1 (1988): 135–51. In fairness to Moran I should make it clear that his purposes are more analytic and far less

speculative than mine, at least about the nature of agency. In fact Moran turns out to develop, in a much finer grain, much the same distinctions between immediacy and description that Rodney Chisholm and John Lyons do, but with the important addition of locating important aspects of the immediacy not in perception but in practical choice, which creates what then can be described. For a very different account of practical choice based on the same concern for self-awareness, see J. David Velleman, *Practical Reflection* (Princeton: Princeton University Press, 1989)

7. Here we find instructive the discussion of Wittgenstein on the self in Saul Kripke's *Wittgenstein on Rules and Private Language* (Cambridge: Harvard University Press, 1982). I cannot do justice now to Kripke's use of the private-language argument for his larger purpose of treating the *Philosophical Investigations* as a response to the skeptical challenge to any guarantee of knowledge holding into the future. But I can briefly indicate how his keen grasp of the asymmetry that Wittgenstein proposes between first- and third-person stances nonetheless does not generate a corresponding appreciation for what is at stake in these reflections Kripke begins by presenting Wittgenstein at his most suspicious and most enabling.

We are supposed to imagine another entity, similar to 'me'—another 'soul', 'mind' or 'self'—that has a toothache *just like this* toothache, except that it (he? she?) 'has' it, just as I 'have' this one. All this makes little sense, given the Humean critique of the notion of the self that Wittgenstein accepts I have no idea of a 'self' in my own case, let alone a generic concept of a 'self' that in addition to 'me' includes 'others'. Nor do I have any idea of 'having' as a relation between such a 'self' and the toothache . . . I have no concept of a 'self' nor of 'having' to enable me to make the appropriate abstraction from the original paradigm The formulation "it toothaches" makes this quite clear: consider the total situation, and ask what I am to abstract if I wish to remove 'myself'. (124–25)

Then Kripke can make a convincing case for what in Wittgenstein must replace talk of a "self" as a discrete entity There remains at least not a nothing because we must be able to account for the fact that it is more difficult to imagine pain I do not feel on the model of pain I do feel than to imagine "ducks which are not in Central Park on the model of the ducks which" I do see there (116). Put crudely, the difference is that in the case of the ducks both sets of objects are treated in third-person terms and must meet distinct criteria for our attributions. But when the first person is at stake it is extremely difficult to separate the subject from the object. Because we cannot locate the "I" within the world of objects, we cannot separate the pain we want to attribute to the other. Similarly, our inability to locate the "I" creates serious problems in interpreting what "having" means for an "I" in pain Does one "have" pain as one "has" a job or two cars? For so long as we dwell in first-person terms the appropriate sense of pain appears inseparable from the subject who experiences it. As Kripke puts it, for the first person "There is no distinction between imagining a pain and imagining my having a pain. To imagine that I am in pain, I do not have to imagine that my pain is connected to anything else" (131), just as for Jones to say he was hungry "does not mean 'Jones said that Jones was hungry,' for Jones need not realize that he is Jones" (144)

Now the problem emerges Kripke stops here. Having located what cannot be put in propositional form about the pain, he refuses to pursue the alternative domain as warranting further philosophical investigation. For Kripke, Wittgenstein's concern in *Philosophical Investigations* for "the special character of the self" "is thought of as deriving from a 'grammatical' peculiarity of the first person pronoun, not from any special metaphysical mystery" (144–45) This is clearly to reduce grammar from an inquiry into forms of life to something excessively linguistic, and it is to equate all mystery with metaphysical mystery, thereby missing the entire point of Wittgenstein's difficulty and his resistance to both empiricism and rationalism. Finally, it is to ignore the fact that this removal of the "self" is not a removal of the subjective agency that expresses pain, an agency that will go on to take actions and develop investments in relation to that pain

Let me add that I have learned a great deal from three recent books on Wittgenstein that do pay attention to questions of psychology and, in the first two cases, to the relations between Wittgenstein's transcendental views of subjectivity and will in the *Tractatus* and his discussions of expression and intention in the second half of the *Philosophical Investigations*. These are *Beyond the Inner and the Outer* by Ter Hark, Michael Hodges, *Transcendence and Wittgenstein's Tractatus* (Philadelphia. Temple University Press, 1990), and Malcolm Budd, *Wittgenstein's Philosophy of Psychology* (London· Routledge, 1989) Yet Budd remains convinced that "it is consistent with Wittgenstein's approach to philosophy that his investigation of the concepts of thought and intention should go only as far as he thought was necessary to undermine seductive misconceptions of the concepts" (144) That may have been Wittgenstein's conception of his relation to academic philosophy, but it simply is not true of his conception of his own writings, which seems to me intent on getting us to change our minds about how we view ourselves and hence open ourselves to particular values One need not go as far as Stanley Cavell does in translating this spirit into new thematic clusters in order to think it important to spell out what these values might be, a task Ter Hark and Hodges accept, but without my specific emphases on how by focusing on intentionality we can develop frameworks for appreciating what is possible for expressive behavior and for something like "will." Finally, the fullest sense of Wittgenstein's ambitions as a wisdom figure emerges from Ray Monk's deep and moving *Ludwig Wittgenstein* (New York: Free Press, 1990)

8. Ludwig Wittgenstein, *Notebooks 1914–1916,* trans G E.M Anscombe (New York: Harper & Row, 1969), 77

9. It is important at least to note how well these commitments to refuse interiority and yet insist on the powers of agency fit with the transcendental notion of subjective agency developed in Wittgenstein's *Tractatus* There the difference between first- and third-person perspectives is located by the argument that the visual field does not emanate from the eye but seems to enclose it In other words, the subject has no privileged access in relation to objects, to what can be known. And, conversely, whatever *Undmg* subjective agency is, it cannot be enclosed within that visual field. All we can say is that what we experience as subjective agency provides the boundary conditions generating values for those fields and determining how the fields wax and wane in correlation with our senses of happiness or unhappiness. For a good summary of this aspect of the *Tractatus,* see Ter Hark, *Beyond the Inner and the Outer,* 83–91; and for a more general connection of this theme to the ethics of the *Tractatus* and the changes Wittgenstein must make in that transcendentalism, see Michael Hodges, *Transcendence.*

10. I offer these speculations on the "as" in my *Canons and Consequences.*

11 Both Ter Hark (*Beyond the Inner and the Outer,* 183) and Monk (*Ludwig Wittgenstein,* 346) note the special force that Wittgenstein gives the "now." But Ter Hark seems content with its neo-Kantian force as a framing device, and Monk with stressing the fact that the "now" in the cases of aspect seeing is not simply a temporal indicator. Neither connects it to the overall issue of intentionality.

12. Ludwig Wittgenstein, *Tractatus Logico-Philosophicus,* trans D F. Pears and B F. McGuiness (London: Routledge and Kegan Paul, 1961).

13 On will in the *Philosophical Investigations,* see Ter Hark, *Beyond the Inner and the Outer,* 252–62. One might also note that Malcolm Budd's otherwise good treatment of Wittgenstein's psychology seems limited by its refusal to link that psychology sufficiently to questions of valuing and willing. At the other pole I want to cite J David Velleman's important *Practical Reflection* because it offers the richest contemporary account of how one can avoid treating subjective agency as lack by beginning with fundamental conditions of self-awareness as an intentional directedness, then moving out to those more capacious modes of subjective desire Velleman treats self-awareness as a conjunction of two processes—the mind's effort to develop momentary self-knowledge in an image and its effort then to flesh out what the image in fact makes visible Then he extends the elements of self-awareness into a full account of how our

decisions are motivated by desires to be able to act in ways that allow consistent self-prediction: "Being an agent is not a neutral capacity for pursuit; it's a substantive commitment to a particular second-order pursuit, that of knowing about one's own pursuits" (*Practical Reflection,* 207). That knowledge in practical reasoning takes the form of developing intentions that "would enhance the agent's self-knowledge by satisfying some self-conception" (198) But brilliant as much of his argument is, Velleman seems to me wrong in concentrating so exclusively on the desire for coherence in the form of self-knowledge as the driving force for all efforts at self-articulation This description may hold for explicit discursive decisions, but as an account of purposive agency it ignores other equally powerful motives. Another basic drive to articulation and to consistency is our desire to be visible to others or to gain identities from others. More generally, I think his stress on self-knowledge and self-prediction defines the content of self-reflection in too narrowly cognitive terms. One could accept his claims but still argue that a richer phenomenology would survey the many ways that we act in order to maximize a cogent sense of the self in power over the direction its activities take. Explicit cognition is one form of that power, but it also takes other less discursive, more conative forms that are less committed to explicit coherence, for example in the feeling of power that having a style gives as one moves through various materials. For me this capacity to move from the sense of power to nondiscursive forms of self-enjoyment and self-recognition is crucial to expressivist values (and to the rejection of narrative accounts of the self as well as cognitive accounts like Velleman's), so in the book I am doing on this subject, I try to link Wittgenstein's remarks on intention to his reflections on style. But for now I think the point is clear if one compares not having a concept of self with not having a sense of one's own style and thinks of how differently each affects us. The lack of style or, more loosely, of a sense of what Spinoza called *conatus* is immediately felt but cannot be thematized except as vague anxiety, whereas we rarely feel the need for explicit self-prediction, except when we worry that we are in fact under the control of some other agent or force Nonetheless, by focusing on a self-interest that is not instrumental but self-reflexive, Velleman serves the crucial role of showing how normative concerns can be basic to the self even where there is no teleology.

14 I have worked out some of the basic features of this expressivist ethics in chapter 6 of my *Canons and Consequences*

15. Henry Staten, *Wittgenstein and Derrida* (Lincoln. University of Nebraska Press, 1984). Staten argues, correctly, that my writing on Wittgenstein belongs in that camp because it relies on the determining force of context rather than on the determinative powers of agency to cut new paths through conventional landscapes. I can only say that one can rely on contexts as shaped by grammar while still allowing agents considerable freedom in what they do within grammars or in the playing of grammars against one another. Therefore, although it is true that most Wittgenstein commentary does not stress the important links between his and Derrida's senses of the malleability of context, we must also recall the quite significant differences between them on the subject of intentionality As I suggested earlier in this essay, whereas Derrida sees all the difficulties Wittgenstein does in traditional treatments of intentionality, he is content to treat those difficulties as constitutive of intentionality. He therefore does not posit a workable alternative like the one we are trying to develop here.

16. Wittgenstein asks avowals to do two quite different kinds of work that are easy to confuse, but they also make it possible to criticize private language since any language that can communicate must be based on criteria for common use. So "I can know what someone else is thinking, not what I am thinking" (*PI,* 222). But, at the same time, understanding the limits of language deepens our appreciation of what remains truly private and requires modes of expression for which the methods of establishing knowledge are not appropriate

17. Ray Monk's biography of Wittgenstein is the work most sensitive to his concern for the power cultural objects give, see especially the link developed between aspect seeing and cultural education (*Ludwig Wittgenstein,* 531).

18. See Wittgenstein's *Philosophical Investigations*. The classic treatment is Stanley Cavell's "Availability of Wittgenstein's Later Philosophy," in his *Must We Mean What We Say?* (New York: Cambridge University Press, 1976), 44–72. And for a good account of how Joyce uses irony in a distinctive way to gain this particularizing effect, see Ralph Rader, "Defoe, Richardson, Joyce, and the Concept of Form in the Novel," in *Autobiography, Form and the Novel* (Los Angeles. Clark Library, 1973), 29–72.

8
Changing One's Beliefs

JACQUES SCHLANGER

We do change our minds. Sometimes changing our minds has to do with what we want, sometimes with what we believe, sometimes with what we do. What is it to change one's mind? What happens to us when we do it? Why do we do it? I will address this issue through the examination of one kind of mind-changing, the changing of our beliefs. We hold certain beliefs, and then, for some reason, or for no (apparent) reason, we change our minds, and we no longer hold these beliefs; instead, we hold others that can even contradict the beliefs we have discarded. What has happened? What has changed? Who has changed?

But first of all, what are those beliefs that we hold and that we discard? There is no simple, direct answer to this question. On the contrary, it seems to me that there are no such things as beliefs per se; there are only situations in which somebody believes something, in which one acts in accordance with what one believes, in which one relates to what one believes. Rather than attempt to answer the very abstract question of what beliefs are, I will examine here the situation of believing: what it is to have a belief; what it is to act in accordance with a belief; what it is to relate to a belief.

I propose to distinguish three main aspects of this situation of believing: a cognitive aspect, which has to do with the contents of our beliefs; a pragmatic aspect, which has to do with how we behave in accordance with our beliefs; and an emotive aspect, which has to do with how we relate to our beliefs. The cognitive aspect has evident ontological connotations in that it pertains to what we think; the pragmatic aspect has ethical connotations in that it pertains to how we act; and the emotional aspect has existential connotations in that it pertains to how we feel. However, we should keep in mind that this distinction is methodological rather than essential and that in actual situations of believing, these three different aspects are thoroughly intermingled, in various degrees of intensity.

THE COGNITIVE ASPECT OF BELIEFS

When we believe something, and we are aware of our belief, we are usually able to express this belief as an object of language, as a set of propositions. I believe that the moon controls the tides. I believe that Julius Caesar crossed the Rubicon. I believe that human beings are equal in rights. Some of our beliefs can be proved to be true or false—and are considered thus to belong to the realm of knowledge. Others cannot be proved true or false although they are meaningful and important for us and have to do with our evaluation of what there is, with what we think should be, with how we think we should behave, and so on. We believe in propositions of the first kind when we believe that the earth is flat—a belief which is false today and was acceptable for as long as it had not been proved to be false. These are factual beliefs that belong to the realm of knowledge inasmuch as they can, theoretically at least, be verified or falsified. We believe in propositions of the second kind when we believe that all human beings are equal in rights, a proposition that cannot be proved true or false, and that we nevertheless consider to be meaningful and extremely important. These are nonfactual beliefs and do not belong to the realm of strict knowledge inasmuch as they cannot be verified or refuted.

As such, our beliefs present themselves as propositions: "The moon controls the tides," "Human beings are equal in rights," and so on, which are expressed by a subject who takes a stand in relation to them, either accepting or rejecting them. It is this stand of the subject in a situation of believing that transforms these propositions into beliefs. From the cognitive point of view, then, beliefs are propositions that relate to a situation of believing in which a subject takes a stand about this or that and is able to express this belief in words, in a proposition.

At this point, I want to introduce the idea of authorities, which I consider essential to many situations of believing. Our beliefs concern what (we believe) there is; what (we believe) should be; the way we appreciate what there is. In this sense, the cognitive aspect of our beliefs designates our extended ontology—not only our actual ontology, namely what for us is, but also our virtual ontology, namely what for us should be. Now, but for very rare occurrences, we do not invent our beliefs. They are handed down to us by what we consider to be authorities: by our parents, our teachers, our friends, the society we live in, our culture. I believe that water boils at 100°C because I have been taught that such is the case. I insist here on saying that I believe it, and not that I know it, mainly because this piece of information has been handed down to me by way of authority. This is generally the case for most, if not all, our factual beliefs: we receive them from experts whose authority we accept.

If some physicist came now and told us that the proposition "Water boils at 100°C" is false and that he can prove it to us and to other experts in his field—and therefore that our belief is wrong—I would readily accept his position because he is, for me, an authority in his field. In the same way, I accept the authority of the physician concerning medical problems, the authority of the lawyer concerning juridical problems, the authority of any expert in his domain—as long as it is not the domain in which I consider myself to be an expert, namely the domain in which I consider my beliefs to be knowledge that can be verified or at least falsified. An important consequence of such an acceptance of authorities in domains in which I am not an expert is that I have no personal commitment to those beliefs. From the start, I have submitted in those domains to the authority of others, and the beliefs I have in those domains are directly dependant on their approval of them.

I insist here on this point because it is directly related to the problem of changing one's beliefs. When I believe through the authority of experts, I readily discard these beliefs if authorities in the matter enjoin me to do so. I do have a problem when there is a clash between experts, and I have to choose the one whose authority I am going to follow without knowing how to justify such a choice. However, in a field in which I am personally knowledgeable, I consider my beliefs in this field as verifiable or at least refutable; they are knowledge for me. When those propositions cease to be true (for me), I stop believing in them. At least, this is the way it should be; as we will see later, this is not always the case because of the emotional relation we sometimes have toward some of our beliefs even when they are factual beliefs that can be proved true or false.

A critical problem here is the problem of authorities for our nonfactual beliefs, for beliefs that cannot be proved true or false, for beliefs that we receive in a subtler, rather more indirect manner. There, the position of the expert is not as clear as it is in the case of a scientific or a professional expert. Who are our authorities when it comes to nonscientific beliefs, to ethical, political, aesthetic, social, religious beliefs? Is a parent, a priest, a guru, a politician, an authority on moral affairs in the same sense in which a physician is an authority on medical affairs and a jurist on legal affairs? For Plato, the philosopher was to be the expert in ethical life, because for him the philosopher was a scientist, the only real scientist, dealing with the only real science, the science of ideas. Most of us do not agree with Plato's view: still we feel that there is such thing as a moral authority and that moral experts have a certain authority over our beliefs—they often make us change our nonfactual beliefs in the same way that the physicist and the physician make us change the factual beliefs we have in the domain of their competence. Remaining on the cognitive level of the situation of believing, what usually happens is that we change our beliefs under the injunction of experts—be they scientific, or professional, or moral—whenever we have greater confidence in their authority than in those beliefs we hold which belong to the domain of their competence.

THE PRAGMATIC ASPECT OF BELIEFS

In a situation of believing, our beliefs generally have a direct influence on our behavior. In this sense, to act in accordance with our beliefs is thus to behave in an ethical way. If I believe that water boils at 100°C, I behave, I have to behave, in a certain way when it comes to heating water. If I believe that human beings are equal in rights, I behave, I have to behave, in a certain way when it comes to social intercourse, and so on. This pragmatic aspect of the situation of believing is absolutely essential to it: it transforms pieces of information, prescriptions, and expectations into beliefs. I believe that something is the case if I act in accordance with it; this is in a nutshell what the philosophical theory of pragmatism is about. I act in a certain way if those are my beliefs; this is in a nutshell what ethics is about. This is true not only of our practical beliefs, be they factual or nonfactual, but also of our theoretical beliefs—such as our beliefs in the existence of imaginary numbers, black holes, or twisted universes. At first glance, they seem to have nothing to do with our behavior, but we learn them, we investigate them, we teach them, we believe in them, we defend them, we do our best to prove them—all of which are very practical activities indeed, to which we commit ourselves very deeply.

This pragmatic aspect of the situation of believing has important ethical corollaries. The "normal" situation obtains when we act in accordance with a belief whose cognitive content we are entirely aware of and to which we wholly adhere. However, we often act in accordance with a belief to which we adhere without being particularly aware of or even interested in its cognitive content. Sometimes we also act in accordance with a belief we do not or no longer hold; we may also act against a belief we hold. Each time, we are in a different ethical situation.

In what we consider the more general situation, we act in accordance with our beliefs, we are aware of them, and we wholly adhere to them. In this case, the pragmatic aspect of our situation of believing fits adequately with its cognitive aspect. However, in order to act in accordance with a belief, one does not have to be wholly aware of it; one does not have to be able to formulate it to oneself or to others. This is what much of our upbringing is about: to have us act in a certain manner, to have us accept acting in this manner even if we do not know explicitly why, to have us act in accordance with beliefs we will thus share with those that inculcate them to us, without even being fully aware of their content. Authorities impose on us beliefs that we consider to be naturally our own. Whenever I receive beliefs in such an authoritative manner, through this kind of educational taming, I adhere to them, I behave in accordance with them although more often than not I am not able to formulate them explicitly.

Another kind of situation occurs when I behave in accordance with a belief I do not or no longer hold. Be it for reasons of convenience, conformism, or fear, we are often inclined to behave in such a hypocritical manner. We do not adhere to those beliefs and still we act in accordance with them. This has nothing to do with the cognitive aspect, with whether or not we know the content of those beliefs, but rather with the emotive aspect, with the manner in which we relate to them. Those are for us beliefs in which we do not believe, and our behavior toward them is a sham, a make-believe—and we are conscious of this fact.

This hypocritical acting puts us often in opposition with beliefs we—cognitively and emotively—hold. However, I consider this kind of misbehavior to be still in accordance with my beliefs as long as I am aware of the fact that I transgress them: this is what in religious language is called to sin. To sin is to act against a belief to which we wholly adhere. This ethical standpoint concerns not only moral or religious issues, but also scientific, aesthetic, political, ideological issues— when one cheats, lies, gives false information, whenever one misbehaves against one's beliefs.

THE EMOTIVE ASPECT OF BELIEFS

There are beliefs to which we cling more than to others, beliefs to which we are emotionally attached, and beliefs toward which we have a more detached attitude. We seem to be more committed to beliefs that are (or seem to us to be) under our own authority than to beliefs that we clearly submit to the authority of experts. I have no emotional relation toward most beliefs I have in the domain of chemistry, of botany, of geology. I will, therefore, readily accept the ruling of experts in those fields and will not even think of arguing with them. In physics, however, there are beliefs that seem closer to me than others, and although I may in the end submit to the opinion of the experts, I still may feel that violence has been done to me. Thus, I am not entirely at ease with the idea developed in quantum mechanics that a particle can be at two different locations at the same time. I have the feeling that this is only a way to point out a certain problem, a way of speaking that does not mean what it literally says. Nevertheless, I accept what the experts say, and I try to adapt my other beliefs—concerning causality, for instance—to what now seems to me a new belief I have to adhere to if I want to go on accepting the physicists' authority.

On the other hand, it seems quite obvious to us that we cling to our ideological beliefs, to which we are deeply committed. This commitment gives us authority over them. We are emotionally involved with our political, social, religious, and artistic beliefs, and many scientists are emotionally involved with their scientific beliefs, with the theories they adhere to and to which they cling as long and as fast as they can. It is this kind of emotional relation to scientific theories that Max Planck had in mind when he said that new theories have their day and say only when the older scientists die. We do not give up easily beliefs that provide us with an inner sense of unity, and that tie us to our group, to our cobelievers—especially if those beliefs have given us a professional and a social status. At the emotional level, the beliefs we cling to seem to be part of ourselves: not only do we know them and act in accordance with them, but we also live and experience them. One can speak here of an existential commitment to the beliefs to which we are strongly connected emotionally in the sense that we may feel ready to pay a price for them, with our comfort, with our careers, sometimes even with our lives.

CHANGES IN BELIEFS

We have seen that a situation of believing manifests itself through a cognitive aspect that has to do with the contents of our beliefs, through a pragmatic aspect as revealed by our behavior in respect to our beliefs, and through an emotional aspect that expresses our relation to our beliefs. Let us now go back to our initial problem: what is it to change our beliefs? What changes, who changes, why does such a change occur—from a cognitive point of view, from a pragmatic point of view, from an emotive point of view? In this essay, I mostly insist on the emotive point of view—mainly because it is the problem of religious conversion that has initiated my interest in belief-changing.

Let us distinguish then between small changes of belief that do not seem very important to us and large changes that transform us entirely, that manifest themselves in a radical transformation of our life.

First, let us look at those small changes in belief. I have believed until now that it is the attraction of the moon that causes tides. Now comes a qualified astronomer, who tells me that I am wrong, that the moon has nothing to do with tides, and that it can be proved. What has changed? From the cognitive point of view, everything has changed. My ancient belief has been shattered, and I have now a new belief concerning the cause of the tides. The opinion of the expert has radically transformed the content of my belief and also my ontology. From now on, I consider that it is false to believe that the moon causes tides; I believe now that the moon has nothing to do with tides. My image of the world has changed. From the cognitive point of view, there has been a dramatic change.

What has happened from the pragmatic point of view? Practically nothing. I am not a seaman, I do not live by the seashore, I am not involved in research concerning tides, and so on. Thus, what causes tides is of no practical importance to me. Nevertheless, we all know that small cognitive changes of belief can be of great practical importance. Until now I have always believed that drinking coffee is harmless. If some expert came now and affirmed very strongly the contrary (as they do at least twice a year in the newspapers), and I accepted this expert's authority, I would have to face a real practical problem: should I go on drinking coffee, acting thus against my new belief, or should I act in accordance with my new belief and stop drinking coffee? In theological language—which seems so appropriate when it comes to beliefs—should I sin or should I comply? And emotions would run very high if I had to give up coffee because of some article in a newspaper.

Here is another example to enhance the emotive aspect of the situation of believing. I have always believed that water boils at 100°C. Now comes some physicist who authoritatively states that water boils at 90°C and that he can prove it. This would be of real cognitive importance to me; it would have some practical influence when it comes to heating water to the boiling point, but it would have no emotive impact on me whatsoever. On the other hand, were I a physicist who had made a career of studying the boiling point of different liquids, and were I to be proved wrong on the boiling point of water, I would accept the evidence if there was no way out—but I would be emotionally very upset. As we see, the changing of our beliefs, even when it is a matter of seemingly harmless and nonessential beliefs, can be a very complex affair.

GREAT CHANGES IN BELIEFS

Let us now examine what I have named great changes in beliefs, be they ideological, scientific, ontological, or religious. It is to those great changes in belief that we have applied the religious term of "conversion." There is a conversion, a thorough transformation in our beliefs and, very often, in the conduct of our lives when we abandon beliefs that have been very important to us and we start holding new beliefs, beliefs that are sometimes opposed to the beliefs we have discarded because of them. Here the three aspects, cognitive, pragmatic, and emotive, are closely knitted together. To have been a materialist and become a spiritualist, to have been a Communist and become a partisan of free enterprise, to have been an atheist and become a religious fundamentalist, to have been a Newtonian and become an Einsteinian, and so on—all these changes of beliefs have to do not only with the contents of the beliefs but also with how we behave in respect to those beliefs and with how we feel toward them.

What happens to a Communist who becomes a liberal? Why does a Newtonian absolutist transform into a Einsteinian relativist? What changes when an atheist converts into a believer in a transcendent God? We have already met with this type of question when we looked at the small changes in beliefs but on a much lower scale. Here, we find the same problems, this time magnified, stretched to their radical edges. Precisely because the impact of conversions is usually very strong on all aspects of the situation of belief-changing, it is particularly interesting to examine them with more attention. In order to get a better understanding of those situations of radical belief-changing, I will present one of those radical conversions, a conversion I experienced myself when I ceased to believe in God. I am perfectly aware that I reconstruct an event that has happened many years ago and that was of great importance in my life: I shall try to be as faithful as possible to my remembrance of this event.

MY CONVERSION

I believed in God, and then, all of a sudden, I stopped believing in him, or rather, I became suddenly aware that I had stopped believing in him. What did it mean to believe in God in the first place? What was it to have stopped believing in him in the second? Let us first look at the cognitive aspect of this situation: as a young teenager—I was fourteen years old at the time—my theology was quite rudimentary, directly drawn from the prayer book and from how I understood the prayers, their language, and their meaning. I had a rather anthropomorphical idea of God, seeing him at the same time as an almighty father, an all-knowing supervisor, a permanent presence, a loving friend. I was concerned with God's presence around me rather than with the problem of his existence. I never felt the need to prove, to myself or to others, this presence of God with me. I was wholly convinced that God was intimately related to me, as a father, as a friend, continuously present with me.

Practically and emotionally, my belief in God suffused my life. I behaved as if being in his presence all the time, as if being looked on and cared for by him all the time. I tried very much to abide by him, to practice his law, to do what I thought to be agreeable to him, to live in accordance with my total belief in his presence. This might seem to be a childish view of a life with God—still this is how I remember it. Whatever I was doing, be it good or bad or morally indifferent, was done in his presence, under his supervision, and for him. From the religious point of view, I was what one might call a God-raptured child. I lived with God. I was emotionally involved with him.

Now, because of circumstances related to the war, great changes occurred in my life. It is important for me to mention this point, because I have no idea what would have happened otherwise, without this enormous turmoil. Anyhow, I discovered one day that I no longer believed in God, that there was no such presence around me, and that this ever-present friend had vanished into thin air. What had happened? What had changed? Who had changed? To stop believing in God meant changing my behavior, experiencing new emotions, having new ideas—but all those changes did not occur at the same time. Thus I remember very clearly that I was already emotionally far away from God when I still behaved ritually in a religious manner. An outside observer would not have guessed from my external behavior that I had already ceased to acknowledge God's presence in me. The pragmatic aspect thus dragged along behind the emotive aspect, and the cognitive aspect—questions about who is this God—came somewhere in between. I am now convinced that it is the emotive change that started it all: first I lost my emotional connection to God, then my cognitive belief in him, and only later my pragmatic behavior toward him.

As I ceased to believe in God, I found myself living in a new world, or maybe I ceased to believe in God because I had discovered a new world, a world without God. This is not just a paradoxical statement. When you have lived with God, to imagine the possibility of a world without God is already to be on the way out. If a world without God is possible, then it is somehow real—and God disappears, because then what keeps him back is only the possibility of his being. How strong is a belief that can be discarded by simply conceiving the possibility of an alternate world in which this belief has no place? What made me abandon a belief that was so essential to me? Had it been proved false? It had not: no one had come to me with sufficient authority and told me that there is no God. I came to it by myself. What exactly did I find out? This seems to be the crucial question.

Until then, I had taken God's existence for granted: nobody ever proved or tried to prove to me that God did or did not exist. What I was told was that I should behave in such a way, because that was what God wanted from me. The belief in God's existence was implied in my behavior toward him: it was only much later, when I went away from him, that I formulated to myself the question of God's existence and nature. I had thus lived with God without being aware of the problem posed by his existence: my religious behavior preceded the formulation of my belief.

Moreover, it was when I started to give myself an account of my belief, that I became conscious of my estrangement from it. I imagine that if, at the time of my belief in God, someone had asked me whether I believed in God's existence, I would have answered yes—although I do not think (now) that I would have really understood the point of the question. It would have been truer for me to say then that I know nothing of his existence, but that I am permanently in his presence. It is only after I had begun to examine my feelings toward God that I got to be aware of the cognitive aspect of my belief in him, including the problem of his existence. I first experienced certain emotions and behaved in a certain way and only afterward did I voice to myself the beliefs that made me act and feel that way.

BELIEFS AND PERSONAL IDENTITY

At this stage, I propose another perspective on the nature of our beliefs in order to understand what happens to us when we change beliefs—especially essential beliefs, beliefs that pertain to what we know, what we do, and what we feel. Let us consider our beliefs as if they were what characterize us, as elements of our personal identities at a given moment in our lives. I am the person who weighs that much, who is nearsighted, who likes to play tennis and drink coffee, and who has such and such beliefs. My beliefs, especially when I express them through my behavior and through my feelings, belong to me, are part of me. I am the man who believes that there is no God in heaven. I am the man who believes that human beings are equal in rights in the same sense that I am the man who is nearsighted, right-handed, and so on. There is no such thing as a belief in itself. There are only believers who behave in a certain way in respect to the beliefs to which they adhere. The problem thus is not whether one is right or wrong to hold a given belief, but rather what makes one hold it now, and why might one eventually stop holding it in the future? A subject is thus characterized by his or her beliefs, and his or her convictions are part of the subject.

I believe in something when I act in accordance with this belief even if I am not entirely aware of its formulated content—in the same sense that I am not totally aware of the meaning of my nearsightedness although I definitely behave as a nearsighted person. A belief that demands a specific behavior and has no impact on our own behavior is not a belief for us. When I ceased to behave as a believer in God, my belief was transformed into the cognitive problem of deciding whether there is a God or not, and the moment the question arose, the answer was of course negative.

A word now on the issue of hypocrisy. In what sense do we change our behavior when we change our beliefs? Although my inner attitude to God had changed, my external behavior was rather misleading. For a long time, I went on behaving as an orthodox Jew—and I do not think that it was out of hypocrisy because of some external social pressure. I lived then in a very open-minded group where my change in religious behavior would at most have raised some eyebrows. I continued to behave externally as an orthodox Jew because this is what I had done all my life, and one cannot get rid so easily of what has been such an essential part of one's everyday behavior. The change of behavior was first of all interior: I stopped talking to God long before I stopped praying to him formally.

SURFACE-BELIEFS AND DEEP-BELIEFS

We come now to the heart of the matter: what is it that makes us change our inner attitude to beliefs that have been so important to us, practically as well as emotionally? How can I lose my beliefs if my beliefs are part of myself? My beliefs are permanently entangled with the events, interior and exterior, that constitute the unfolding of my life. In the same way that the warp of a fabric retains its weft, my beliefs at a given moment of my life retain the events I go through and twist them in accordance with their own lines. What happens to me fits in with what I am. The events of my life, whether imposed by the outside world or provoked by myself, yield to the beliefs of my nature. The events that mark my life are filtered through my beliefs and those beliefs—whether acquired by education, by immersion in a culture, or in reaction to other beliefs—constitute a steady fixture as the threads of the warp that retain the weft of the fabric.

We all know, however, that the threads of the warp can snap under the pressure of the weft. In other words, events can undo beliefs as they sometimes undo other parts of ourselves, our limbs, our properties, or even our lives. The question then is not why some beliefs snap, but rather how is it that some beliefs do not?

Beliefs that are easily discarded are necessarily surface beliefs. To discard those beliefs implies no profound change in us, and discarding them has no real influence on our emotional life even when it has an impact on our knowledge and on our behavior. We are not emotionally attached to those surface beliefs, and we generally discard them at the injunction of specialists that we consider to be authorities in their fields. This goes not only for professional experts—scientists, physicians, lawyers, and so on—but also for moral and spiritual authorities. If I submit to the authority of a guru, a rabbi, a priest, then all the beliefs I hold in the spiritual field in which I consider him as an authority are surface beliefs for me—since his authority will be sufficient to make me abandon those beliefs. In such a case, I believe more in his authority than in the beliefs I have put under his authority.

The question then is, how can one discard one's deep, essential, vital beliefs? And the answer now seems obvious: we cannot discard our deep beliefs as long as they remain deep beliefs in the same way that we cannot discard our heart or our brain as long as they act as our heart and our brain. For a deep belief to be discarded, it has to be transformed into a surface belief, because only a surface belief can be discarded harmlessly.

Such a transformation is possible only if we suppose that our beliefs can change their status, that deep beliefs can become surface beliefs as we look at them with a colder eye, and that surface beliefs can become deep beliefs as we get more and more emotionally committed to them. To be a deep or a surface belief is thus a temporary state, which can change under the pressure of exterior or inner events. The belief I get rid of, the belief that seems to leave me, is necessarily a superficial one—otherwise the price to pay to let it go would be too high. A deep belief that leaves us is necessarily not deep any more; it is like a flake of dead skin, that leaves without hurting too much: at times with a feeling of discomfort, the feeling of being seen for a moment naked behind this dead cover that we take away, and at times with a feeling of relief, of being born anew.

This is what conversions are about, be they religious or ideological—

and the loss of God is also a conversion: a slow, subterranean transformation that appears as if out of the blue but has been emotionally prepared for a long time. Saint Augustine and Pascal after him, say that they would not have searched for God if they had not already found him, and I say that I would not have left God if we had not already been separated for a long time.

Things happen within us, under the pressure of events or thoughts. Essential beliefs get slowly undermined before we are even aware of it. One day we wake up, knowing what has happened, and we dare tell ourselves that we no longer believe in what we had believed before. The deep belief has been pushed aside, has been ousted, in the name of another deep belief that has taken its place in us. I stopped believing in God because a new deep belief took possession of me, a belief in a world without God, a world in which I preferred to live, and which seemed to me to be more adequate to reality. My belief in God ceased to be a deep belief for me. It transformed itself into a surface belief, which I now examined with a critical eye and found to be erroneous—to be discarded as we do discard erroneous surface beliefs. But this time, nobody told me what to do. I was my own authority for this discarding.

The former deep belief becomes a surface belief: we look at it and we discard it—sometimes with a feeling of shame, of sorrow, of nakedness, at others with a feeling of triumph, and most often, as in the case of most factual beliefs, with no specific emotions whatsoever. Conversion, when the moment arrives, is just a brutal manner to acknowledge and to assume a situation that had been latent for a long time. Yes, this had been one of our deep beliefs. We clung to it; we loved it; we acted in accordance with it, but this is no more the case, and we are ready to pay the price of the abandonment. We are ready to lose friends, to lose our social status, to lose an inner peace of mind. And when the time has come, and nevertheless we do not want to pay the price, when we behave as if we still believed although we believe no more, we play at make-believe and become hypocrites.

This moment of emotional transformation, this feeling of shame or of relief, is an important indicator of what happens when we change our deep beliefs. On the one hand, we feel neither shame nor relief when we change surface beliefs: (1) because we have accepted from the start the authority of experts for all beliefs for which we consider ourselves noncompetent; (2) because from the start, we had no emotional commitment toward them. On the other hand, we feel profoundly committed to our deep beliefs, and even if we partly accept the authority of others, be they religious, scientific, political, or ethical, our commitment to those beliefs is nevertheless personal, and we are not willing to discard them just on account of an authority. We have made those beliefs ours and to abandon them has an emotional impact on us even after they have become surface beliefs.

Why this moment of shame, this feeling of discomfort when I lost my belief in God? Why was I not simply relieved for having abandoned a false belief, for knowing now better than I knew before? To change one's beliefs, especially one's deep beliefs, seems often to us, and to others that observe us, to be a weakness, a lack of character, even a betrayal. You who have believed with all your fervor believe no more. What has happened to you? When we lose a deep belief, it is as if we had shattered our idealistic foundations. Even more, it is a blow to our personal identity. I am not the same man who has believed in God and who now no longer believes in him. I behave otherwise. I feel otherwise. I know otherwise. Not only has my world changed for me, I have also changed within my world. I started to disbelieve in God when I found out that I had stopped loving him, and I stopped loving him when I found out that there could be a world without him. But it took me some time to admit it, first to myself and then to others. My belief in God, one of my vital beliefs, had become a dead skin that I was ashamed to remove, because, like Adam in his lost paradise before he went out into the "real" world, I felt naked and vulnerable without it.

9

Theories of Gender

ROSI BRAIDOTTI

I think it important at this stage of women's studies research to explore as wide a range as possible of different feminist theories and especially to take into account theoretical ideas coming from different cultural contexts. This is no mere cultural pluralism, but rather the awareness of the equal relevance of theoretical traditions that may appear to be very far from each other. Remaining in western Europe, for instance, one can compare theories of "sexual difference" to theories of gender; whereas the former are mostly French-oriented, the latter are mostly English-speaking. Through the feminist 1970s, this difference in cultural background led to mutual mistrust and serious communication problems,[1] but of late new orientations have emerged that seem to approach cultural differences in Western, white feminist theory as a positive source of theoretical debate.[2]

Furthermore, "gender" deserves special attention precisely because of the new interesting developments that have taken place in this field of late. I also want to suggest that the notion of gender, in its feminist redefinitions, can be relevant and inspiring for other disciplines in the humanities. The starting point for the feminist analysis is that the notion of gender challenges the pretense to universality and objectivity of conventional systems of knowledge and of accepted norms of scientific discourse. It introduces the variable of sexual difference at the very heart of theoretical research. Insofar as gender attempts to articulate an alternative to the pretense to objectivity, neutrality, and universality of scientific knowledge, it can play a revitalizing function in other scientific areas.

Recent developments in gender theory show that attention to gender results in renewed emphasis being placed on the situated, that is to say, local structure of knowledge. That one cannot speak on behalf of humanity as a whole, that the intellectual or academic position cannot claim to represent universal values, but rather extremely specific—class-, race-, age-, sex-specific—ones. But the recognition of the partiality of scientific statements, their necessary contingency, their reliance on concrete mechanisms that are overdetermined by historical and socioeconomic factors, has nothing to do with relativism. It marks rather a significant change in the ethics of discursive and intellectual style. The rejection of old-fashioned universalism in favor of more attention being paid to the complexity of "situated knowledges"[3] calls for more flexibility in research, especially in the field of the humanities, and for a new sensitivity to differences.

Differences of class, race, sex, age, culture, and nationality require an intellectual or academic recognition that the old-style-humanist, universalist mode does not grant. Speaking on behalf of "mankind" today without recognizing that this umbrella term fails to account for people other than white, male, adult, professional, Western individuals is a historical aberration. Research on gender is one of the areas in which constructive alternatives to the old universalist mode are being developed. I believe this kind of experimentation is of great value to the whole field of the humanities and to all intellectuals who reject nostalgic attachment to the old universalism and reactionary appeals to the *status quo ante*.

I intend to trespass one of the least visible and consequently most effective boundaries of outmoded thinking, that which separates "high" or university culture from "low" or popular culture.[4]

I stopped believing in such a distinction even before I became a feminist. I always saw the belief in an ivory tower of higher cultural pursuit in opposition to the vulgarity of common culture as a sign of what is known in ministerial circles as "the crisis of the humanities." There is no denying that university-based knowledge today struggles to keep up with what is happening in the world around it. The most outspoken apologists of French postmodernism, such as Derrida and Lyotard,[5] do not hesitate to confront the challenge that contemporary culture throws open to the rather sedate tradition of university knowledge. They claim that the humanities must prove again their relevance to an increasingly managerial, technocratic, chronically bureaucratized social context. In other words, relevance is not to be taken for granted—it must be earned again (and again) by hard work.

Moreover, within women's studies, relevance is less of a problem than gaining access to the very segregated clubs of academic respectability. Born of a social movement, fueled by one of the most intense shudders of rebellion that Western culture experienced in modern times, women's studies is implicitly connected to the currents of ideas, to the movements of thought of late post-industrial patriarchal society.

In my own feminist work, therefore, I have given up the distinction between high and low culture, and I treat with a great deal of respect and curiosity the works of art, even of pop art, the kind of ideas or theories that are being developed outside the university. I sometimes think that there is more vitality, less depressed reliance on the past, less inertia outside our venerable institutions than within them. Accordingly, I approach with equal interest texts—written, visual, or performed—of a nonacademic nature.

On this point I may be permitted to quote the crucial work accomplished by some of the poststructuralists, especially Michel Foucault and Roland Barthes, on equalizing all texts within a general theory of discourse.[6] Discourse is the network of circulation of texts, meant both as material, institutional events and as symbolic or "invisible" effects. A text is a term in a network that creates meaning, values, and norms and distributes them in a social context. Within contemporary French philosophy, therefore, the study of popular culture has quite an intellectual tradition, which distinguishes it from the British and American approach to "cultural studies."[7]

Since feminist women have been particularly active in popular culture, especially in the music industry, and have used it creatively and intelligently, I have opted for music as the ideal illustration for the rather theoretical ideas I defend here. Let this also be a tribute to intellectuals of the caliber of Laurie Anderson who have had the courage to experiment with different forms of expressions without falling into the model of the engagé intellectual,[8] and who are writing informed, refined, and lucid analyses of what the embodied life of the mind is like in late patriarchy.

THE SEX/GENDER DISTINCTION

Gender is not originally a feminist concept: it has a previous identity derived from research in biology, linguistics, and psychology.[9] This multi-layered history makes it unreliable as a concept, and the subsequent feminist appropriations and adaptations of gender add even more layers of complexity.

The feminist adoption of gender as a ruling notion occurs through the intermediary of Simone de Beauvoir. Her study of the philosophical and material structure of "otherness" as a fundamental category in human experience led her to assert the constructed, rather than biologically given nature of identity. "One is not born, one becomes a woman" is the synthesis of her analysis.

In this sentence, the emphasis falls on the word "born": in fact, central to de Beauvoir's concerns is the critique of the naturalistic, that is to say, biologically deterministic arguments for the inferiority and the subsequent oppression of women. By stressing the role played by history, tradition, and culture in conditioning women into inferior roles, de Beauvoir drew a distinction between natural sex and the cultural gender roles that one is expected to play. In so doing, she attacked misogyny by disclosing its brutally reductive basis.

By giving the issue of woman as other a central position in her philosophy of liberation through transcendence, de Beauvoir also laid the foundations for a critique of sexist or misogynist biases in science and scholarship. In *The Second Sex*, de Beauvoir shows both the extent of the depreciation of women and the ubiquity of the figure of woman in intellectual and psychic life. She stresses the crucial role played by woman as the site or location of otherness: it is by negation of this privileged "other" that the male subject can construct himself as the universal standard of normality and normativity.

The central aim of de Beauvoir's analysis of gender is, however, not critical but creative: she aims at providing a foundational theory for the reappraisal and redefinition of female subjectivity. Her proposed solution is the path to transcendence, which means that any woman can and should overcome the contingency of her particular situation as the other in order to gain access to the position of subject. In other words, women will not be liberated until they can make statements that are received as representing human values, ideas valid for the whole of humanity and not only for the "second" sex. De Beauvoir demands the same rights and entitlements for women that men have always been granted by virtue of their sex.

De Beauvoir's emphasis on the cultural bases for the alleged inferiority of women and the corresponding program of liberation through transcendence inaugurate the sex/gender distinction that was to give feminism its *titre de noblesse*. For singers like Aretha Franklin and Carole King before her, identity is acquired in a relational link to the other, as in their lyrical expressions of personal relationships and denaturalization. Acquiring an identity is therefore quite an achievement, as Freud reminds us in his work on the psychopathology of the subject. This achievement, and the hard work required to construct oneself as a woman—or a man—proves that sex and gender are not to be confused, but that the unity between the empirical and the symbolic—between being male and a man, being female and a woman—is acquired at a high cost. As Judith Butler puts it in her witty analysis:

> "I feel like a woman" is true to the extent that Aretha Franklin's invocation of the defining other is assumed: "You make me feel like a natural woman." This achievement requires a differentiation from the opposite gender. Hence one is one's gender to the extent that one is not the other gender, a formulation that presupposes and enforces the restriction of gender within that binary pair.[10]

Butler puts her finger on one of the crucial aspects of de Beauvoir's gender-theory: its dualistic structure ("One is one's gender to the extent that one is not the other gender"). This binary way of thinking is in keeping with de Beauvoir's Cartesian assumptions, which lead her to separate mind from body and build the gender/sex distinction on this binary foundation. For de Beauvoir, gender is to culture as sex is to nature and mind to body.

De Beauvoir's intellectual hostility to naturalism spilled over to issues such as the body and, by extension, sexuality and motherhood, which she tended to dismiss as part of the "facticity" of women's lives, that is to say, as that which a feminist ought to try to transcend.

It took feminists a long time to become critically aware of the fact that de Beauvoir's dualism and her consequent Cartesian dismissal of the body, combined with her adaptation of Hegelian dialectics to the differences between the sexes, while making the emancipation of women theoretically representable, created as many problems as they solved.[11] Although this realization led to bitter disappointment on the part of some,[12] it seems to me inevitable that younger generations of women had to come to terms with the legacy of de Beauvoir's binary definition of gender, that is, its subordination to the dialectics of conflicting consciousness.

Back to Aretha Franklin, the second point she makes about gender identity concerns the denaturalization of the signifier woman. Again, Judith Butler comments: " 'Like a natural woman' is a phrase that suggests that 'naturalness' is only accomplished through analogy or metaphor. In other words, 'You make me feel' like a metaphor of the natural and, without 'you,' some denaturalized ground would be revealed."[13] In other words, the constructed, relational structure of female identity is such that "nature" can only signify a displaced and infinitely deferred horizon, accessible only metaphorically. If "feeling like a woman" expresses the struggle for identity, and the consequent hiatus between sex and gender, "feeling like a natural woman" comments on the denaturalized structure of human subjectivity.

An important and related point here is the role played by desire as a relational category that discloses the fundamental structures of the self: the pointedly highlighted *You* defines the speaking—in this case the singing—subject, and calls her object of desire into question. You could translate this into the statement that it takes a man as object of desire to make one feel "like a natural woman." In a double-barrel shot, the institution of sexuality and the force of heterosexuality are singled out. I shall return to this.

These seemingly abstract notions and subtle intellectual distinctions between sex and gender, self and other, nature and culture had immediate and rather wide-ranging practical consequences. De Beauvoir's sex/gender distinction and her program for the emancipation of women paved the way for the second wave of the feminist movement. Central to what the media nicknamed "women's lib" and the bra-burning brigades of the 1960s was the conviction, elevated to the rank of a political creed, that anatomy is no destiny and that a woman's human potential and the related socioeconomic roles are not exhausted by her function as wife and mother.

In other words, the notion of "gender" accompanied and highlighted the struggle of the "second sex" to state their radical vindications about her social, economic, intellectual, and political position in a male-dominated world. This explosion of women's vindication, demands, hopes, and aspirations took many different forms. Many volumes of feminist scholarship have been devoted to analyzing the intellectual and political climates of the sixties. I shall not even attempt to enter this debate.[14]

I just want to stress that what made the second wave significant in the history of feminist struggles is that it posited a common link among women, insofar as they are constructed as the second sex, subjected to the authority of fathers and husbands—linked by a bond of oppression, of servitude. The positive side of this analysis is that women become valid and trustworthy interlocutors for other women. The novelty of the sixties was that women started talking to other women and comparing notes on their respective conditions. The "other" for a woman ceased to be necessarily the other sex. To illustrate this extraordinary moment, I single out a few aspects of it that strike me as significant: anger, ambition, and political separatism.

Janis Joplin exemplifies the healthy anger generated by the movements for the liberation of women. She is the singer who symbolizes for many of us the passion, the political vigor of the sixties and also sadly embodies its limitations. Joplin's anger captures both the lucidity of vision of the women in the late sixties and also a sort of powerlessness[15]—Joplin only just missed the feminist wave—she died of an overdose just as Kate Millett's *Sexual Politics* and Shulamith Firestone's *Dialectics of Sex* went to press. And yet, in a way unique to artists, she felt the spirit of the times and knew that this was the age of the new women.

You will find a great deal of this anger in all the texts written by the women who triggered off the second wave. That most of them dedicated their books explicitly to Simone de Beauvoir testifies not only to the importance of her book, but also to the speed with which women were setting up a theoretical tradition of their own: a new intellectual genealogy for women.[16]

For an example of the ambition generated in women by the lifting, or rather, the overthrow of ancient taboos about their "natural inferiority" and social subordination, let us turn to the real Janis Joplin. In the song "Mercedes-Benz,"[17] she addresses an appeal to the good Lord to please provide her with this car as a quintessential status symbol, so that she can keep up with her friends (and with the Joneses!) and not lose face.

This prompts a word of warning: ambition is a rare and difficult quality for people who have long been oppressed. It is taking women a long time to set the standards of their ambition to a number of variable goals and targets. At first, as often is the case with decolonized nations, ambition took a straight and relatively simple form: "Give me, too!" Give me jobs, give me goods, give me that great equalizer, that great compensation—give me symbolic worth, give me money, give me a Mercedes-Benz!

Money—which Joplin spent as quickly as she earned it, though she actually drove around in her legendary silver Porsche—points to one dimension of the liberation of women that was to grow in complexity over the next two decades: the issue of the symbolic system. That money is a major symbol in our society is not only a commonsense notion but also a concept that structural anthropology and psychoanalysis have developed into a theory of how social order is established and maintained. Georges Dumézil points out that the symbolic functions in our civilization are quite constant: the divine, the military, and the transmission of knowledge. That women are traditionally excluded from the social administration of the symbolic functions (the church, the army, the university) shows the masculine structure of our culture. That Janis Joplin addressed her request for symbolic compensation to God shows just as strongly that she understood how the symbolic works.

I will return to this. For the moment suffice it to say that it took some time for feminists to extricate the issue of the symbolic from monetary issue and to confront it in all its other aspects.

Patti Smith is an example of political separatism, whose lyrics represent not only feminism, but many other liberation struggles. She was the high priestess of rock modernism crossed into funk: erudite, setting Rimbaud's texts to music, she brought popular culture as close as it could go to performance art. A great artist—not the least of her achievements is, quite simply, to have survived the end of the sixties and seventies, alive and still creative. Her lyrics embody the basic elements of the sixties' political revolt: the author attacks the dominant ideology of her social context, emphasizing the racist, class-conscious, and sexist practices that make Western culture into a dominant, regulatory, and exclusionary system.[18] The accent is put on the practices of exclusion that are implicit in such a system. That the rebellious intellectual may want to secede from this system seems to follow quite logically.

With Patti Smith, millions of women chose the way out, in a gesture of political feminist separation that struck patriarchy where it was most vulnerable: at home. Reversing the liberal distinction between the public and the private, feminists politicized the private and, declaring that the personal is the political, questioned and problematized that which is the key to patriarchy: the power of the father and, secondarily, that of the husband. The "second sex," conscious of the power games of the gender system, set as its target the institution of the family, that is to say, the political economy of heterosexuality.

COMPULSORY HETEROSEXUALITY

The next moment in the feminist redefinition and analysis of gender includes Gayle Rubin's classic reading of the sex/gender distinction in the light of cultural anthropological analysis about the exchange of women. This was to have enormous consequences for the feminist analysis of the political economy of sex.[19] Following Lévi-Strauss's work on kinship structures, Rubin studied the material and symbolic function of women as objects of exchange among men. By focusing on the phenomenon of exogamy, she identified the circulation of women in a patrilinear society as the key to the gender system that sustains the patriarchal order.

This pointed out a number of interesting features: that women are merchandise to be used by men as a medium of exchange,[20] but also and more important, that the social order such as it exists is a male homosocial contract. In other words, the gender system that constructs the two sexes as different, unequal, and yet complementary is in fact a power system that aims at concentrating material and symbolic capital in the hands of the fathers, that is to say, older men, by controlling the younger men and the women. The family is thus the power unit that seals the wealth of men and establishes heterosexuality as the dominant political economy for both sexes. As such, heterosexuality is the institution that supports the gender system.

Gayle Rubin radicalizes de Beauvoir's analysis by showing how central the objectification of women is to the material but also symbolic upkeeping of the patriarchal system and the forms of knowledge, representation, and scientific investigation the system perpetuates. The sex/gender distinction is turned into a political economy in which the institution of heterosexuality supports the male homosocial bond by ensuring that women are exchanged, losing the father's name to gain the husband's.

Adrienne Rich builds on Rubin's work by introducing the notion of "compulsory heterosexuality" into the gender debate. She draws a much stronger connection between the condition of women and the structures of the family, motherhood as an institution and the normative enforcement of one model of sexual behavior: reproductive heterosexuality.

Rich's work is extremely important in that it also constitutes an innovative rereading of de Beauvoir–style feminism. In her poetry even more than in her essays, Rich presents an in-depth analysis of the paradoxes of female identity, especially of motherhood as an experience that determines a woman's sense of sexual identity while remaining an institution that enforces the law of the fathers.

Another significant innovation that Adrienne Rich draws from black feminism[21] is the idea that gender is not at all a monolithic category that makes all women the same, but rather that it is the mark of a position of subordination that is qualified by a number of powerful variables. Central among them is the variable of race or ethnicity. Through her notion of "the politics of location," Rich emphasizes the importance of situating oneself in the specificity of one's social, ethnic, class, economic, sexual reality. "Situating" for Rich does not have the same resonance as it does in the existentialist call for being situated in the world. It aims rather at bringing to the fore the importance of a lucid analysis of the material conditions that overdetermine one's speaking position.

The fact of being a woman is no longer taken by Rich as sufficient evidence of a common position. In a transmutation of values, Rich recommends that feminists try to define the female condition not in a reactive but in a creative manner, that is to say, not only in terms of oppression but also in the light of the positive values associated with being a woman. In her analysis, sexuality and race intersect to produce a complex vision of gender as a system that creates differences and subjects them to power relations. "Gender" thus turns into a complex network of power formations as opposed to the binary model of domination proposed in earlier versions.

As an illustration of this theoretical style, which is also known as the "woman-identified" approach insofar as it emphasizes the positive aspects of female identity, I would refer to the music of Helen Reddy, which is composed with disarming candor.[22] Her music sounds old-fashioned in its slightly utopian celebration of the new possibilities now opening up for women. Beyond grief and complaints, it is the strength, the intelligence of woman that gets celebrated.

The next significant development in gender theories is also prompted by Gayle Rubin's pioneer work, but it takes a more sociological turn. The neomaterialist thinkers, Christine Delphy, Monique Plaza, and Monique Wittig,[23] interpret the political economy of heterosexuality in a number of interesting ways.

First, by referring to a much more orthodox brand of de Beauvoir's thought, they develop the notion that women are a social class, that is to say, that sexuality is to feminism as labor is to Marxism: a fundamental concept on which one can build a revolutionary consciousness. Being a class means that all women are subjugated through the political economy of reproductive heterosexuality; it follows that the task of feminism is to overthrow the terms of this class relation and change the material conditions that engender them. There follows a very unqualified emphasis on materialism in the Marxist mode: as the material conditions that structure both social relations and theoretical practice.

One of the effects of this approach was the violent rejection of the celebratory mode in feminist theory, especially the movement known as *écriture féminine*,[24] which stressed the importance of language and the unconscious and made extensive use of psychoanalysis, semiotics, and philosophy in order to reevaluate female identity.

In a move of radical rejection of all identities created in the patriarchal system, Monique Wittig opened the era of suspicion about the very notion of "woman," which she takes as the ideological construct of a male-dominated gender system. For Wittig "woman" as concept is imbued with masculine projections and imaginary expectations; it is therefore epistemologically unreliable and politically suspicious. Wittig's radical critique of "woman" rests on her rejection of "essentialism"; Wittig argues that in patriarchal ideology "woman" stands for a normative model of reproductive heterosexuality: she stands for nature, motherhood, the male-dominated family. Such notions are essentialist because they pass off as natural and therefore as inevitable or unchangeable conditions that are in fact socially induced and culture-specific.

By extension, Wittig turns upside down de Beauvoir's distinction between sex and gender, radicalizing the terms of the opposition. For de Beauvoir, the differences between the sexes are part of the fundamental dialectic that structures human consciousness; they rest and build on a biological given: sexually differentiated bodies. Gender roles are therefore caught in a law of dialectics and negation, in which the male stands for the human and the female for the other-than-human. Wittig changes this around: the gender system is not the cultural recoding of a biological reality, but rather the expression of a patriarchal ideology that requires binary oppositions between the sexes in order to assert male dominance.

Consequently, the gender system for Wittig functions by a dualistic logic of binary oppositions that create sexed identities ("man" and "woman"). These identities provide an essentialist basis to patriarchal power; that is to say, they support a belief in the "natural," that is to say, historically inevitable structure of the institutions, values, and modes of representation, especially the vision of the subject, of the patriarchal social system. For Wittig the gender system constructs the female as sexed, conflates the male with the universal (man = mankind) and sets both sexes up in the social framework of compulsory heterosexuality. It is important to emphasize this point: that for Wittig, as for de Beauvoir, only women have a gender, men are exempted from such mark of specificity insofar as they represent the human.

It thus follows that the term "woman," far from being the foundational category it was for de Beauvoir, is a culturally determined notion. Taking her distance from Adrienne Rich's reevaluation of the terms, Wittig proposes that feminists abandon this mystifying, essentialist notion and rather take as their point of assembly and identification a much more subversive figure: "the lesbian." In her highly controversial statement, "a lesbian is not a woman," Wittig argues that the lesbian represents a form of political consciousness that rejects male-dominated definitions of woman and calls into question the whole gender system with its conveniently arranged sexual bipolarization. In other words, the lesbian is like a third pole of reference: she is neither "non-man," nor "non-woman," but rather radically other.

In other words, the lesbian marks the overcoming of identities based on the Phallus and consequently the bypassing of the gender system. This radical change in perspective takes gender as an instance of male dominance; it organizes sexuality through a power system in which control is exercised by men. Control is exercised through this objectification of women, but also, as object-relation feminist psychoanalysts point out, by eroticizing the act of control itself.[25] The link between sexuality and power thus provides the groundwork for a critique of masculine desire for power, that is to say, the eroticizing of control by men.

This shift in perspective also corresponds to a change in political climate: a much sharper sense of separatism comes into place. As an example of the intensity of this particular moment of feminist theory, I refer to the deconstruction of feminine identity by women punk-rockers of the early 1980s. Few moments in popular culture can match the punks such as Nina Hagan or the British band Crass in iconoclastic rejection of stereotypes, uncompromising criticism, and political determination.

THE INSTITUTIONALIZATION

From the early eighties, the main factor that influenced the growth of gender theories was the institutionalization of women's studies in the universities. This resulted in a major output of research on this field; the added quantity corresponds also to qualitatively higher demands for a more systematic approach to feminist theory.[26]

Institutionalized research in women's studies has a twofold aim: on the one hand, to consolidate the wealth and range of knowledge produced by women and, on the other hand, to refine the methodological accuracy of the key notions in feminist theory. An added incentive to the systematization of the founding notions of feminist methodology is the pedagogical factor. With the institutionalization of women's studies courses, the need emerged to ensure effective transmission of the range, depth, and variety of feminist forms of knowledge. Experience shows that no matter what the subject may be, the best teaching practice is to lay one's convictions open to the critical scrutiny of younger generations. The students are one's most valuable critics. This is particularly strong within women's studies where the question of intergenerational exchanges is crucial to the issue of how to establish a genealogy of feminist theories.[27] This institutionalized phase of feminist theory and the generational problem it creates strike a positive note. Women teaching and studying their own cultural traditions, that woman be the measure of knowledge, is a welcome relief from the monotony of androcentric scholarship as well as an occasion for joy and intellectual excitement.

Over the last few years women's studies research on gender has concentrated on the notions of relation. Joan Scott encourages feminists to approach gender as marking a set of relations, thereby developing one of Rich's insights. Sex, class, race, and age are fundamental axes or variables that define the gender system. Using extensively the poststructuralist analysis of power and discourse, Scott takes her distance from Wittig's idea of gender as an ideological system and leans toward a notion of gender as a network of power relations.

Central to this approach is the idea of the coextensivity of power and discourse, that is to say, the notion that the struggle for naming, the epistemological struggle, is at the heart of feminist theory and politics. The central question now becomes how to redefine the female subject after the certainties of gender-dualism have collapsed. How can we think about the complexity of the differences—of class, race, age, sexual preference—which separate women while postulating a commonness of situation and vision? Previous work on gender has in fact shown that female identity is a site of differences and that a woman occupies different subject positions at different times.

The paradox that emerges out of this is that feminist theory in the nineties is based on the very notion of gender that it problematizes, complicates, and, in some cases, undermines. One very important effect of this new awareness of gender as a network of relations is that a new state of mind has come into place within feminism. Less emotional and intellectual energy is spent on opposition, complaint and naive self-celebration. What is emerging instead, also thanks to the impact of younger generations of women, is a calmer determination about achieving the aims of improving the status of women and the forms of representation that are reserved for women. Otherness is not necessarily taken as a mark of inferiority but rather as the starting point for positive differences for something new and better.

Another theoretical development that needs to be stressed is the work of Teresa de Lauretis on what she calls the technology of gender.[28] Relying on Foucault's notion of the "materiality" of discourse, de Lauretis approaches the construction of female identity as both a material and a symbolic process. Gender is a complex mechanism, a "technology" that defines the subject as male or female in a process of normativity and regulation of what the human being is expected to become.

The key notion in de Lauretis's idea of the regulative function of gender is that this notion produces the very categories that it purports to explain. Gender as a process of constructing the subject produces such categories as men, women, heterosexuals, homosexuals, perverts, and so on. De Lauretis's idea that gender constructs certain sexed identities leads on to a second crucial statement: that the process of gender intersects with other normative variables, such as race and class, to produce a formidable power system. Innovating on both Wittig and Scott, de Lauretis sees gender as a process that organizes differences on the basis of race and other crucial variables for the purpose of constructing socially normal subjects. As a consequence, she calls for feminists to destabilize the normativity of the dominant forms of sexed identity and to find new definitions for the female feminist subject.

Judith Butler takes a slightly different orientation: she takes up Wittig's analysis of "woman" and innovates on de Lauretis's insight about gender as a technology. Butler's question becomes, if gender as a process constructs the very categories of identity that it purports to explain, is it still useful to feminists?

Concentrating her critique on the dualistic nature of the sex/gender opposition, Butler argues that "woman" as a category constructed by this binary opposition is both normative and exclusionary: normative because it enforces compulsory heterosexuality; exclusionary because it conceals the multiplicity of differences that constitute the subject. Butler's analysis, in other words, focuses on the "woman" part of de Beauvoir's famous: "One is not born, one becomes a woman." Attacking the normative fiction of heterosexual coherence, Butler calls for feminists to produce a whole array of new, noncoherent genders.

TOWARD A FEMINIST GENEALOGY

In this short overview of the development of gender theories, I have tried to sketch the evolution of the notion from the substantive value that de Beauvoir granted it to the recent view of gender as process, technology, or even performance. This evolution parallels another: whereas in earlier versions the masculine represented the human, recent gender theories are more optimistic about women's entitlement to speaking as subjects. Language, however manmade, has shown remarkable plasticity and adaptability to the requirements of the female feminist subjects. One clear trend over the last ten years is the increasing recognition of the importance of differences among women, especially those based on class, race, and sexual orientation. In the final section of this essay, I indicate some of the directions in which I would like to see feminist theory grow.

What has already become clear, through this rapid growth of theories about the status, structure, and political significance of the female feminist subject is that the challenge for women's studies in the 1990s is to assess and systematize the different methodologies of gender. Donna Haraway suggests the expression "feminist figurations" to describe these different ways of representing the subject in feminism.[29] The challenge today is to find new images of thought to help feminists think about the changes and changing conditions that they have helped to bring about.

I would like to argue that the quest for adequate representations of the feminist subject is part and parcel of a feminist theoretical genealogy: I am a great believer in the usefulness of a feminist intellectual tradition. Why? Because, although the stock of cumulated feminist knowledge has grown considerably, women still have no codified tradition of their own. It will take time and hard work to bring such theoretical capital into being; women must have the means by which to bring about such transformations.

The central point remains: very few women are in a position of symbolic power, that is to say, in a position to systematize, codify, and transmit their own intellectual traditions. In such a situation, women of a feminist inclination have had to revise upward their own relationship to ambition. Gone is the candid, simplistic longing for a Mercedes-Benz. A new kind of realism has set in of which the singer Madonna is the best example: for the women of today, being material girls living in a material world is not the aim, but only the starting point.[30]

In other words, the symbolic recognition female feminists aspire to today is that of being entitled to elaborate their own forms of scientific discourse and to have them recognized as scientific. This point is particularly relevant if you take into account the forms taken by contemporary antifeminism. Whereas earlier on the standard antifeminist line was that women's studies is a mere ideological construct, at best a politically motivated critique or satire of patriarchy, the line in the nineties is that feminism does have its theoretical bases. These, however, are usually seen as disrespectful of tradition, iconoclastic, even nihilistic. Feminists are regularly accused of destroying tradition, upsetting the canon, criticizing but offering nothing in return.

Another version on this theme merges with the misogynist traditions of anti-intellectualism and female underemployment to produce yet another antifeminist line: women's studies scholars are found to be too theoretical, abstract, jargon-ridden, even obscure. Their difficult notions and elaborate prose are compared to the crystal-clear lucidity of good old homemade common sense and dismissed in the name of pragmatic, down-to-earth realism.

The "clarity fetishists"[31] who thus dismiss feminist theory have never bothered to read any of the founding texts of this tradition, and they add arrogance to ignorance by sitting in judgment on a field they are not qualified to assess. What remains constant in the antifeminist line is that women are judged insufficient either by lack (not enough theoretical power) or by excess (too much theory): the result is the same.

I consequently support the establishment of a systematized feminist theoretical genealogy, a tradition of female feminist theorists and critics to counterbalance the continuous antiwoman line that so many of the learned institutions promote and support. There is such a thing today as feminist theory, and it is other than the critique of sexist biases in science and scholarship; it is other than protest, rebellion, anger. It is a theoretical movement with its own assumptions, ruling principles, criteria, and intellectual histories. Feminist theory is a radically non-nostalgic and forward-looking form of thought: for female intellectuals, the past is not such a great model and there is no way for us to go but up.

Although there is a great variety of approaches within women's studies, there is consensus on a number of crucial points. The first is that new ideas, new theories, different ways of thinking—if they are to be something more than mere utopianism—must be born of careful, caring repetitions of old ideas. Parthenogenesis is hardly a viable option. Far from being nihilistic destroyers of past traditions and traditional wisdom, feminists are lucid readers and diagnosticians of their political and cultural implications for women and for the gender system that constructs them. As analysts of this system, feminists are very much part of it; linked to patriarchy by negation of its very premises, feminists know that only patterns of studied repetition, only a strategic form of mimesis such as Irigaray proposes, can generate authentic differences. In other words, you do not reinvent the subject "woman" by sheer willpower: the process requires rather the deconstruction of the many, often contradictory meanings and representations of "woman." Only through such a process can a new definition of "woman" emerge, because language is endowed with amazing resilience and complexity.

As Laurie Anderson puts it, language is a virus! Consequently, the powers of language are incalculable and you just do not know whom you may have contaminated with messages, ideas, texts, that may well appear obvious and even tired-out to the author.

That language is a fabulous prison-house is a truth that women learned at their own expense well before the electronic avant-garde art of today. One of the great masters of modernism, Virginia Woolf, in her speech on BBC radio in the thirties, made us aware of the viral, contaminating nature of language and gave her answer to it:

> ... only after the writer is dead do his words to some extent, only to some extent, become disinfected, purified of the accidents of the living body. Now this ... suggestion is one of the most exciting and most mysterious properties of words. Most exciting if you are a person in having to use them. Everyone who has ever written a sentence must be conscious, or half-conscious of it. Words, English words, are full of echoes, memories, associations, naturally. They have been out and about, on people's lips, in their houses, in the streets, in the fields, for so many centuries. And that is one of the chief difficulties in writing them today. They are stored with other meanings, with other memories. And they have contracted so many famous marriages in the past. The splendid word *incarnadine* for example, who can use that without remembering *multitudinous seas*? In the old days, of course, when English was a new language, writers could invent new words and use them. Nowadays it is easy enough to invent new words, they spring to the lips, whenever we see a new sight or feel a new sensation. But we cannot use them, because the English language is old. You cannot use a brand-new word in an old language because it is a very obvious yet always mysterious fact that word is not a single and separate entity, it is part of other words. Indeed it is not a word, but it is part of a sentence. Words belong to each other, although of course only a great poet knows that the word

incarnadine belongs to "multitudinous seas." To combine new words with old words is fatal to the constitution of the sentence. In order to use new words properly you'd have to invent a whole new language, and that is....—we shall come to it—is not at the moment our business. Our business is to see what we can do with the old English language as it is. How can we combine the old words in new orders, so that they survive, and so that they create beauty, so that they tell the truth? That is the question.

Just like new language is born of patient repetitions, caring, and frequent encounters with the old, so equally history is not a four-lane highway, but a discontinuous line, where progress is often achieved by twisting and turning, repeating and going back. History as repetition is a genealogical cycle, the careful sifting through of old notions, to improve them, to make them less regulative, more beautiful. Teleologically ordained historical "progress" in the eighteenth-century sense may not be available to us as a historical option, but this does not mean that no progress at all is possible and that nihilism is around the corner.

Walter Benjamin warned us that the angel of history moves on by walking backward toward a future that s/he neither controls nor predicts.[32] Stumbling on to a new age, we are all like Benjamin's angel.

NOTES

1 One example of this communication breakdown was the debate on equality versus difference; another was the never-ending discussion on essentialism For a lucid discussion of the former, see Joan Scott, "Deconstructing Equality versus Difference: or the Uses of Poststructuralist Theory for Feminism," *Feminist Studies* 14, no. 1 (1988): 33–50. On essentialism, see "The Essential Difference," *Differences* 1, no. 2 (1988). See also "Rosi Braidotti" in the *Dictionary of Feminism and Psychoanalysis*, ed. Elizabeth Wright (forthcoming).

2. See the new collection of articles on Dutch feminism in English edited by Joke Hermsen and Alkaline van Lemming, *Sharing the Difference*, (London Routledge, 1991). See also the collection of texts on Italian feminism edited by Paola Bono and Sandra Kemp, *Italian Feminist Theory* (Oxford: Blackwell, 1991).

3. See Donna Haraway, "Situated Knowledges," in *Simians, Cyborgs and Women* (London. Free Association Books, 1990), 183–202.

4 For an example of crossing high and low cultures, see my analysis of Laurie Anderson in "Dies Irae," *Copyright* 1, no. 1 (1987)· 119–24

5 See Jacques Derrida, *Qui a Peur de la Philosophie?* (Paris· Flammarion, 1979) See also Jean-François Lyotard, *Le postmodernisme expliqué aux enfants* (Paris Galilee, 1982), "Some of the Things at Stake in Women's Struggles," *Wedge* 6 (1984): 3–12, and *La condition postmoderne* (Paris: Minuit, 1979). For a feminist reply to Lyotard, see Seyla Benhabib, "Epistemolo-

gies of Postmodernism, a Rejoinder to J. F Lyotard," in *Feminism/Post-modernism*, ed. Linda Nicholson (New York. Routledge, 1990), 107–32.

6. See Michel Foucault, *L'ordre du discours* (Paris: Gallimard, 1977). See also Roland Barthes, *Mythologies* (Paris. Seuil, 1967).

7 For an illuminating account of this approach, see *Off-Centre Feminism and Cultural Studies*, ed. Sarah Franklin, Celia Lury, and Jackie Stacey (London: HarperCollins, 1991). Before the poststructuralists, Walter Benjamin had already perfected what is now becoming known as cultural studies, or the serious analysis of contemporary culture. The revival of scholarly interest in Benjamin is also linked to the boom of cultural studies in the institutions, especially in the United States

8. Juliette Greco embodied the existentialist prototype of the engagé intellectual as well as, if not better than, Jean-Paul Sartre and Simone de Beauvoir

9 This point is made strongly by Donna Haraway in her article on the history of this concept: "Gender for a Marxist Dictionary: The Sexual Politics of a Word," in *Simians, Cyborgs and Women*, 127–48. For a more detailed historical account, see also on this point Teresa de Lauretis, "Eccentric Subjects Feminist Theory and Historical Consciousness," *Feminist Studies* 1 (1990): 115–50. At the moment critical surveys of the notion of gender seem quite needed in feminist theory

10 In *Gender Trouble* (New York: Routledge, 1990), 22

11 For intelligent and generous criticisms of de Beauvoir, see Butler, *Gender Trouble*, and Elizabeth Spelman, *Inessential Woman* (Boston. Beacon, 1989).

12. Particularly poignant here was the disappointment about and disapproval of de Beauvoir by the *écriture féminine* theorists, especially Hélène Cixous

13 Butler, *Gender Trouble*, 154 n 34

14 See, among others, Hester Eisenstein, *Contemporary Feminist Thought* (Boston. G K. Hall, 1983).

15 I have analyzed the paradox of female performers in popular culture, together with Anneke Smelik, in an audiovisual lecture, "The Eternal Feminine Revisited."

16 In addition to Millett and Firestone, Ti-Grace Atkinson also dedicated her classic *Amazon Odyssey* (New York: Link Books, 1974) to de Beauvoir.

For a discussion of the notion of "genealogy," see Luce Irigaray, *Le temps de la différence* (Paris. Grasset, 1989) See also the text of my inaugural lecture, *The Subject in Feminism* (Utrecht, 1990); reprinted in *Hypatia* 6, no. 2 (1991) 155–72 See also the text of Teresa de Lauretis's inaugural lecture, "Feminist Genealogies" (Utrecht, 1991).

17 From the album *Pearl* (Strong Arm Music/CBS, 1971)

18 See her album *Easter* (Arista)

19 The expression "compulsory heterosexuality" was coined by Adrienne Rich; see her "Compulsory Heterosexuality and Lesbian Existence," *Signs* 5 (1980) 631–60 Concerning the political economy of sex, see Gayle Rubin, "The Traffic in Women: Notes on the Political Economy of Sex," in *Towards an Anthropology of Women*, ed. R. Reiter Rapp (New York. Monthly Review Press, 1975)

20. Luce Irigaray devoted a brilliant study to this question in *Ce Sexe qui n'en est pas un* (Paris Seuil, 1977) J. J. Goux also studies the analogy between women and money in *Les iconoclastes* (Paris. Seuil, 1977).

21. Adrienne Rich, "The Politics of Location," in *Blood, Bread and Poetry* (London: Virago, 1987). For the impact of black feminism, see Audre Lorde, *Sister Outside* (New York: Crossing, 1984), Bell Hooks, *Ain't I a Woman: Black Women and Feminism* (Boston: South End, 1981); Gloria Hull, Patricia Bell Scott, and Barbara Smith, eds., *All the Women Are White, All the Men Are Black But Some of Us Are Brave* (New York. Feminist Press, 1982)

22. See her album *I Am Woman* (Capitol, 1972).

23. See Christine Delphy, *Close to Home—a Materialist Analysis of Women's Oppression* (London: Hutchinson, 1984), and "Pour un féminisme matérialiste," *L'Arc* 61 (1975). See also Monique Plaza, "Pouvoir phalle morphique et psychologie de la femme," *Questions Féministes* 1 (1977), and "Nos dommages et leurs intérêts," *Questions Féministes* 3 (1978) See also Monique Wittig, *Le corps lesbien* (Paris: Minuit, 1973); *Les guerrillères* (Paris: Minuit, 1968); "The Straight Mind," *Feminist Issues* 1 (1980): 103–11, and "One Is Not Born a Woman," *Feminist Issues* 2 (1981): 47–54.

24. The movement of *écriture féminine* saw creative writers such as Hélène Cixous, Annie Leclerc, Marguerite Duras, and others join hands with theoreticians such as Luce Irman, Julia Kristeva, and others in exploring specific forms of feminine writing, theory, or expression. For a detailed analysis, see my *Patterns of Dissonance*, trans Elizabeth Guild (Cambridge: Polity, 1991).

25 See especially Jessica Benjamin, *The Bonds of Love* (New York: Pantheon, 1988), and Jane Flax, *Thinking Fragments* (Berkeley and Los Angeles University of California Press, 1990)

26 See Sandra Harding, *The Science Question in Feminism* (Ithaca Cornell University Press, 1986) and *Feminism and Methodology* (Milton Keynes Open University Press, 1987).

27. For a discussion of the impact of the institutionalization of women's studies, see Alice Jardine, "Notes for an Analysis," in *Between Feminism and Psychoanalysis*, ed Theresa Brennan (London: Routledge, 1989) See also Evelyn Fox-Keller and Marianne Hirsch, eds, *Conflicts in Feminism* (New York: Routledge, 1990)

28. See Teresa de Lauretis, *Technologies of Gender* (Bloomington: Indiana University Press, 1987).

29 See my "Promises of Monsters" (Paper delivered at the graduate school for women's studies, Arts faculty, Utrecht, October 1990).

30. The reference is to Madonna's song "Material Girl," from the album *Like a Virgin* (Warner Brothers, 1984).

31. The expression was coined by Gayatri Spivak in a public lecture at the University of Utrecht, 16–17 May 1990.

32 In "Theses on the Philosophy of History," in *Illuminations* (New York: Schocken Books, 1968), 253–64: "A Klee painting named 'Angelus Novus' shows an angel looking as though he is about to move away from something he is fixedly contemplating. His eyes are staring, his mouth is open, his wings are spread This is how one pictures the angel of history. His face is turned towards the past Where we perceive a chain of events, he sees one single catastrophe which keeps piling wreckage upon wreckage and hurls it in front of his feet. The angel would like to stay, awaken the dead, and make whole what has been smashed. But a storm is blowing from Paradise; it has got caught in his wings with such violence that the angel can no longer close them. This storm irresistibly propels him into the future to which his back is turned, while the pile of debris before him grows skyward This storm is what we call progress" (257–58).

10

Stories of Gender

SARAH WESTPHAL

Once I asked my students to construct an image of the angel of history exactly as Benjamin describes it. Someone volunteered to draw the image on the blackboard as members of the class offered various details. The angel emerged in profile, facing paradise on the left, its useless wings stretched behind by the blast. In front of the angel we drew the debris of history, which resembled an exploding junk shop.

I then showed the class a copy of the etching by Klee called *Angelus Novus* that Benjamin had owned, which had served as his source for this emblem.[1] When the class discovered that the etching depicts only the angel gazing at the viewer, their shock was palpable. As readers we had performed the "god trick," locating ourselves outside the frame, looking in as wholly detached observers.[2] But if we reconstruct Benjamin's text starting with the attitude of Klee's image, then we must position ourselves in the blast of history, in the ever-growing pile of wreckage, staring straight into the angel's visage.

The threshold of the twenty-first century is a moment ripe for retrospection as well as for visions of what will come, and of what we need to accomplish. In Christa Wolf's phrase, now is the time to remember the future.[3] The eerie temporality of her double vision is also expressed by Benjamin's dialectical image in which the viewer looks toward the future to see history's allegorical representation. In Rosi Braidotti's "Theories of Gender," I would like to consider how alternative futures are visible through shifting reconfigurations of what has already occurred; but also how the viewer is positioned within the frame of reference, since "where one speaks from affects the meaning and truth of what one says, and thus ... one cannot assume an ability to transcend one's location."[4]

Gender is one of those words that has "been out and about, on people's lips, in their houses, in the streets, in the fields" (Virginia Woolf; quoted in Braidotti, "Theories of Gender," 149). Gender theory is like the "new language" that Woolf envisioned, but whose possibility she doubted in the 1930s.[5] I agree that the feminist redefinition of gender has had a significant impact on nearly all academic disciplines during the past decade and a half. One index is the volume of publishing. More than one hundred English-language journals are devoted entirely to feminist research.[6] Many journals based in the disciplines regularly publish feminist work, including special issues on gender or women's studies.[7] University presses in the United States have series for book-length research on gender; some presses, such as the Women's Press in Toronto, Beacon in Boston, and Virago in London, specialize in feminist research and women's writing. The reach of this transformation is suggested by some randomly selected titles: *The Poetics of Gender,* edited by Nancy K. Miller; *Science and Gender* by Ruth Bleier; *Gender and the Politics of History* by Joan Wallach Scott; and from philosophy, *Gender/Body/Knowledge,* edited by Susan R. Bordo and Alison M. Jaggar. Significantly, each of the above-mentioned books forges its own understanding(s) of how gender works as a category of analysis or as a critique of knowledge. Thus the dissonance over time you describe also characterizes the synchronic slice of gender research in 1993.

I am sympathetic with your claim that women's studies needs a fuller account of gender theory. Yet the concept of genealogy does not fit easily with this idea of double vision, nor with a temporality that is not strictly chronological. One reason is that the word *genealogy*, having contracted "so many famous marriages in the past," is "stored with other meanings, with other memories" (Woolf; quoted in Braidotti, "Theories of Gender," 149). One set of meanings arises from the history of the patriarchal family: the "traffic in women" established by nonconsensual marriage; coverture; the severance of the bride's ties of kinship and the loss of the mother's name, all to ensure the orderly transmission of property and title through the legitimate paternal line. Today's social institutions continue to define and defend themselves through discourses of legitimation, and to concentrate their resources in the hands of "rightful heirs." A genealogical method whose goal is to authorize and transmit feminist intellectual "property" to a new generation would have to acknowledge these meanings, and how they position women both historically and today.

Traditionally, the idea of a genealogy implies a definite origin and a process of historical development that is something like the unfolding of a genetic code, with underdetermined contextual input. Foucault's genealogical method, with its attacks on the founding subject, on continuous history, and on totalizing philosophies, repudiates these traditional assumptions. Many feminist theories have found a resource in Foucault's theory of sexuality and his history of bodies. And gender itself, understood as a "tacit project to renew a cultural history in one's own corporeal terms," is an apt object for genealogical analysis.[8] But gender is not only a technology of power, and not entirely analogous to the medical gaze or punitive surveillance. There is a tension between the range, depth, and variety of feminist research on gender, and the kind of object or "True Discourse" that a genealogy would seem to demand.[9] A gendered standpoint is itself a methodological stance, commensurate in its analytical power with Foucauldian methodology. I would argue, therefore, for gender as theory, along with genealogies of gender.[10]

Traces of traditional genealogy remain, particularly in your discussion of origins. The state of productive openness that characterizes the synchronic slice of 1993 has to do, in part, with the absence of founding figures, or to put it positively, with the multiplicity of beginnings. Who would want to claim the same relation to feminist gender theory that Marx has to Marxist theory, or Freud to psychoanalysis? In the place of a founder or a "big picture," I would argue, as many others have done, that gender theory has a politics. The long history of feminist activism is part of its knowledge system, though the forms and locations of feminist politics are as diversified as its theory.[11]

The long history of activism—in my own field of medieval studies, to be a feminist is to claim a history buried in often surprising places; to discover that deeply held notions of family and sexuality were under active construction, for Western Europe, in the eleventh and twelfth centuries; and to unravel the contradictions between what historical women did, and how they were represented in art and literature. Second-wave theory, which shapes my understanding of the past, has grown and continues to grow in many and tangled paths. What I am describing is not exactly the same as the "systematization of the founding notions of feminist methodology" that you discuss (Braidotti, "Theories of Gender," 145). My emphasis here is on the long view backward, but also on the gaps and contradictions, the idea that history is like a mass of fragments whose links are constructed through an exercise of remembering. As Katie King observes: "Feminists too easily believe 'we' already know the 'history' or even histories of feminism."[12]

Along with "genealogy," I offer the story. Stories have the capacity to perform many cultural functions. As shapings of the past that tell us where we are going, they are comparable to the image of the angel. They are conscious constructions, obviously and openly partial in their claims, with a deliberate choice of elements, whose structures will create an illusion (but only an illusion) of coherence.[13] In addition, stories are partial in the sense that "each writer writes the missing parts to the other writer's story."[14] In the production of multiple stories, time and space are deliberately confused (King, "Producing," 83). And good storytellers are always aware of what their listeners may be thinking. Stories will not convert anyone to feminism, but they may raise consciousness, and they are serviceable in certain situations that arise in academic life.

In the classroom, for example, since "with the institutionalization of women's studies courses, the need emerged to ensure effective transmission of the range, depth, and variety of feminist forms of knowledge" (Braidotti, "Theories of Gender," 145). Those of us who have put together a course syllabus on feminist theory already have a story on hand. The filling in of missing parts, though, is accomplished by students themselves as they make their way from one feminist course to another. Students at my university tell me that women's studies, in its far-flung departmental settings, gives a focus and coherence to their learning that is not available in a more traditional, departmental major, nor in any individual course.

I would like to hear much more about how intergenerational exchanges are crucial to establishing a genealogy of feminist theories (Braidotti, "Theories of Gender," 145). I am reminded of Audre Lorde's observation on how the "generation gap" is an important tool of repression, for if one generation views another generation as "contemptible or suspect or excess, they will never be able to join hands and examine the living memories of the community."[15] As you point out, in the university it is the student generation who often have little input in the classroom setting. One way this silencing occurs is through the disconnection of formal learning from other aspects of students' lives, including family relations, eating disorders, sexual identity, date rape, and sexual or racial harassment. It is one thing for individual professors to learn from individual students in the course of teaching or advising, but quite another to ground our teaching in "an appreciation for the knowledge, diversity, and intellectual strengths of those who take our classes." The latter is a far more radical approach and challenges the "authority relations of faculty (the class of knowers) to students (the recipients of knowledge) by developing a student-based critique of teaching and learning."[16] Your intergenerational exchange helps overcome this repressive disconnection, moving as it does from younger to older, crossing the boundary of "high" and "low," of feminist theory and popular culture, of what belongs in the classroom and what supposedly does not. This crossing taps the subjugated knowledge of learners and gives a more inclusive picture of women as idea makers and agents in the diverse settings of their lives.[17]

Other forms of women's cultural production could be included as well. Women, after all, had stories, poems, and songs long before they were admitted to the university as students and teachers. The entire scope of women's music and poetry, past and present, is a source—not simply an illustration—for theory. The definition of theory becomes more elastic, accessible, and connected to lived experience. On the close relationship between feminist theory and creativity, it is amazing to consider that de Beauvoir, Wittig, Millett, Walker, Lorde, and Rich (and others as well) are important creative writers whose combined generic range includes poetry, drama, prose fiction, epic, and autobiography. As you observe in *Patterns of Dissonance:* "The transition between the critical, reactive moment, and that of active creation, is almost imperceptible. Feminism demands this continual reflection, this calling into question of its own theoretical and practical modalities of operation."[18]

I need a different story about gender theory when called on to represent feminist research to nonfeminists or antifeminists "to counterbalance the continuous antiwoman line that so many of the learned institutions promote and support" (Braidotti, "Theories of Gender," 148). Like you, I am extremely impatient when confronted with people who have never read any of the numerous source texts and who would dismiss academic feminism as either too theoretical or not sufficiently theoretical. Frequently it is not feminist theory, but feminists themselves who are stereotyped and discounted. If lack of respect is constant, it may become a form of direct discrimination.[19] Thus one of the more urgent teaching challenges we face is to educate our colleagues who may be older, more powerful, or better established in the universities where we work and in the discipline as a whole. I am convinced that a broader-based understanding of feminist theory is connected to the goal of equity for women as university employees and students. Women will be more highly valued by our learned institutions when feminist theory finally gets the respect that it deserves.

Yet the urgency of this teaching assignment does not mean that we should smooth over the contradictions of feminism by offering a culinary account to those who oppose its goals.[20] The transatlantic disconnection, for example, succeeded to some extent as an easily digested image of "where feminists are at." Among its drawbacks was its tendency to subsume the differences within the national cultures. I like the way you tell this part of the story, contrasting the American theories of gender with the more Eurocentric theories of sexual difference. But you surprise the reader by putting de Beauvoir at the beginning of the American stream.[21] A story about sexual difference might begin with Woolf, whose attention to "the women's sentence" and the workings of the unconscious configure with some second-wave French thinking.

The Second Sex was available in English in the United States in 1952. Following this moment in your reconstruction are the radicals of the 1960s, especially Millett, who learned from de Beauvoir's powerful confrontation of history and literature; Gayle Rubin, the self-defined exegete of Lévi-Strauss, Engels, and Freud; Monique Wittig, whose "lesbian" offers a "radically subversive location in a heterosexual culture" (Fuss, *Essentially Speaking,* 42), and whose relocations between Europe and the United States destabilize any notion of the nation for theory; and Christine Delphy, whose opposition to "Psych et Po" cracks the stereotype of French feminism even as her materialism resists accommodation on the American side; and many other theorists as well. The Canadian location offers another story of dis- and reconnections between anglophone and francophone feminists that again subverts the transatlantic binarism. Bitter controversy is also part of this story or a dovetailing story that might have a biographical and institutional focus. But my point is simply that yours is a better account of how ideas and people grow and travel because it is not based on language and nation as hidden determinants, nor does it reify the received divisions within feminism by suppressing the differences within either of these strands.

I would like to return to Benjamin's angel, picking up another aspect of what it means to find oneself inside the frame, rather than safely positioned outside of it. The "god trick" is a comforting illusion of authority and control. But having exposed it for what it is, the question arises, how, precisely, does the speaker's location begin to have a bearing on the meaning of her utterance? Though this relationship between social location and textual or spoken meaning is "uneasy, underdetermined, and contested," it is evident that a university is an immensely conflicted location for a feminist (Alcoff, "Problem," 17). The speaker is beneficiary of a progressive past of women's activism in education and actor in an often elitist status quo, at once excluded and allied with structures of exclusion.

I agree therefore that we are "linked to patriarchy by negation of its very premises," even though "as analysts of this system [we] are very much part of it" (Braidotti, "Theories of Gender," 148–49; my emphasis). But an institutionalized feminism whose aim is systematization, either of founding notions or of research methodologies, appears to be overly isomorphic with its supporting structure. Women who have been excluded from the university because they are older, lesbian, of recent immigrant or First Nations origin, disabled, or black have made this point urgently and repeatedly. Bell hooks, for example, writes: "As institutional structures impose values, modes of thought, ways of being on our consciousness, those of us who work in academic settings often unwittingly become engaged in the production of feminist theory that aims to create a new sphere of theoretical elitism."[22] For this reason, I do not find Irigaray's idea of strategic mimesis, of undoing by overdoing, a very persuasive way of thinking about how our university location bears on the meanings of our theory-making. Feminist academics may aspire to "symbolic recognition"—to "being entitled to elaborate their own forms of scientific discourse and to have them recognized as scientific" by learned institutions (Braidotti, "Theories of Gender," 147–48). We also challenge the authority of learned institutions to recognize what discourse counts as scientific. This means using our own academic authority wisely "to make common cause with those others identified as outside the [university's] structures" (Lorde, *Sister Outsider,* 112). Lorde continues with the warning that "the master's tools will never dismantle the master's house."

This is my most pressing criticism: that a systematized feminist theoretical genealogy, as a text or as a knowledge system, threatens to create its meanings through the exclusion of ideas as well as people. A related issue is how the process of citation and publication reify theory whose insights depend on whole communities *theorizing* (King, "Producing,"

91). Aretha Franklin's language mediates the tension between art and theory, high and low, and older and younger feminist generations.[23] But the specificity of her art draws on meanings in black American English and the blues tradition, for example, in her use of the word "natural."

Another story might begin with Sojourner Truth's question, Ain't I a woman? which resonates through contemporary gender theory. This story could continue with Frances M. Beal, who published her essay "Double Jeopardy: To Be Black and Female" in 1970. She affirmed black women's independent standpoint in the struggle against racism, sexism, and economic exploitation. White feminism, she said, has been largely middle class, and unless it examines its own racist and classist assumptions, it is unwittingly part of the problem for black women.[24] *Sexual Politics* appeared in the same year. There, Kate Millett uses the word *gender* to talk about the arbitrary advantaging of one group of human beings over another, showing how the question of difference was an issue of power. Millett's discussion of Jean Genet's play *The Blacks,* though relying too heavily on the race-sex analogy, is, to my knowledge, a pioneering attempt by a white, second-wave feminist to theorize how the exclusionary processes of race and gender reinforce each other in literature and society. In 1970, the political context for both texts was the civil rights and antiwar movements. My purpose is not to achieve a more objective account of feminist theory through a pluralist dream of inclusion. Nor am I reaching for some defining theme of the whole.[25] My question is, how can feminist academics consolidate their intellectual tradition and also be responsible to feminist theorizing that happens where dominant-group women are not at the center? What I am arguing for is a fuller understanding of how social location of the reader or writer affects the meanings of the text. Linda Alcoff, whose ideas I am citing here, goes on to explain that there is no way to draw a boundary between one's own location and all others: "Even if the speaker offers a dozen caveats about her views as restricted to her location, she will still affect the other woman's ability to conceptualize and interpret her experience and her response to it. And this is simply because we cannot neatly separate off our mediating praxis that interprets and constructs our experiences from the praxis of others" (Alcoff, "Problem," 21).

I close with another theme from the emblem of the angel of history, the fragment. The story of gender that you tell might be seen as a string of fragments, each one an account of yet another feminist text. Given the current fragmented state of the feminist movement, the idea of the fragment seems appropriate for talking about gender theory. Fragmentation multiplies the movement's potential sites of resistance. Thinking in terms of fragments means thinking in terms of choice and accountability within a vast range of possibilities, which enables the feminist thinker to sustain ambivalence in the face of inherently conflicted situations, rather than resorting to premature closure.[26] One may even hope that overlooked fragments of the past may provide a more utopian image of the future. In this way, Christa Wolf's idea of remembering the future expresses a process of change connected to one's location in the present, and one's connection to other people.

I was in the audience at the plenary session of the Conference on Change (Montreal, May 1991), when you presented your paper. The expectant laughter that arose in the gaps between text and music, as the tapes were cued up, was restorative. The musical passages had a remarkable effect on the audience at the end of a long conference day. There seemed to be an understanding that academic speaking had been transformed into something more generous and more liberating.[27]

NOTES

1. Klee's *Angelus Novus* is reproduced in Gershom Scholem, "Walter Benjamin and his Angel," in *On Walter Benjamin: Critical Essays and Recollections,* ed. Gary Smith (Cambridge: MIT Press, 1988), 60 Rosi Braidotti quotes in full Benjamin's description of the angel of history at note 32 to her "Theories of Gender," on page 152.

2. Donna J. Haraway defines the "god-trick" as "being nowhere while claiming to see comprehensively," in *Simians, Cyborgs, and Women: The Reinvention of Nature* (New York Routledge, 1991), 191.

3 The idea is central to her novel *The Quest for Christa T.,* trans. Christopher Middleton (London: Virago, 1982).

4. Linda Alcoff, "The Problem of Speaking for Others" (*Cultural Critique* 20 [Winter 1991–92]: 6–7). I find it easiest to speak in the first person, from the standpoint of my own experiences as a feminist researcher and university teacher Since a response is a piece of dialogue, I would like to address Rosi Braidotti in the second person, although we have never met. This will dismantle the uncomfortable illusion that I am speaking as a disembodied authority on Feminist Theory or Women's Studies (and those who produce it).

5 Jane Flax states that "the fundamental purpose of feminist theory is to analyze how we think, or do not think, or avoid thinking about gender" ("Postmodernism and Gender Relations in Feminist Theory," in *Feminist Theory in Practice and Process,* ed. Micheline R. Malson et al. [Chicago University of Chicago Press, 1989], 56). Accordingly, I will be using "feminist theory" and "gender theory" interchangeably.

6. For a frequently updated listing, see "Feminist Periodicals," published by Phyllis Holman Weisbard, Women's Studies Librarian at the University of Wisconsin System, 430 Memorial Library, 728 State Street, Madison.

7 On patterns of feminist publication in representative journals in the disciplines, see Ellen Carol DuBois et al., "Ten Years of Feminist Scholarship: The Response of the Disciplines," *Feminist Scholarship: Kindling in the Groves of Academe* (Urbana University of Illinois Press, 1985), 157–94

8. Judith Butler, "Variations on Sex and Gender: Beauvoir, Wittig, and Foucault," in *Feminism as Critique*, ed. Seyla Benhabib and Drucilla Cornell (Minneapolis: University of Minnesota Press, 1987), 131.

9. Isaac D. Balbus, "Disciplining Women. Michel Foucault and the Power of Feminist Discourse," in Benhabib and Cornell, eds., *Feminism as Critique*, esp. 111.

10. Compare Kathy E. Ferguson, "Interpretation and Genealogy in Feminism," *Signs* 16 (Winter 1991): 322–39.

11. "It is politics which feminism cannot do without, politics that is essential to feminism's many self-definitions" (Diana Fuss, *Essentially Speaking: Feminism, Nature, and Difference* [New York: Routledge, 1989], 37)

12. Katie King, "Producing Sex, Theory, and Culture: Gay/Straight Remappings in Contemporary Feminism," in *Conflicts in Feminism*, ed. Marianne Hirsch and Evelyn Fox Keller (New York: Routledge, 1990), 83.

13. Jane Flax offers a droll overview of Enlightenment philosophy as a story with hero, moral plot, etc. in *Thinking Fragments: Psychoanalysis, Feminism, and Postmodernism in the Contemporary West* (Berkeley and Los Angeles: University of California Press, 1990), 30–31.

14. Alice Walker, *In Search of Our Mothers' Gardens* (San Diego: Harcourt Brace Jovanovich, 1983), 49.

15. Audre Lorde, *Sister Outsider: Essays and Speeches* (Trumansburg, N.Y.: Crossings Press, 1984), 117. Mature students often experience ageism at the hands of both students and faculty.

16. Jean O'Barr and Mary Wyer, eds., *Engaging Feminism* (Charlottesville: University Press of Virginia, 1992), 1 and 9.

17. Debbie Louis highlights another potential for intergenerational exchange. The increasing levels of "denial" among young women on campus is taking its toll among young feminists who are trying to mobilize for action on critical issues. Louis reflects on her own memory of fear and apathy on campuses in the 1950s, concluding that at this complex moment in the history of American feminism, there is "an urgent, *political* need for intergenerational connection . . . that could be facilitated by the Women's Studies network more effectively than any other available to us at present." See Debbie Louis, "National Office Update," *NWSAction* 4 (Winter 1991): 10.

18. Rosi Braidotti, *Patterns of Dissonance: A Study of Women in Contemporary Philosophy*, trans. Elizabeth Guild (New York: Routledge, 1991), 172.

19. Colleen Sheppard and Sarah Westphal, "Equity and the University: Learning from Women's Experience," *Canadian Journal of Women and the Law* 5 (1992): 17–19.

20. Teresa de Lauretis, "Feminist Studies/Critical Studies. Issues, Terms, and Contexts," in *Feminist Studies/Critical Studies*, ed. Teresa de Lauretis (Bloomington: Indiana University Press, 1986), 15.

21. In 1987, Elaine Marks noted that "neither Luce Irigaray nor Julia Kristeva has written about Simone de Beauvoir. Given the kinds of questions in which they are interested, this can hardly be an oversight" ("Introduction," in *Critical Essays on Simone de Beauvoir*, ed. Elaine Marks, Critical Essays on World Literature [Boston: G. K. Hall, 1987], 5).

22. bell hooks, *Talking Back: Thinking Feminist—Thinking Black* (Toronto: Between the Lines, 1988), 37.

23. See bell hooks, *Talking Back*, on feminist theory course syllabuses that include "theory" by white women, "and then *The Color Purple*. Often novels or confessional autobiographical writings are used to mediate the tension between academic writing, theory, and the experiential" (37–38).

24. Frances M. Beal, "Double Jeopardy. To Be Black and Female," in *Sisterhood Is Powerful: An Anthology of Writings from the Women's Liberation Movement*, ed. Robin Morgan (New York: Vintage Books, 1970), 382–96.

25. The full context of this phrase "Within feminist theory a search for a defining theme of

the whole or a feminist viewpoint may require the suppression of the important and discomforting voices of persons with experiences unlike our own" (Jane Flax, "Postmodernism," 63)

26. On sustaining ambivalence, see Flax, *Thinking Fragments,* 11

27 Thanks to Christie McDonald, Gary Wihl, and Colleen Sheppard for their helpful responses to an earlier draft of this paper I am grateful as well to Linda Alcoff, for her conversation on some of the topics I discuss here

11

Three Renaissance Madonnas: Freud and the Feminine

MARY BITTNER WISEMAN

In the anonymous publication in 1914 of an interpretation of Michelangelo's statue of Moses ("the Moses of Michelangelo"), Freud tells of having heard about a Russian connoisseur, Ivan Lermolieff, who had caused a stir in the art world by calling into question the authorship of many paintings.[1] Lermolieff's way of

---

Portions of this article are published elsewhere The author wishes to thank the following for permission to reprint: Oxford University Press for what appears in "Two Women by Giovanni Bellini," *British Journal of Aesthetics* 33 (July 1993), and *Hypatia: A Journal of Feminist Philosophy* for what appears in "Renaissance Madonna and the Fantasies of Freud," *Hypatia* 8 (Summer 1993) Also, several sections repeat what is forthcoming from Routledge in "Renaissance Paintings and Psychoanalysis: Julia Kristeva and the Function of the Mother," in *Ethics, Politics, and Difference in Julia Kristeva's Writings: A Collection of Essays*, edited by Kelly Oliver

determining whether or not a painting really was the work of the artist to whom it was attributed was to attend not to its "general impression and main features" but rather to "the significance of minor details, of things like the drawing of the finger-nails, of the lobe of an ear, of aureoles and such unconsidered trifles which the copyist neglects to imitate and yet which every artist executes in his own characteristic way" (271). The anonymous Freud says that he subsequently discovered Lermolieff to be a pseudonym concealing the identity of an Italian named Morelli and straightaway observes that Morelli's "method of inquiry is closely related to the technique of psycho-analysis. It, too, is accustomed to divine secret and concealed things from unconsidered or unnoticed details, from the rubbish-heap, as it were, of our observations" (271). The interpretation of Moses that follows this observation is a psychoanalysis of the statue that turns in large part on the seemingly minor detail of the exact disposition of the fingers of Moses' right hand.

This kind of interpretation is interesting because we typically think that only people can be psychoanalyzed, and what it suggests is that whatever has an unconscious can be so analyzed and, moreover, that wherever there are things "secret and concealed," there may be said to be an unconscious. A comparison between the work of the anonymous author of "The Moses of Michelangelo" and that of the pseudonymous Lermolieff suggests further that the subject of psychoanalysis must have a history as well as an unconscious and that historical details are in complex ways related to the burying and unearthing of things secret and concealed. The statue was produced under historically specific conditions, which Freud invokes in order to account for his interpretation's making Michelangelo's *Moses* discrepant with biblical accounts. First he justifies his account's departure from the biblical on the grounds that modern evidence shows the Bible to have been "clumsily put together from various sources" and so to be discrepant with itself. His interpretation, then, need not be faithful to an original whose coherence is itself in question. Freud goes on to cite as motives informing Michelangelo's particular portrayal his temperament and that of Pope Julius II for whose tomb the statue had been commissioned, as well as the relationship between sculptor and pope.

The philosophically important move made by Freud is from the psychoanalysis of people to that of texts in general rather than to works of art in particular. Accordingly, I take proper names, case histories, titles, well-entrenched concepts, and figures of speech to be like anonyms, pseudonyms, and disguises, and as such the proper subjects of psychoanalysis or the application of Morelli's methods. I interpret them without privileging the guise over the disguise, for the two are connected no matter how labyrinthine the paths between them and neither would be what it is without the other. Moreover, what the interpretation yields— the meaning of the work, the unconscious sealed off from consciousness, the truth of the matter—cannot be separated out from the interpretation itself, where the interpretation is the argument, the movement from what is given to what is concluded. Just as the same conclusions can issue from different premises and the conclusions of a given argument themselves figure in innumerable other arguments, so different minor details can yield the same interpretations and interpretations can themselves be interpreted. In light of this I propose to interpret Freud's concept of the feminine by two "unconsidered trifles" or "unnoticed details." One is a simile that Freud uses to describe his discovery that contrary to what he had thought, something of moment does happen in the life of an infant girl before the appearance of the Oedipus complex; the other is his dispensation of the theme of the Madonna in the case histories *Fragment of an Analysis of a Case of Hysteria* and *Leonardo Da Vinci and a Memory of His Childhood*. The theme is raised by two paintings, Raphael's *Sistine Madonna* (Gemäldegalerie, Dresden) and Leonardo's *Madonna and Child with Saint Anne* (Louvre, Paris). Freud's treatment of this theme marks out two paths. One leads to Freud's characterization of the Oedipal fantasy of the little girl according to which the Madonna is a figure for what the girl must want to be, whereas the other leads to Julia Kristeva's analysis of Giovanni Bellini's *Lochis Madonna* (Accademia Carrara, Bergamo). Finally, the *Lochis Madonna* under Kristeva's interpretation bears the stamp of places to which Freud could not directly go, even anonymously, but to which he went by indirection and under a spate of different names: Dora, Leonardo, Oedipus, the Madonna.

In the first full discussion of the Oedipus complex in *The Interpretation of Dreams* (1900), Freud assumes a parallel between the sexes, "a girl's first affection is for her father and a boy's first childish desires are for his mother."[2] This is to say at least that the time in a girl's history before her father becomes the object of her love is a time empty in the sense that her affections have no object. Even though Freud was led to say in 1919 that "the expectation of there being a complete parallel [between the two sexes] was mistaken,"[3] he still held as late as 1923 that the overcoming of the Oedipus complex was "precisely analogous" in each sex.[4] By 1925, however, in "Some Psychical Consequences of the Anatomical Distinction Between the Sexes," he had revised his account of the roles played by Oedipal desire and the fear or anger occasioned respectively by the threat or fact of castration.[5] There he says that the infant boy's desire for unending and exclusive intimacy with the mother is "smashed to pieces by the shock of [the] threatened castration," whereas the girl's desire for her father need never end. The temporal order of the complexes of feelings was reversed in the two sexes: the threat of castration followed and "smashed to pieces" the boy's Oedipal desire; the fact of castration preceded and caused the girl's Oedipal desire for her father, really desire for a child by him, a child that would be the penis she lacks. By 1925 he holds that her desire for the father is not original but is formed in the time of intimate connection with the mother. Something had to have happened in that time to turn the girl's desire from her mother to her father. The pre-Oedipal time is not empty time for the infant girl after all, and in "Female Sexuality" (1931) Freud admits, "Our insight into this early, pre-Oedipus, phase in girls comes to us as a surprise," like the discovery, in another field, of the Minoan-Mycenean civilization behind the civilization of Greece."[6] Freud's absorbing interest in ancient civilizations provides some clue to how momentous he would find such a discovery, and yet the realization that something happened before classical Greece and before the seductions of the father did not lead to the uncovering of what is buried there in Crete, in Mycenae, in the place where mother and daughter meet. The momentous discovery bore no fruit because the place where mother and daughter meet is precisely the place to which Freud could not directly go.

DORA

Freud had difficulty in seeing mothers as other than the objects of a son's desire; he resists them and as a result they remain elsewhere. This, together with his blindness, is manifest in "Fragment of an Analysis of a Case of Hysteria" (1905), his account of the analysis of the eighteen-year-old Ida Bauer, whose pseudonym was Dora.[7] Dora's own mother and the Madonna who appears in Dora's recital of her experience in the picture gallery in Dresden, where she "remained two hours in front of the Sistine Madonna, rapt in silent admiration," appear obliquely at best. Freud's interpretations of Dora's symptoms and dreams include any number of identifications with her mother, and his analysis of her remains a fragment not only for the reasons he seems endlessly to iterate but also because the *figure* of the mother (real or idealized as the Madonna is) appears in his text in only the most marginal way. After the introduction of Raphael's *Sistine Madonna* in Dresden's picture gallery (Fig. 1), the Madonna is spoken of by Freud only three times, once in a statement of Freud's future intention and twice in footnotes: "I should [also] like to

Fig. 1. Raphael, *The Sistine Madonna*. Dresden, Gemäldegalerie (photo: Foto Marburg/Art Resource, New York).

single out, *with a view to subsequent investigation*, the theme of the 'Madonna', of the virgin mother" (116, my emphasis). The first footnote reference is to the "phantasy of defloration... and the stress which the dreamer was so ready to lay upon her virginity—a point alluded to in another place by means of the Sistine Madonna" (120). The second appears after Freud's victorious announcement that "Dora disputed the fact [that he had unearthed the cause of her symptoms] no longer," emboldened him to, in the footnote, "here add a few supplementary interpretations to those that have already been given: The *'Madonna'* was obviously Dora herself.... Moreover, the notion of the 'Madonna' is a favourite counter-idea in the mind of girls who feel themselves oppressed by imputations of sexual guilt,—which was the case with Dora" (125).

Just as the question of what goes on within the time before the girl turns to her father remained "veiled in an impenetrable obscurity," so the promised investigation of the theme of the Madonna as such never came about. What it would have shown remains veiled. But the reader can make her own investigation by looking in less than obvious places, in "minor details and unconsidered trifles," and in unexpected juxtapositions. For example, a second Renaissance Madonna appears in Freud's work, this time more centrally than it does in his case history of Dora. It is Leonardo's *Madonna and Child with Saint Anne* (Fig. 2), which Freud analyzes in *Leonardo da Vinci and a Memory of His Childhood* (1910).[8] In this painting, according to Freud, the mother exists for the sake of the son and is, therefore, a wholly satisfying object of his desire. The painter Leonardo is the child, the identification driven by Leonardo's love for his mother or, more accurately, by his love of her love for him. Just as the *Sistine Madonna* is a stage on which Dora enacts her love for her mother and the analysis a stage on which she enacts her revenge against Freud and her father for not seeing her, for their suffering the blindness of Oedipus, so too is *Madonna and Child with Saint Anne* a mirror in which Leonardo sees himself and the analysis a mirror in which Freud himself is reflected and diffracted.

The Madonna that Freud did not confront in his analysis of Dora is buried deep within Freud's "Some Psychical Consequences of the Anatomical Distinction Between the Sexes" (1925) and "Female Sexuality" (1931), in which it is figured as what the daughter wants to *be* rather than, as in the analysis of Leonardo, as what the son wants to *have*. In each case (the figure of) the Madonna is the *object* of the infant child's desire, the difference between the sexes lying in and being constituted by the relation in which the child stands to the object mother, the one

Fig. 2. Leonardo da Vinci, *Madonna and Child with Saint Anne*. Paris, Louvre (photo: Alinari/Art Resource, New York).

desiring to replace, the other to possess, her. In these articles Freud announces the discovery of the period of infantile development before the Oedipal, but lacking Ariadne's thread to lead him through the labyrinth from birth to Oedipus, he makes no headway in describing the time before the infant girl takes her oppositely gendered parent as the object of her desire. What Freud does instead is to give an account of the complex in the girl that is such that her Oedipal fantasy is perfectly realized by the Madonna. The complex begins with the girl's recognizing her anatomical difference and being forced "on to new lines which lead to the development of femininity.... But now the girl's libido slips into a new position along the line—*there is no other way to put it*—of the equation 'penis-child'. She gives up her wish for a penis and puts in place of it a wish for a child: and *with that purpose in view* she takes her father as a love-object. Her mother becomes the object of her jealousy. The girl has turned into a little woman" ("Some Psychical," 256). The Madonna has a child by God, the archetypal father from whom all goods flow, and the child she has by him is what shall enable all of God's children to regain paradise. There could be no more powerful nor more desirable father or child. Moreover, there is no heavenly mother of whom Mary need be jealous; she is henceforth the archetypal mother and the sublime fulfillment of a girl's Oedipal dream.

The Madonna is, then, a most powerful inducement *against* giving up the Oedipus complex, as powerful in the imagination of the girl as the threat of castration is in the imagination of the boy. So completely is the fantasy given up by the boy that in ideal cases it "exists no longer, even in the unconscious; the super-ego has become its heir," whereas in girls "the motive for the demolition of the Oedipus complex is lacking;... it may be slowly abandoned or dealt with by repression, or its effects may persist far into women's normal mental life" ("Some Psychical," 257). It is, however, not merely that the motive for giving up the complex is lacking but rather that there is a powerful reason for *not* giving it up. The reason reaches as far as does the esteem in which Mary or any figure that bridges the distance between heaven and earth is held, as far as the sway of the Madonna in her many guises. In Freud's account of the desire of the little girl, the Madonna is what the girl must want to be, and in his announcement of what it is that she wants, he puts himself into the picture as the angel Gabriel who tells Mary who she henceforth is. Even though the origins of the girl's desire are by his own admission veiled in an impenetrable obscurity, their place a dark continent for which there are as yet no signposts, Freud makes his annunciation. In the story of the annunciation told by Luke, Mary is troubled at first because she does not understand the angel's message but ends up acknowledging it, saying, "Let it be done unto me according to thy word."

Freud failed where Gabriel succeeded, however, for although he says that Dora "disputed the fact no longer" as though it were with her too according to the announcing angel's word, she nonetheless told Freud at the very next session that she was stopping the analysis, because, Freud believes, he "did not succeed in mastering the transference in good time" (*Dora*, 140). He should have said "transferences"; for there were two he did not master, Dora's feelings toward Herr K *and* toward Frau K. The result of this failure was that what Freud discovered and Dora no longer disputed (her love for Herr K) was *not* what he had sought, namely, "the strongest unconscious current in her mental life" (142), "the operation of a single, simple factor" "behind the almost limitless series of displacements which [the analysis]... brought to light" (126), where this factor would be connected with the "most deeply buried group of thoughts" (133). This was what Freud unearthed only after Dora stopped the analysis, namely, the deep-rooted love of Dora for her father's mistress, love buried as deep as the Minoan-Mycenaean civilization behind the civilization of Greece. The analysis failed because this early civilization was to Freud a dark continent, and since he could not see what was there, he could not reveal it to Dora. What he did descry after Dora's leaving "smashed to pieces" the transferences and countertransferences whose unrecognized presence gave the lie to the unusual clarity of the analysis, he described as homosexual, gynecophilic. For everything he saw and said was diffracted through his theory of the Oedipus complex according to which everyone is always already gendered and the little girl before she becomes a woman is a little man. If this early civilization is one in which the distinction between masculine and feminine is not yet made, then neither infant nor mother is gendered and the concept mother is not linked as a matter of necessity to the concept feminine.

Freud wrote up Dora's analysis as an application of the theory presented that same year in *The Interpretation of Dreams*, and as such it was more or less successful. The analysis lasted a little more than three months during which two dreams were interpreted, and although Freud could not get down to Dora's most deeply buried thoughts, it was not because of any flaw in the technique of interpretation but because he was blind to Dora's having transferred her feelings toward two of the characters in her family romance onto him. After the analysis had ended, he realized that Dora had made of him a "new edition" of a family friend, but he seems never to have considered the possibility that she transferred onto him her feelings toward the friend's wife as well. That would be to have made of him a very new edition, indeed; it would be to have made of him a woman and, moreover, one who was the object of desire of another woman. And this in his iconography could only be homosexual, gynecophilic desire.

This fragment of an analysis ends with Freud struggling with the technique of *mastering* the patient's transference. This, he says, is by far the hardest part. "It is easy to learn how to interpret dreams, ... for these the patient himself will always provide the text" (*Dora*, 138) whereas the analyst's mastery of the transference depends on his knowing what the patient is making of him, what role she is casting him in, and knowing also how he is responding to her from within that role. The first is the patient's transference, the second the analyst's countertransference. Freud introduces the term "transference" halfway through the postscript to his fragment of an analysis with a metaphor about publishing new editions, a metaphor apt for one whose works saw so many reprintings and revisions. Transferences are, he says:

> New editions or facsimiles of the tendencies and phantasies which are aroused and made conscious during the progress of the analysis; but they have this peculiarity... that they replace some earlier person by the person of the physician.... Some of these transferences have a content which differs from that of their model in no respect whatever except for the substitutions. These, then... are merely new impressions or reprints. Others are more ingeniously constructed; their content has been subjected to a moderating influence—to *sublimation*, as I call it—and they may even become conscious, by cleverly taking advantage of *some real peculiarity in the physician's person or circumstances* [my emphasis] and attaching themselves to that. These, then, will no longer be new impressions, but revised editions. (*Dora*, 138)

They comprise, Freud goes on to say, a class of mental structures created by the unconscious. Psychoanalysis did not invent them; it accounts for them in its theory and in the practice of its art destroys them by bringing them to consciousness. One can, then, "replace some earlier person" by another only so long as one is unaware of doing so, but an interpreter can "almost without assistance and with only the slightest clues to go upon" (*Dora*, 138) trace the substitutions, identifications, replacements, displacements. A detail, an unconsidered trifle, serves as the point at which thoughts or feelings, memory or desire, switch from one line of associations to another. The switchpoint is some "real peculiarity in the [substitute's] person or circumstances," ignorance of which would leave the juxtaposition of associations unexplained.

Move now from Freud's treatment room to the museum in Dresden and position Dora with respect to the figures in the *Sistine Madonna*, which include the saints Sixtus and Barbara along with the Madonna and child and two angels. It need first be known that Dora was the (empty) center of a constellation made up of her mother and father and another couple identified only as Herr and Frau K, that she "looked down on her mother and used to criticise her mercilessly, and she had withdrawn completely from her influence" (*Dora*, 35), that she had as rich a relationship with Frau K as she had an impoverished one with her mother, that she had been courted by Herr K who made a proposal to her and received a slap in return, and finally that she had been brought to Freud by her father for having become increasingly insistent that he end his affair with Frau K. Freud was to bring her around to accepting the affair. It need be known also that in the last few pages of the postscript Freud tells us that at first "it was clear that I was replacing her father in her imagination" (140), but that after hearing the first dream he ought to have said, "Now, ... it is from Herr K that you have made the transference onto me" (140). Then, he said, her attention would have been directed to "some detail in our relations, or in my person or circumstances, behind which there lay concealed something analogous but immeasurably more important concerning Herr K" (140–41).

The end of the story told in the body of the account of the analysis is the discovery that despite Dora's conscious beliefs and feelings to the contrary, she loved Herr K. However, the story told in the footnotes (notes 20 and 26 of the account proper and note 2 of the postscript) ends with her love of Frau K. Whereas much is made of the roles played in Dora's mental life by her father, Herr K, and Freud, both by her father having handed her over to Herr K and then to Freud, and by her displacing one by the other in her unconscious mind, little is made of the roles played by her mother, Frau K, and the Madonna, and the displacements made among them. The reason for this is that Freud could not recognize Dora's transferring her feelings for Frau K onto Freud, from which it follows either that she did not do it or that she did it, but Freud could not perceive it. On the first alternative, Dora's not making the transference is her resistance to Freud just as a woman's not saying "we" with an author when he is talking about males is the reader's resistance to the author. On the second, Freud's not recognizing the transference is tantamount to his exclusion of her from the scene of the treatment rather as an author's use of "we" in talking about men excludes whomever is reading as a woman. Suppose the second alternative and suppose further that the revenge Freud finds concealed in Dora's dreams and acted out in her leaving the analysis is for his failure to recognize the transference of her feelings toward Frau K onto him.

Freud had to fail Dora. He had to fail to play the part of a woman loved by a woman. For to assume such a role would be to lose the difference between the sexes. This would be to lose knowledge and power, men's knowledge of what they are as reflected in the mirror that is woman and men's power to rule over what is itself incapable of reason or will, woman, as conceived by philosophers from Aristotle to Kant. Freud had to fail Dora because he could not conceive the love of woman for woman that was not homosexual. He could, then, not speak it. Nor could Dora, but for a different reason. For there was no language in which it could be said, neither at the time of her analysis nor in the time before the Oedipus complex turned her from her mother. There was barely language at all in that ancient early time. Dora could, however, displace the object of her love, transfer the feelings, substitute one love object for another, substitute Frau K for her mother, resort to anonyms, pseudonyms. Frau K becomes a "revised edition" of the mother and the name Frau K a pseudonym hiding the identity of the mother on whom Dora looked down and from whose influence she "had withdrawn completely." Freud's indifference to the maternal function was such that whereas he challenged virtually all of Dora's assertions assuming that what they concealed was truer than what they said, he did not analyze her assessment of her mother and their relationship. There is reason to suspect that the influence of Dora's mother on her was not inconsiderable. Nonetheless, the mother's identity is submerged and she becomes anonymous, and her influence is made into a minor detail by Dora and Freud, her unwitting coconspirator.

One enters the scene of a psychoanalysis by transferring feelings onto the analyst; the patient subject puts the analyst, seriatim, in place of various objects of her emotions. Dora has feelings, more and more deeply buried, toward her father, Herr K, Frau K, and her mother, and she would transfer them onto Freud, but he could recognize only the first two (and master only the first). The names of the characters in the scenes, the objects of her love, were not proper, and she could not find them or herself in the scene. When the price of admission to the play is too high, as when Dora had either to leave her love deep buried or to become a man (to love a woman is to turn oneself into a man) in order to participate in Freud's analysis, one may as Dora did refuse to pay the price and become instead a stranger, a spectator.

THE SISTINE MADONNA

On the day before the second dream important to her analysis some circumstance of complete indifference to Dora reminded her of her first visit to the city of Dresden. "On that occasion she had been a **stranger** and had wandered about, not failing, of course, to visit the famous picture gallery.... [A] cousin... had wanted to act as a guide and take her round the gallery. *But she declined, and went alone*, and stopped in front of the pictures that appealed to her. She remained *two hours* in front of the Sistine Madonna, rapt in silent admiration. When I asked her what had pleased her so much about the picture she **could find no clear answer to make**. At last she said: 'The Madonna' " (*Dora*, 116, boldface added). Reading these words as Morelli would, one can see concealed behind certain of them "something analogous but immeasurably more important" than what at first sight they say. Dora was a *stranger* to the analysis because Freud, being blind to what goes on in a female's life before Oedipus appears, had to leave in darkness "the strongest unconscious current in her mental life" (142), the "most deeply buried group of thoughts" (133). Not able to find herself in the conception of woman that informs psychoanalysis, she could not recognize herself in the analysis. A stranger to the language also, Dora *could find no clear answer to make* to Freud's question about the painting because she had no way of thinking or talking about what went on when she looked into the picture. Let us interpret the painting in terms of what might go on when one looks at it from the position in which Freud put Dora. It is not Freud or Dora but his two stories of her case history (one in the main body, the other in footnotes and postscript) and the painting that are being psychoanalyzed, where the psyches in question are the objects' histories and whatever interpretations can plausibly be made of them. Dora and Freud appear only as fragments inscribed in the stories of the analysis and in the painting.

Painted by Raphael in 1512, his twenty-ninth year, the *Sistine Madonna* (see Fig. 1) presents Mary standing on a billow of clouds between velvet curtains pulled back to reveal her and the child she holds lightly. Two angels lean on a balustrade at the bottom of the painting, upon which rests the papal tiara of Saint Sixtus, who kneels below and to one side of the centered Madonna while Saint Barbara kneels on the other side. Mary's veil swirls out to her left describing a circle that continues with the fold of her mantel on which the infant weightlessly rests and is completed by the curve of his right arm and head which touches her cheek. Mother and child are self-contained; no earthly thing seems able to touch them: queen of heaven, she displays her prince. The backs of the saints' voluminous garments are cut off at the edges of the painting, their feet hidden in the indifferent whirl of robes and clouds. Only Mary and infant are shown whole. Her feet touch the clouds, her hands the infant, but her eyes touch nothing. Barbara, eyes cast down and hands clasped to her breast, looks down and away from Madonna and child in dramatic contrast to Sixtus who looks up at them and points out of the painting into our space, the same space into which the infant looks. There is then a triangle whose apexes are the eyes of the baby boy, the old man, and the viewer. Redeemer and pope, men both, command the space, whereas the women's eyes and hands point to nothing outside themselves.

Another triangle is described within this nonnatural theatrical space by the two women and the man who can stand in variously for Dora and her mother sharing (exchanging, competing for) her father, her mother and Frau K sharing Dora's father, Dora and Frau K sharing Herr K. One of the women in the painting is a mother, the other (Saint Barbara) is not, and by identification with the other woman, a viewer can resist the assimilation of the feminine to the maternal. Barbara defied her father for the sake of her faith, and by identification with her the viewer can resist the father, "smashing to pieces" Freud's Oedipus fantasy. But Freud's Dora would have nothing of the other woman, for Dora was the Madonna. Among what he calls supplementary interpretations added in a footnote is that "the '*Madonna*' was obviously Dora herself; ... because she had won Herr K's love chiefly by the motherliness she had shown towards his children and lastly because she had a child though she was still a girl (this being a direct allusion to the fantasy of childbirth).... If the analysis had been continued, Dora's maternal longing for a child would probably have been revealed as an obscure though powerful motive in her behavior" (*Dora*, 125). Dora, then, by Freud's soundings wants to be the Madonna because then she will be a mother, the mother of a son by her father. There are, however, a myriad of other possible ways to put Dora into the painting.

MADONNA AND CHILD WITH SAINT ANNE

One way to put Dora into the painting is to be found in Freud's interpretation of Leonardo's *Madonna and Child with Saint Anne* (see Fig. 2) according to which the painter is the painted child and the painting a mirror in which Leonardo sees himself. Executed in 1508 when Leonardo was fifty-six, it takes Mary down from heaven's stage and puts her on her mother's lap in a landscape of rocks, the rocks as solid as the clouds were not. As dense as rock is the spatially descending group whose line goes from Anne to Mary to Jesus to the lamb. The tree in the upper right of the canvas balances the gentle slope of the group of figures toward the lower right along the curving right arms of Mary and Jesus and the sight lines of Anne and Mary. The tree pulls the viewer's eye back up onto the canvas, and the lines along which child and lamb look draw the eye to the place where the eyes of Mary and Jesus meet. They look at each as do none of the characters in the *Sistine Madonna*, and although the child moves away from her onto the lamb, he looks back at her. The eyes of Anne and the lamb repeat the gaze of Mary and her son, underscoring the bond between them while the child is bound not only by his mother's look but also by the tangle of lower limbs—the legs of Mary and the lamb enfold the child's. Anne, impassive as the mountains of rock that are the near background, witnesses the drama of the son's loving and eventually having to leave his loving mother, even as she holds her own grown daughter on her lap. Freud spins out the story of the son so as to leave it open to two endings: either the father's threat of castration will "smash to pieces" the Oedipal fantasy or the boy's desire for his mother will go underground henceforth to emerge only in disguise. Leonardo's fantasy emerges in the painting, disguise for his too-great love for his mother, a painting from which no one looks out into a different and a more real world.

Blind or indifferent to what a young girl sees in the painting of the Madonna, Freud cares and takes care to see what Leonardo put into *Mother and Child with Saint Anne*. On Freud's reading, the figures in the painting are Leonardo and his mother and stepmother. Born in 1452 as the illegitimate son of Ser Piero da Vinci and a woman named Caterina, Leonardo's name was included in a Florentine land-register of 1457 as part of the Vinci family. In 1452 Ser Piero had married Donna Albiero, who remained childless, and at least by the time Leonardo was five years old he had become her child. Freud concludes from his analysis of the work and what is known of Leonardo's history that Leonardo had two mothers and was tenderly loved by each. Impressed by cases in which the father is absent and an infant boy is "left entirely under feminine influence," Freud notes that in such cases the "child's love for his mother cannot continue to develop consciously any further. . . . The boy represses his love for his mother: he puts himself in her place, identifies himself with her, and takes his own person as a model in whose likeness he chooses the new objects of his love. In this way he becomes a homosexual.... He finds the objects of his love along the path of *narcissism*" (*Leonardo*, 55). A painting like a dream can represent what has been repressed, and in this painting Freud finds Leonardo figuring his early love for his mother(s). Could a girl find herself in the painting if she had access to the time before she recognized her difference and "was forced onto new lines which lead to the development of femininity"?

Where the case history of Dora saw the beginning of the theory of transference, this history of Leonardo is the beginning of an account of narcissism, the substitution of oneself for an object (of love), which is structurally similar to transference, the substitution of one object (of any sort of feeling) for another. But there is a difference between one's replacing an object by oneself and replacing one object by another *when gender is in question*. Notice that under Freud's description the homosexual love of a man for a man is mediated by the homosexual's having identified himself with his mother. This is to say that it is only as a woman that one can love a man. Similarly, only as a man can one love a woman. Freud says in the last footnote of the *Fragment* that "we can see the action of the ... most deeply buried group of thoughts—those relating to her love for Frau K—in the fact that the fantasy of defloration is represented [in the dream] *from the man's point of view*" (133; my emphasis). In the indifferent exchange of objects allowed by psychoanalysis, then, one exchange is impossible: the gender of the object of one's love. What cannot be breached is the law that one cannot love the same (gender as oneself). What bears on an interpretation of Dora's rapture before the *Sistine Madonna* is that whereas psychoanalysis allows the conceptual possibility of one's transferring feelings toward a man or woman onto a woman or a man, it denies the possibility of a woman qua woman loving or being loved by a woman. How, then, can psychoanalysis find its way about in the dark continent that is the time in a girl child's life before she turns from her mother?

Dora the spectator and Leonardo the painter are not evenly matched in Freud's hand, his interpretations of their encounters with the Madonna having been made against the background of his admission in 1905 that the sexual life of women "is still veiled in an impenetrable obscurity."[9] On Freud's account of the development of a little girl into a woman, Dora can only want to *be* the Madonna. She cannot love the Madonna or want to be the child without identifying herself as a man. If she loves the Madonna, the love is homosexual, and through it Dora has identified either herself or the Madonna as a man. And to want to be the child is to want to be a little man both because women want only boy children since they have what women lack and because girls are only little (deficient) men until they turn from mother to father in early childhood and from the penis-like clitoris to the proper source of female pleasure in puberty. Dora had said that it was the Madonna that had so interested her about the painting, but Freud has stopped the chain of interpretations of the relation between Dora and the Madonna with the difference (between masculine and feminine) that is fundamental to his theory with the law that one cannot love the same. The supposition is that if there is no difference to begin with, there never can be difference, and Freud's further supposition is that if there is no difference between man and woman, between masculine and feminine, there is no difference whatsoever. His theory, then, can make no sense of love that is not modeled on the love of man and woman and, therefore, can make little sense of love between mother and daughter or between mother and child before the child is gendered. *For the mother is already feminine, and everything else masculine.* Here is the place where a great knot is tied, but the net woven from its threads could not keep Dora in Freud's analysis and could not keep her from loving the Sistine Madonna or from wanting to be the child in its arms.

THE LOCHIS MADONNA

Julia Kristeva suggests a way to untie this knot, to free the feminine from the maternal by identifying the mother not as *object* of the child's desire to be or to have but as a *function*. Becoming a mother replaces the wanting to be a mother that Freud takes as constituting a girl's becoming a woman. The object mother gives way to the maternal function and the relation between feminine and masculine to the relation between maternal and paternal where the paternal function consists in the father's acknowledging his child by giving it a name and thereby inaugurating it into language and the social order, both systems of names. Kristeva works the ground of the maternal function in the course of which she assimilates the body of the mother to the ground of a painting. The article in which she does this, "Motherhood According to Giovanni Bellini," characterizes the kind of pictorial representation of which Bellini was master as the cause of a jouissance that results in "a shattering of figuration and form in a space of graphic lines and colors, differentiated until they disappear in pure light."[10] She traces the course of his career and concludes that finally what he achieved was works that enabled their spectators to witness the dissolve of the world into a field of color and light out of which the languaged world of masterable forms has been produced.

This dissolve, this jouissance, is, Kristeva suggests, homologous to what occurs in the maternal body when the symbolic destiny of the speaking animal is superimposed on its archaic basis, the unconscious of the maternal body wherein the biological and social program of the species is written ("Motherhood," 241). The symbolic destiny of the speaking subject superimposed on the biological *seals off* this archaic base, and "psychotic" moments, or whatever induces them naturally, thus become necessary if the biological and the instinctual are not to be sealed off, inaccessible, to consciousness. Maternity induces them, as does art. "At the intersection of sign and rhythm, of representation and light, of the symbolic and the semiotic, the artist speaks from a place where [the mother] is not, where she knows not" (242). The artist "bears witness to what the unconscious (through the screen of the mother) records of those clashes that occur between the biological and social programs of the species. This means that through and across secondary repression (founding of signs), aesthetic practice touches upon primal repression (founding biological series and the laws of the species). At the place where it obscurely succeeds within the maternal body, every artist tries his hand" (242–43).

The wife of Jacopo Bellini, the painter father of Giovanni, seems not to have counted Giovanni as a child of hers, and the painter son's portrayals of the Madonna and her child corroborate the suspicion that he, unlike Leonardo, was not the beloved son of a loving mother. Kristeva takes the two painters' different relations to their mothers to account not only for their opposite ways of associating Madonna and child in their paintings but also for their prefiguring "two destinies within the very economy of Western representation," the difference turning on their attitudes toward the maternal body. For Leonardo, there is "worship of the figurable, representable man," for Bellini, the "integration of the image accomplished in its truth-likeness within the luminous serenity of the unrepresentable" ("Motherhood," 243). Leonardo, whose mothers' love for him was so satisfying an object of his desire that it was impossible for him to love another, paints mothers who exist for the sake of their children. His art too exists for the sake of the forms that he masters as his mothers mastered him. Bellini, who had no mother whose love could secure him, paints mothers who like his own are elsewhere. He goes to this elsewhere, to the place where no one is identified, no forms are figured or represented, to where there is color, light, planes, spaces, the raw material out of which masterable forms will be constructed, out of which objects and therefore subjects will be formed. The luminous, chromatic differences productive of volume, the volumes engendering separate other volumes rising out of the same surface, the sense of space created by the juxtaposition of colored masses in Bellini's paintings are all homologous to the drives and their rhythms. It is out of these drives, their pulsions and energies, that the speaking subject will be formed when the symbolic is imposed on the biological base in the individual. This union of symbolic and biological is in turn homologous to what goes on in the maternal body, in which is repeated the impossible "I am there and I am not there," "it is there and it is not there," the impossible union of instinct with language, of chromatic, luminous spatial intensity with masterable forms. This, Kristeva suggests, is what is repeated in Bellini's art. "A unique biographical experience and an uncommon, historical intersection of pagan-matriarchal Orientalism with sacred Christianity and incipient humanism was perhaps needed for Bellini's brush to retain the traces of a marginal experience, through and across which a maternal body might recognize its own [experience], otherwise inexpressible in our culture" (242).

The four human figures of the *Sistine Madonna* and the three of the *Madonna and Child with Saint Anne* give way in the *Lochis Madonna*, (Fig. 3) to two, who exhaust the space of the painting. No one else witnesses the drama enacted in the shallow space between the flat background of dark squares that replace Raphael's heavenly stage and Leonardo's landscape of rocks, and the parapet on which the child kneels and from which he almost tumbles out of the painting. He does not, however, because the Madonna holds him as firmly as ever a maternal body has held its parasite, its guest. But she is not there. Abstracted, inward-looking, beautiful fragile face beneath the Byzantine wimple, a woman as absent as her maternal hands are present. Face and hands move along different axes: one axis, left inclining, goes along her body from his left knee to the top of her head, the other, more sharply right inclining, goes from his right foot to the top of his head. Her hands are positioned along the axis of his body which is twisting away from her, whose own body is cut off by the parapet, making of it the partial figure of the icons beloved in Byzantium, icons in which the holy person represented is supposed to be present. No mother is present here, however. Kristeva's suggestion is that not only is the mother not present in Bellini's life or his Madonna paintings but also the woman mother is not the *subject* of motherhood and therefore does not become an *object* of

184   Transformations in Personhood and Culture

Fig. 3. Giovanni Bellini, *Madonna and Child*. Bergamo, Galleria Carrara (photo: Alinari/Art Resource, New York)

the child's desire (to have or to be) until the appearance of the languaged world of forms figurable and representable, masterable and graspable. Neither subject nor object, the woman mother is a function, a field of color, light, air, space, the place where everything solid melts into air.

This field plays through and across the paintings of the Venetian Renaissance, at whose beginning Bellini stands and to which he "contributed a completely new element: the luminous density of color" ("Motherhood," 243). No person is present in the *Lochis Madonna* as in an icon but what is there is that out of which the world of named things, including man and woman, will be made masculine and feminine. And the world will be fashioned by cuttings, by the markings of differences, but the first split will not have been, as Freud would have it, between masculine and feminine. It will have been in and from the maternal body in which cells split and split again, "within the body, growing as a graft, indomitable, there is an other. And no one is present, within that simultaneously dual and alien space, to signify what is going on. 'It happens, but I'm not there'. 'I cannot realize it, but it goes on'. Motherhood's impossible syllogism" (237). Maternity itself is neither masculine nor feminine, and neither man nor woman is the subject of gestation.

The figure of Dora traces a path from the *Sistine Madonna* in the fragment of her analysis by Freud, through his analysis of the *Madonna and Child with Saint Anne* by Leonardo, to branching paths in the later essays on female sexuality. One branch goes to his discovery of the archaic civilization behind the civilization of Greece, Dionysius behind the veil of Apollo, the mother as a function behind the mother as object of the desire of the child either to be or to possess her. This branch led Freud to an ancient place where he could not make his way, not able to recognize the mother before gender difference turned her into an object nor able to recognize himself in the absence of a feminine that could reflect him as masculine, the division fundamental to his thought had not yet been made. There was only the maternal body, and although the "maternal body is the place of a splitting," the splitting is not into masculine and feminine. The *Lochis Madonna* figures the divisions that occur in the body of the mother between part and whole, one and many, same and other, presence and absence, as the line of filiation goes from Freud to Kristeva, who can make her way about in that ancient place and who finds all of metaphysics in the relation between bearing mother and child being born. The other branch goes to the figure of the Madonna concealed within Freud's description of the Oedipal fantasy of girls, the Madonna having had a child by God the father. Yet because of the peculiar genderlessness of the Madonna and her child and because of the absence of a rival father with whom either has to contend, the Madonna and child as well figure the time before the coming of Oedipus as they do the realization of the girl's fantasy after Oedipus has appeared on the scene.

How can we speak the connection between the body of the mother and the body of its child before the child becomes a son or daughter? How can we make sense of a child's connection with its mother that does not make of its mother an object? How can Dora have loved the Sistine Madonna or wanted to be the child in its arms without making herself into a man? Answers to these identity questions lie buried in the time before Oedipus, buried with the Minoan-Mycenaean civilization, within the body of the mother.

NOTES

1 Sigmund Freud, "The Moses of Michelangelo," in *Collected Papers* (New York: Basic Books, 1959), 4:257–88.

2. Sigmund Freud, *The Interpretation of Dreams*, in *The Standard Edition of the Complete Psychological Works of Sigmund Freud*, ed. James Strachey (London: Hogarth, 1953), 4:257. [The *Standard Edition* is henceforth abbreviated in the notes as *SE*.]

3. Sigmund Freud, "A Child Is Being Beaten," in *SE*, 17:196.

4 Sigmund Freud, "The Ego and the Super-Ego," in *SE*, 19:32

5. Sigmund Freud, "Some Psychical Consequences of the Anatomical Distinction Between the Sexes," in *SE*, 19:248–58.

6. Sigmund Freud, "Female Sexuality," in *SE*, 21:226.

7. This is the title of the article in *SE*. I cite *Dora: An Analysis of a Case of Hysteria*, ed. Philip Reiff (New York: Collier-Macmillan, 1963).

8. Sigmund Freud, *Leonardo da Vinci and a Memory of His Childhood*, introduction by Peter Gay (New York: Norton, 1964).

9. Sigmund Freud, "Three Essays on the Theory of Sexuality," in *SE*, 7:135–243.

10 Julia Kristeva, "Motherhood According to Giovanni Bellini," in *Desire in Language*, ed. Leon S. Roudiez (New York: Columbia University Press, 1980), 269

Notes on the Contributors

Charles Altieri, professor of English at the University of California, Berkeley, has written *Painterly Abstraction in Modernist American Poetry* (1989) and *Canons and Consequences: Reflections on the Ethical Force of Imaginative Ideals* (1990). His essay in this book states the basic argument of his forthcoming book on expressivist agency.

Nancy Austin is assistant professor of art history at Brown University.

Rosi Braidotti is chairwoman of the Women's Studies Program, Arts Faculty, State University of Utrecht. She is the author of *Patterns of Dissonance* (1989).

Mary Ann Caws is Distinguished Professor of English, French, and Comparative Literature at the Graduate School of City University of New York, past president of the Modern Language Association, and a translator of Hugo, Mallarmé, Reverdy, Desnos, Breton, and René Char. She is the chief editor of the *HarperCollins World Reader.* Her recent titles include *The Eye in the Text* (1981), *Perception from Mannerist to Modern: Reading Frames in Modern Fiction* (1985), and *Women of Bloomsbury* (1990).

Karsten Harries is Mellon Professor at Yale University. He has written *The Meaning of Modern Art: A Philosophical Interpretation* (1968) and *The Bavarian Rococo Church: Between Faith and Aestheticism* (1983).

Christie McDonald was professor of French at the University of Montreal until 1994, and is professor of Romance Languages and Literatures at Harvard University. She is the author of *The Dialogue of Writing* (1985), *Dispositions* (1986), and *The Proustian Fabric* (1991).

Nancy Partner, associate professor of history, McGill University, is the author of *Serious Entertainments: The Writing of History in Twelfth-Century England* (1977) and editor of *Studying Medieval Women: Sex, Gender, Feminism* (1993).

Jacques Schlanger teaches philosophy at the Hebrew University of Jerusalem. His main research deals with cognitive phenomenology. His books include *Objet idéels* (1978), *Une Théorie du savoir* (1978), and *L'Activité théorique* (1983). His latest books are *Solitude du penseur de fond* (1990) and *La Situation cognitive* (1990).

Judith Schlanger teaches at the Hebrew University of Jerusalem. She has published many books in France about the intellectual and cultural dimensions of thought and thinking. Among her books: *Les Métaphores de l'organisme* (1971), *Penser la bouche pleine* (1975), and *L'Invention intellectuelle* (1983). Her latest book is *La Mémoire des oeuvres* (1992).

Isabelle Stengers teaches at the University of Brussels. Her books include *La Nouvelle alliance* (1979) and *Entre le temps et l'éternité* (1988), written with I. Prigogine; *Les Concepts scientifiques: Invention et pouvoir,* written with Judith Schlanger; *D'une science à l'autre: Les concepts nomades* (1988), *La volonté de faire science* (1992), and *Histoire de la chimie* (1993).

Sarah Westphal is associate professor of English and Women's Studies at McGill University. She is the author of *Textual Poetics of German Manuscripts, 1300–1500* (1993) and co-editor of two volumes: *Feminist Theory in Practice and Process* (1989) and *Sisters and Workers in the Middle Ages* (1989).

Gary Wihl, associate professor of English at McGill University, is the author of *Ruskin and the Rhetoric of Infallibility* (1985) and *The Contingency of Theory* (1994).

Mary Bittner Wiseman is professor of philosophy at Brooklyn College and of philosophy and comparative literature at the Graduate School of City University of New York. She is the author of *The Ecstases of Roland Barthes* (1988) and is writing a book on Renaissance Madonnas and conceptions of the feminine.

Index

Alcoff, Linda, 160
Anderson, Laurie, 135, 149
Aristotle, 6, 63, 176

Barthes, Roland, 135
Bauer, Hermann, 72
Bauer, Ida (Dora), and Freudian definitions of gender, xii, 167, 168–70, 172–73, 175–78, 180–81
Baumgarten, Alexander, 63
Beal, Frances M., 160
Beauvoir, Simone de, xi, 136–39, 141, 142, 144, 147, 157, 158
Bellini, *Lochis Madonna*, xi, 167, 181–85
Benjamin, Walter, on history, xi, 150
Breton, André, 80
Butler, Judith, 137, 146

Cartesianism, 87, 137
Comte, August, 15, 22, on "trente ans," 15–16
Cornell, Joseph, 83
Courbet, Gustave, ix, 39–42, 46, 57n2, 66
cultural studies, 135

da Vinci, Leonardo, *Madonna and Child*, 170, 178–81, 183, 185
de Lauretis, Teresa, 146
Delphy, Christine, 142
Derrida, Jacques, 86, 88, 135
Duchamp, Marcel, 75; on modernist art, 66, 67
Dumézil, Georges, 140

Eco, Umberto, 68, 69, 72, 81

feminist theory, 133, 144, 145, 147–48, 157, 158, 159
Finlay, Ian Hamilton, 82

Finley, Moses, on historiography, 7, 9
Firestone, Shulamith, 139
Flax, Jane, 144, 161n5
Foucault, Michel, 135, 146, 155
Franklin, Aretha, 137, 138, 160
French postmodernism, 135
Freud, Sigmund, xi, 137, 155, 167–76, 178–81, 185

Gadamer, Hans-Georg, 22–23
gender: multiple theories of, xi, xii, 9, 133–34, 142–44, 145, 146, 147, 154, 155, vs sex, 136, 137, 138, 141
genealogy, xi, 139, 145, 147, 148, 150, 154–56
Goethe, on architecture, 71, 72
Gould, Stephen Jay, on Martin Rudwick, 28–30
Green, Nicholas, on artistic consumption, 37, 48, 49

Hark, Michel Ter, 89
Hegelianism, 138
Heidegger, Martin, 74, 81, 82
Herodotus, 8
history, 1, 17, 24, 26–27, 36, as cultural artifact, 5–6, 13; and epistemology, 4, as narrative, 2, 3, 6–8, 28, 30, 31, 33
Hobsbawm, Eric, 23
Hodges, Michael, on Wittgenstein, 103
Horace, on the definition of a classic, 13, 14, 15, 22, 23, 31
Husserl, vs. Wittgenstein, 94, 96

Impressionism, ix, 37

James, Henry on fiction vs history, 1–2, 5, on imitation, 81
Joplin, Janis, 139–40

Kant, Immanuel, 20–21, 63, 71, 76, 97, 99, 108, 176
King, Carole, 137
King, Katie, 156
Kripke, Saul, 113n7
Kristeva, Julia, on Bellini, 167, 181–83, 185
Kuhn, Thomas, 31, 33

L'Illustration, 47, 50, 51, 52; and leisure and travel, 45, 46
Laugier, Marc-Antoine, 70, 71, 82
Lermolieff, Ivan. *See* Morelli
Lodoli, Carlo, 73
Lorde, Audre, 156, 157
Lukács, Georg, 22
Lyons, John, 89, 91

Madonna, 147
Mainardi, Patricia, 37
Marxism, xi, 142
Milizia, Francesco, on imitation, 71
Millett, Kate, 139, 157, 158, 160
Monet, Claude, 46, 51; and the Salon, 35–36, 53–55, 56
Moran, Richard, 91, 92, 98
Morelli, and Freudian analysis, 165–66, 177

Nancy, Jean-Luc, 86
novel. influence of Zola and Flaubert, 19, 20; and literary history, 18, 25
Novick, Peter, 3, 4

Oedipus complex, 167–68, 171–73, 185

Panofsky, Erwin, on aesthetic appeal, 62, 80
Pevsner, Nikolaus, on architecture, 62, 64, 69, 75, 76

Plato, 71, 120
Plaza, Monique, 142
Pope Julius II, 166
punk-rockers, 144

Raphael, *Sistine Madonna*, 167, 169, 170, 175, 177–78, 180, 183, 185
Reddy, Helen, 142
Rich, Adrienne, 141–42, 144, 145, 157
Rorty, Richard, 4, 86
Rousseau, *L'Emile*, 19–20
Rubin, Gayle, 141, 142, 158
Ruskin, John, 73, 79, 82

Scott, Joan, 145, 146, 154
Scruton, Roger, 67, 68
Smith, Patti, 140

Tafuri, Manfredo, on architectural language, 67, 81
Thucydides, 8
Tzonis, Alexander, and Liane Lefaivre, 63, 64

Venturi, Robert, and Brown and Izenour, 65–67, 70, 80, 81

Whiteley, Jon, on the Paris Salon, 37
Wittgenstein, Ludwig, x, 85, 93–96, 99–102, 105–11; on intention, 87–89, 96–99, 102–4; vs Derrida, 88
Wittig, Monique, 142, 143–44, 146, 157, 158
Wolf, Christa, 154, 161
Women's Studies and psychoanalysis, 155
Woolf, Virginia, 80, 149–50, 154, 158